Gripped by Guyana

Gripped by Guyana

A Memoir of Purpose and Adventure

Merle Kindred

Pincushion Publishing

Penticton, BC, Canada

The views and opinions expressed in this book are those of the author and not of any organization with which she is, or has been, affiliated.

Editor: Joyce Gram

Cover batik art: Merle Kindred

Cover image: © Photos by Pharos

Cover design: Jim Bisakowski, www.bookdesign.ca

ISBN 978-1-7387853-0-8 (Paperback)

ISBN 978-1-7387853-1-5 (Kindle Edition)

Memoir, Travel, Adventure, Volunteering

Pincushion Publishing

1-197 Dauphin Ave.

Penticton, BC, V2A 3S3, Canada

CONTENTS

FOREWORD

Gripped by Guyana: A Memoir of Purpose and Adventure is an invitation to explore a fascinating country with a violent past and an uncertain future. Guyana is rich with natural beauty, flush with oil, timber, and gold—a land of bounty with much potential. Part travelogue and part survivor's manual, this memoir conjures up the tropical scents, sounds, and tastes of a nation in rapid transition, a place that quickly becomes familiar, and—like family—is often dysfunctional.

Kindred's story resonates as she introduces us to a troubled society fractured politically along ethnic lines, haunted by its history, and a playground for drug traffickers and crooked politicians made bold with impunity. Once a hotbed of socialism, now a forgotten victim of the Cold War, Guyana is weakened by corruption and impoverished by decades of mass emigration to Canada, the US, and the UK. This isn't a destination for the fainthearted, yet Kindred jumps right in upon her arrival in the below-sea-level capital of Georgetown and within days becomes comfortably familiar mapping the streets of rough neighborhoods and exchanging quips with the touts and louts.

Both funny and informative, Kindred's narrative contains valuable insights into volunteering and international development, especially projects implemented through civil society organizations that specialize in sending overseas mostly young, but increasingly seasoned professionals, from all walks of life. Some volunteers succeed, some fail, and some become consular cases. Others soar, like Kindred, when she quits the city and hangs her hammock in remote settlements. Like so many aboriginal nations destroyed by colonialism, Indigenous people are the poorest and most marginalized in Guyana.

Under the most basic living conditions that border on the line of what is deemed too insecure for foreign volunteer placement, Kindred is exposed to the same dangers her neighbours experience every day.

She takes the ups and downs of challenges and cultural misunderstandings in stride, self-aware, generous in sharing knowledge and experience, a sympathetic listener, and ultimately a practical doer. Using unorthodox tools for community development, such as craftivism and birding, Kindred is a born storyteller, adventurer, and a natural educator. Unusually, but effectively, she recognizes the role that fibre arts—embroidery and beadwork—can play in instilling confidence through self-expression and as a means for forging connections with strangers. By sharing something creative that becomes larger than it could be by itself, Kindred makes a difference.

Gripped by Guyana is a true account of a deeply committed and courageous woman who believes in paying it forward and inspires the rest of us to follow.

Jan Sheltinga, Charge d'affaires and Head of Aid, Canadian High Commission, Co-operative Republic of Guyana (2016-2018)

Guyana on NE coast of South America © Freeworldmaps

© Nations Online Project
GUYANA
VENEZUELA
BRAZIL
SURINAME
ATLANTIC OCEAN
N
Mabaruma
Kaituma
Baramanni
Five Star
Matthews' Ridge
Charity
Anna Regina
Spring Garden
Georgetown
Vreed en Hoop
Cuyuni River
Arimu Mine
Bartica
Fort Wellington
New Amsterdam
Rosignol
Rose Hall
Peters Mine
Mazaruni River
Mara
Nieuw Nickerie
Linden
Rockstone
Corriverton
Kamarang
Imbaimadai
Issano
Kumaka
Takama
Ituni
Potaro Landing
Orealla
Kwakwani
Mount Roraima (2,810 m; 9,219 ft)
Mahdia
Apoera
Epira
Kaieteur Falls
Orinduik
Kurupukari
Surama
Apoteri
Good Hope
Normandia
Rupununi River
Rewa River
Essequibo River
Courantyne River
Lethem
Boa Vista
Dadanawa
Aishalton
Kwitaro River
Disputed Area
Biloku
Masekenari
National capital
District capital
City, town, village
Major airport
International boundary
Main road
Secondary road
0
50
100 km
0
50 mi

To all who urged me to tell this story, especially Julie

Part One

2017

If you have come here to help me, you are wasting your time. But if you have come because your liberation is bound up with mine, then let us work together.

Lilla Watson, Australian Aboriginal activist, academic, and artist

Chapter One

How It All Began

I gazed at the dusky rose and pale orange dawn that brightened the dark green carpet of rainforest below. Georgetown appeared in the distance built on coastal floodplains. I arrived with an umbrella and high rubber boots.

An ancient seawall and canal system provided some protection, but the Atlantic and the rainy season would always threaten flooding. With a city that was six feet below sea level at high tide, Canada's aid organization—Cuso International—had rented apartments only above ground level. I'd be living in the working-class neighbourhood of Campbellville. Home would be in the backhouse, a second building on one of the city's deep and narrow lots established by the original colonists.

I dragged my bags up the long flight of concrete steps and heard, "Hi! I'm Caroline" as the grill that protected a hardwood door swung open. This young woman with long blond hair and sharp blue eyes grabbed my duffle bag and dragged it into the bright and breezy apartment. I followed with a small carry-on bag and my daypack filled with tech gear. Caroline hefted my bag into a small room furnished with a bed, a nightstand, and a wooden wardrobe.

"You can have the bigger room when I leave in a month," she said. Cheery greeting. Simple space. I liked it.

We swapped the usual introductory information as I unpacked, and she went back to preparing lunch for us both. We spanned Canada with my arrival from British Columbia and her upcoming departure for home in Nova Scotia. I also realized she was exactly the age I'd begun my international career fifty years ago—twenty-one. This was a sobering thought as I settled down for a welcome Caribbean meal of rice and vegetables.

"I have a meeting downtown," said Caroline. "The neighbourhood is safe, so go ahead and walk around, if you like."

As she headed out into the bright afternoon sunlight, I studied the immediate area. At the raggedy old house across the street, a sullen woman half-sat, half-hung on the crumbling steps while rambunctious children tore through the debris-strewn yard. I waved, but she didn't respond. Men in natty dreadlocks, the twisted long hair of Rastafarians, were wandering around the yard smoking what I recognized by its sweet smell as ganja—marijuana.

I'd learned decades ago about this Jamaican religious and social movement when I was on my first Cuso assignment in Montego Bay at a teacher training college. Rastafari believed Emperor Haile Selassie of Ethiopia was the messiah. Blacks were the chosen people and would eventually return to Africa. The dreadlocks were uncut hair, which they called natty, and we would call knotty. Such hair was like a mane and was homage to the Lion of the Tribe of Judah, the emperor.

I heard the twitter of a tiny songbird in a cage atop a car wreck nestled in tall weeds in front of the house. I stepped forward for a closer look. A man ambled over sporting a knit cap with the Rasta colours of red, yellow, green, and black holding the abundant plaits of his hair. He introduced himself as Judah. I recognized it as the common Old Testament moniker offered to strangers by the Rastafari.

"You wanna bird?" Judah asked.

"I prefer my birds in the wild, like in the rainforest," I said.

"Yeh, me too. But maybe dis bird like most o' we—in a cage." His speech was what I also recognized as Rasta talk.

Later, I learned that just as Haitians bet on cock fights, like the one that I had stumbled upon when working in the Bahamas, Guyanese held songbird competitions. Sizeable bets were placed for best pitch and longest song. The country's diaspora scattered around the world, especially in English-speaking places, paid high dollar for smuggled songbirds. It was an illegal but lucrative trade.

Wildlife trafficking is the fourth most prevalent illegal trade in the world. Drugs hold first place, then guns, and people. Guyana was notorious for trading in Colombian drugs along with guns and wildlife.

Across the street, next to the Rasta house, was a party rental business. Big cube vans moved tables and chairs and other party equipment in and out of the storage building day and night. Sometimes traffic on the narrow street was stopped. I didn't mind the wait. These were people engaged in meaningful, legal business. Folks getting together socially at family or community celebrations was called liming or gaffing. This was big business in Georgetown. Hurrah!

I never did meet our neighbour, the drug lord, who lived on the next block in what I called a starter castle. It was painted pistachio green with windows framed in white. The black wrought iron fencing that encircled the building was edged with gold-coloured trim. The house filled the depth of the entire long lot, and a fleet of new cars was always parked in front. Sometimes the police came by for what looked like a friendly visit. All was usually quiet. Transactions were conducted behind closed doors. I never felt threatened and just strolled by on my way to the main street. The drug lord tended his business, while I minded mine.

Sometimes hymns rippled over the rear boundary wall of our property from a church on the street behind my backhouse. I also saw the domes of a Hindu building across the street from the church but never heard anything, though I'd hoped for the melodic pattern of raga—traditional Indian music. I felt comfortable in my neighbourhood and liked my apartment. Life was good.

I also enjoyed Caroline, my spirited apartment mate, and considered her an asset. She and other young volunteers knew musicians and spoken word poets who addressed cultural issues and often blasted the status quo. She invited me to attend a small gathering of young Guyanese performers in a courtyard just off a downtown main street.

The event showcased vocal and instrumental talent of contemporary music in many genres. Songs included Caribbean classics that I knew from the 1960s in the US Virgin Islands and especially reggae that had pounded from every rum bar in villages outside Montego Bay. There was original music by Guyanese composers, which had hints of Trinidadian rhythms. I appreciated this early introduction to some of the cultural life of the country and tapped my foot to many a melody.

Another evening, Caroline and I had headed over to the National Park for the World Wildlife Federation's Earth Hour, scheduled globally every April. A packed audience of all ages filled a big tent that was erected in a parking lot and applauded speeches and a presentation on energy conservation. That was what my work was all about from the 1980s until now—energy conservation in the built environment.

I'd never attended an Earth Hour celebration and was grateful for the experience here in Georgetown. When the power was switched off, the audience moved to the nearby pavement and helped light the votive candles arranged to read 60+. It was a reminder to "Turn Up the Dark" for sixty minutes this night.

A camera drone hovered overhead. I was surprised at my initial experience of this technology in a country in the Global South. It reminded me that technology transfer was occurring everywhere. I then remembered the glow of cell phones, called mobiles, in India a decade earlier when my work was centered in the subcontinent. Homeless people in Mumbai were sleeping on sheets of cardboard on sidewalks and clutching mobiles with the telltale bright blue screens. Why wouldn't some Guyanese, probably connected with media companies, have camera drones? I wasn't in some backwater swamp. I was in one of what had been the richest colonies of the British West Indies when the empire was at its zenith. I was now living with the descendants of builders of imperial might in this part of the world.

I was overjoyed with all these encounters, large and small. I stuffed myself with every experience possible that gave me insight into daily life in the big city. I was intrigued by Georgetown's vibrancy on these special occasions and captivated by the bright lights and music that animated urban spaces. I felt the pulse of Caribbean culture, which was a homecoming of sorts. Memories of island life and past events in India would wing themselves into the midst of my Guyanese experiences and I'd just smile to myself.

This small, thumb-shaped coastal country in South America characterized itself as the "Land of Six Peoples". These were Amerindian or Indigenous, Afro-Guyanese, Indo-Guyanese, Chinese, European—especially Portuguese, and Brazilian. It was a kaleidoscopic blend of backgrounds.

Along with the sights and sounds of Caribbean life, the scents of tropical vegetation tingled my nose with aromas that celebrated life near the Equator. Sometimes I stuck my nose into tropical flowers, mindful of insects that might already be busy with nectar collection or dusted with pollen. Other times I just stroked flower petals and leaves. I also stroked trunks of tropical trees and savoured textures that ranged from silky smooth to ragged and rough. I was not a tree hugger; rather, a tree rubber.

As I continued settling into life in Georgetown, I reviewed the basic survival list we all share: food, clothing, and shelter. I had brought enough loose cotton pants and Indian cotton kurtas or loose-fitting shirts to start the assignment. I'd also packed khaki cargo pants with ample pockets and buttoned cotton shirts for more rugged excursion wear. Cuso took care of shelter. That left food and water.

We ordered big jugs of bottled water. Any other water was suspect. For food, I wanted fresh provisions from open-air markets and a return to the weekly ritual that I'd experienced in Jamaican markets. Cuso staff and my gracious landlady, Miss Lam, offered marketing tips. Soon I was on a quest to learn the food ways of Guyana. I was eager for the colourful, pungent, and lively world of Caribbean markets that rooted me to the earth.

Every Saturday morning, I made my marketing pilgrimage. I would tote a big cloth bag and walk half an hour through neighborhoods from rough to the equivalent of Guyanese royal to stock up with provisions for the week. The two biggest sites were Stabroek Market on the bank of the Demerara River to the west and Bourda Market in the centre of the city. Both were huge wooden warehouses of Guyanese timber built in the nineteenth century. These structures exuded post-colonial decay. Even the outdoor stalls that surrounded both markets were crowded and unappealing.

Bourda, however, also contained a market area with contemporary, canvas-covered stalls erected over a nearby canal that had been filled in to provide more market space. I gravitated to this airy venue for most of my marketing mindful of the conversation one older gentleman shared with me one Saturday. Shoulder-to-shoulder in a conspiratorial whisper, he said, "Wonder what dem gonna tink da day of da big flood when no way to carry city water west to da Demerara and out to da ocean."

Georgetown's outdoor Bourda Market

At Bourda Market, produce was spread out on tables and hanging in mesh bags overhead. I filled my bag with yams and carrots, fresh pineapple, onions, wedges of melon, oranges, and other tropical fruit. I pawed through rough-skinned tubers and enjoyed the textures. I didn't mind the dirt that clung to the roots and just brushed my dusty hands onto my old marketing pants. Eddo root was my first choice despite its ugly skin. The bright pink underlayer was bitter and needed cutting away. I would then slice or cube the white flesh below and cook it slowly revealing its rich, earthy promise of good taste.

I indulged in my favourite food, plantain, which looked like a banana but was boiled, baked, or fried like a vegetable. It was my choice of lunch when at home. I'd slice it, season with just salt and pepper, and fry it in coconut oil. It was a satisfying meal with its firm texture and mild taste.

I also loved the squishiness and sweetness of papaya, so messy that I'd eat it at home while leaning over the kitchen sink. Cassava was a staple of especially Indigenous life. I'd pop into a Guyanese specialty food store near Bourda Market as part of my shopping routine and collect a package of thin, cracker-like cassava bread with its crunchy texture.

Another weekly stop was for midmorning refreshment. The man who always had a huge bag of coconuts smiled when he saw me coming. "G'mornin', miss. The same?" he'd ask.

"Yes, please," I'd reply as I settled my bulging market bag on the packed ground and sat on the single rickety chair provided. He'd select a coconut, heft it, then whack—cut an end off with his cutlass and hand it back to me with a plastic straw. The other Caribbean countries that I was familiar with called his tool a machete, but here in Guyana, it was a cutlass and conjured visions of pirates.

When I'd slurped all the rich coconut water, I would return the nut. Whack—he'd slice it open, hand me half, and cut a chip out of the other half before giving it back. I'd use the chip to scoop the mellow, cool flesh.

While I was sipping and slurping, I'd watch my lean, gap-toothed vendor fill plastic bottles provided by customers who wanted only the water. Done with my coconut, I'd tossed the empty shells and, alas, the plastic straw onto the heap of discards. "Till next week," I'd say with a wave. He'd wink as he split another coconut for a customer.

Oh, the fresh fruits and vegetables at the market were to drool for! Mango season meant sweet juice that would drip down my chin and make a happy mess. Rambutan or Thai lichee looked like a bright red, spiny sea urchin. When I cut it open, out would pop a juicy white seed. I'd slip it into my mouth, suck it until the sweet pulp yielded all its juice, and then spit out the seed. This was another food for me to eat at home.

Later, I read about research that revealed the healthiest dietary patterns on the planet. The sub-Saharan African countries such as Chad, Mali, and Cameroon ate what was rated as food of the highest nutritional quality. Their diet was sorghum, maize, millet, and teff in stews and soups along with relishes of local vegetables. These countries may have lacked an adequate quantity of these foods for their citizens, but the quality was rated superb for human beings.

Guyana came in fourth place, and I knew why. Its markets overflowed with an abundance of tropical fruits, a wide range of vegetables and root crops, herbs and spices, legumes, local rice, and numerous medicinal plants. Was it organic? Maybe. Maybe not. I never asked and kept to my vision of fresh, pure food.

Getting provisions was no problem, but what about preparation? I was a moderately successful cook who preferred vegetarian fare but with no great enthusiasm for kitchen craft from years of solo living. I did, however, become interested in what the Guyanese called Cookup as a variation on what I knew of the protein-rich rice and legume combinations from other Caribbean countries.

Jamaicans prepared what they called Rice and Peas with onion, thyme, allspice, and coconut milk. Bahamians had a similar dish but called it Peas and Rice and used a tomato base. Both versions provided high-quality nutrition at low cost. In the US Virgin Islands, we ate Fish and Fungi—salted cod plus cornmeal and okra mash. These were ingredients allotted to slaves when the islands were the Danish West Indies before World War I at which point the US purchased the islands for defense purposes. As Volunteers in Service to America or VISTA people, we'd received large wooden crates of salted cod for the preschools we were establishing in an era before the closing of the Canadian cod banks. Our cook prepared this dish regularly for students. I ate it but never cooked it after leaving the islands. It was good but not that good.

Now I was poised for Guyanese cooking as I dashed into our kitchen with the scent of cumin, cinnamon, and cloves setting my nose twitching with delight. "Caroline, how did you produce such a great aroma? It's the best smell that I've ever experienced coming from a kitchen! How did you do it?" This was meatless Caribbean cooking with the added flair of Indian spicing.

I was transported straight back to happy times and the dishes that nourished my body and spirit those many years I'd spent in India. I never mastered Indian cooking. Grandmother Salome in our home never relinquished her throne room, the kitchen. However, I certainly distinguished myself in adoration of eating Indian food, which I'd eat in traditional manner with fingers as a scoop and thumb as a thruster.

Meanwhile, back in our kitchen, Caroline, with beads of sweat on her face and elbows thrust out for greater power, continued to scrape the frying pan with a wooden spoon. Without looking up or changing the rhythm of her spoon stroke, she said, "First garlic cloves diced and mashed up with the back of a wooden spoon. Then into the pan with oil and stir till they start getting brown but not burned."

"What else?" I asked as I peeked through the steam rising from the pan.

"Thinly sliced onion with a little water to keep the pan moist," she said, still scraping. "Then salt and pepper to taste, half a tablespoon of garam masala, and one tablespoon of curry powder. Now help chop those vegetables over there," she said pointing to the counter with her elbow.

"You mean these carrots, the eddo root, and the bora greens?" I asked, proud that I recognized the tuber and the half-metre long local equivalent of green beans.

"Yep, and chop fine. I need the carrots first, the longest to cook." I'd soon chopped those vegetables along with bok choy and some eggplant into bite-size morsels. "Into the pan and now you stir," said Caroline handing over the spoon.

It was a tasty meal, and Caroline and I took turns cooking more cookup and curry combinations. She was vegan and determined to share more of her training from Captain before she left the country. Captain was the owner and chief cook at the House of Flavours near Bourda Market. His nickname was from his days as a fisherman and his restaurant was our go-to lunchtime destination on Saturdays.

With market bags stuffed, we'd trot over to see Captain. My order was always, "Fill up the ol' calabash bowl with rice and a sampling of today's curries, except the fake meat." I enjoyed the scent of all the spices that he would mix and match for the various curry dishes but didn't like the one with soy-based so-called meat.

"Sure nuf," he'd say with his ever-present smile. His white baseball cap was turned backwards, and a surgical mask covered his chin whiskers for demonstration of food safety awareness.

I never achieved Caroline's level of culinary skill. However, after her departure, I tinkered with even more curry and cookup combinations. My first big success with Guyanese cuisine was memorable.

I had wrestled with beans and rice, vegetables and spices all afternoon remembering tips from Caroline and Captain. I wanted this cooking caper to be at least passable. I was tackling Cookup, the first to make a public appearance. I didn't know if I was brave or foolish to try the classic Afro-Guyanese dish along with an Indo-Guyanese curry. Together, the combo would be a tasty meal, or so I hoped.

After my cooking frenzy where I chopped, mixed, and steamed up the kitchen, I wrapped my casserole dish and headed down the dirt path beside a nearby narrow paved street. I was off to a potluck hosted by two Cuso colleagues a short distance away. When passing several shops, I heard roadside voices across the way.

"Miss, that sure do smell fine," said one of the grey-haired regulars on this route. He was dressed in his usual tatty shirt and shorts. He roosted on what looked to be his favourite bench across the street from a food shop and added, "Will you marry me?"

"Not him, miss! He eat too much," said his neighbour, of similar vintage, also tattily dressed, on the bench under the coconut palm. He poked his friend in the ribs and said, "I have much mor' manners."

"Sorry, fellows," I replied with a grin as I clutched my towel-wrapped casserole. "Haven't time to get married today—maybe tomorrow."

"We be waitin'," said the first fellow as both laughed and slapped their thighs. Then he added, "And that dog followin' sure do like da smell of yo' cookin' too." I laughed over my shoulder and trotted onward along the dusty path. Crossing the bridge over the weed-choked canal to my destination two blocks away, I continued chuckling over the marriage proposals based on scent.

The potluck was a gathering of Cuso volunteers, Guyanese musicians, spoken-word poets, and expats. Bountiful selections for sipping and nibbling were spread over the dining table and kitchen counter. At one point, when standing near the serving table chatting with someone, I heard a Guyanese fellow ask, while filling his plate with a second helping of my Cookup, "Who made this great dish?"

"Oh, just this Canadian," I said with feigned modesty, "but it did rate two proposals of marriage and a most attentive dog."

A friend whom I met later, posted with another Canadian aid organization in Guyana, shared a comment that she'd heard when announcing her assignment back home. Someone had said, "But nobody goes to Guyana." I didn't share that sentiment. This country was as rich and vibrant an experience as I'd had anywhere in the world. I was committed to listening, pitching in, and providing whatever assistance possible.

With food, clothing, and shelter settled and feeling comfortable walking around much of the city, I was able to focus on work as a strategic planning advisor. My partner organization was Volunteer Youth Corps with headquarters in a rough section of Georgetown not far from my apartment. I could walk the distance in twenty minutes. It was no farther than the Cuso office, but it required that I follow a main road with wild drivers, a curious mixture of vehicles, and no place for pedestrians. What to do?

Chapter Two

Georgetown Encounters

"You don't want to walk around Lodge," said Indranie, our Cuso staff member who handled accounts and oversight of volunteer accommodations. So, following the standard transportation practice recommended for volunteers to get to work, I called a taxi. The fare was GYD400 or $2.66 Canadian and $2 in US currency. Soon I was whisked along the main road and off onto a residential street with a garbage-strewn canal in the centre of the boulevard.

I arrived in front of a nondescript, two-storey building surrounded by a high chain-link fence with Volunteer Youth Corps painted in big letters on the front wall. I opened the creaky iron gate and walked across a narrow plank, one foot in front of the other, over the soggy grass. Maybe this was a Guyanese version of a medieval moat. Georgetown was in Region 4 bordering on the Atlantic and conditions of the coastal floodplains were constant, even when it wasn't the rainy season.

I rang the bell, and someone peeped through the curtain. Then I heard the click of the lock release. The fence, the moat, now the locked door. Guess it was a bad neighbourhood.

"Come on in," said a muscled woman with a welcoming smile but a manner that said don't mess with me. "Our director is waiting for you upstairs." When I reached the top of a steep staircase of Guyanese hardwood that I admired as I was climbing slowly, I heard a cheerful voice.

"Welcome!" said a woman in a form-fitting, polyester business suit despite the tropical heat. She extended her hand accompanied by a big smile and said, "Just call me Goldie." Shaking hands, I matched her smile as we stepped into her office with an air conditioner humming behind her ergonomic desk chair.

The background study that I'd done for this assignment showed youth unemployment was forty percent. That was a whopping number until I read the fine print and learned that the government officially considered people as youth up to their mid-thirties. My Global North conditioning calculated that age to be half the biblical three-score-and-ten, or on the downside of heading for dead. When I did more research, I saw that much unemployment was from lack of education. This was doubtless painful for a country that had once boasted having the best educational system in the Caribbean region.

VYC After-school Program

I knew that Volunteer Youth Corps, or VYC, had logged almost twenty years of experience in enriching the after-school lives of youth in Lodge and other rough areas of Georgetown. Goldie was quick to outline what programs were operating and hopes for the future.

"Our oldest program, Big Brothers Big Sisters of Guyana, is after-school mentorship with activities to combat destructive behaviour. That means we're dealing with alcohol and substance abuse, risky sex, criminality, and often gang violence."

"That's a huge undertaking," I said noting the wide range of focus. "How long has the program been running and what's the source of funding?"

"It's over a dozen years old with Guyana Goldfields providing support. We need to include more teenagers and do more HIV/AIDS education. That means recruiting social workers, upgrading volunteer teacher training, and building more community support."

What a huge mandate, I thought as I wondered how such a patchwork fix offered in a few down-at-the-heel communities could succeed. What hope was there in counteracting an implosion of the educational system and obvious social repercussions following the collapse of the colonial structure at independence in 1966? How much could I reasonably accomplish in a six-month posting? "What are other areas of operation?" I asked as I realized Big Brothers Big Sisters was also going to be a big challenge.

Goldie leaned forward with eagerness to introduce the next program. "Our National Career Guidance program helps teenagers in the secondary schools learn what knowledge and personal traits they'll need for various careers. We also revise teacher and student materials and it's Cuso that funds and runs this whole program."

I nodded and, even though I was just learning about VYC, I wondered if this program wasn't relying too heavily on Cuso. Were there any plans for the Ministry of Education to take over?

Goldie shifted in her chair and startled me with an answer to my unspoken question. "We depend too much on Cuso. The program has been successful for four years, but it needs to expand beyond Georgetown and be operated by the Ministry of Education."

When Goldie introduced VYC's next program, she spoke with an even greater uptick in enthusiasm. "Our After-school Interactive Math and Science program, including STEM education, is funded by

ExxonMobil. It's been five years and they're planning to expand offerings."

Now it was my turn to shift in my chair and note that I was sweating into my embroidered Indian cotton blouse despite the air conditioning. I wondered how much real science, technology, engineering, and mathematics could be conveyed and worried about involvement with ExxonMobil. I wasn't going to get any time off from the fossil fuel issues that we were battling in Canada, especially in the west and my province of British Columbia.

Pay attention, I ordered myself. Now wasn't the time to get sidetracked into my personal feelings or possible complications for Cuso. My Canadian nongovernment organization, or NGO, received ninety percent of its funding via the Canadian government and raised ten percent itself from donors, including the two thousand dollars each volunteer was to provide through fundraising or personal contribution. Funding couldn't be seen as colluding with corporations.

Goldie went on to describe the fourth and final program under the umbrella of VYC management. "We're also involved with an organizational consultancy project called Guyana Civil Society Leadership and funded by USAID. Twenty-six NGOs here are learning to become more effective. We're hoping to keep this coalition financed and networking beyond the funding period, which lasts one more year." Goldie then leaned back in her chair.

I realized that this program wasn't focused on youth. USAID probably needed an established Guyanese organization to provide formal oversight. How was I going to fit this into an updated strategic plan for VYC? "I'm impressed with the history and range of your programs. Let's see what useful roadmap we can construct for future operations." Now it was my turn to lean back in my chair as we chitchatted our way to the end of our first meeting.

I retraced my steps on the plank over the squishy lawn, watched an after-school session at the side of the building, and waited for the taxi that I'd summoned. I needed time in the natural world, which was part of my personal strategic plan for my stay in this country. I now wanted to experience some of Guyana's wealth of over nine hundred bird species. More than half were endemic, roughly a quarter migrated annually from the north escaping winter, and the remaining quarter migrated from countries in the southern region of this continent. Guyana provided bountiful birdwatching.

The Botanical Gardens were halfway between VYC and my apartment. Preparing for a birding break, I'd tucked my camera and binoculars into an unremarkable cloth bag, slung it over my shoulder, and walked the short distance south to the gardens.

The back gate was locked to motorized traffic, but there was space for me to squeeze through. An asphalt road ran straight through the park and was lined with scrubby grass and a few large trees. I trudged down the pavement inhaling the scent of the grasslands. The nose knows. I was reminded of semiarid regions of my life—home in the Okanagan Valley of BC, areas in India's subcontinent, and the Saskatchewan prairies where all my Finnish grandparents had homesteaded.

Veering off the road to a narrow canal dappled with lily pads, I'd spotted my first bird stepping across the flowerless pads with its long, greyish toes spread wide. It had a black head and chestnut body and wings. The base of its yellow bill was bright red. When it flew, I saw bright yellow on the underside of its wings. I'd snapped a picture for record purposes and wondered how I was ever going to get a copy of the Guyana birding bible, *Birds of Northern South America*, whose lead author was Robin Restall. Yes, really Robin. The book would provide colour plates of the cornucopia of all the species that lived in or migrated through the country.

I had learned about this book the day before I left Canada. I was having coffee with our member of parliament, Richard Cannings, a biologist with world-class birding credentials and a dozen books published on the natural history of British Columbia.

"I have a book on the birds of Trinidad and Tobago," I piped up.

"Wrong book," he said. "You'll be in rainforests and savannahs—not Caribbean islands. You'll need Restall's book." Too late for ordering. Getting it would be a problem to be solved in Guyana.

Wattled Jacana

When I walked home from the Botanical Gardens on my maiden outing, I spotted a mottled-brown bird on a fence. It was near a ditch with the bank strewn with snail shells, the same shells that I'd spotted on the banks of the Lodge canal near the VYC office. Its strong, curved beak was ideal for plucking snails from their shells. Who are you? I then sent photos back to British Columbia to one of my ace birding friends. She said that I'd seen a Wattled Jacana on the lily pads and a juvenile Snail Kite near the ditch. Hurrah! I was birding, albeit with remote help.

Another species that I saw and heard every morning and evening consisted of a flock of chatty parrots that emitted what sounded like—cm-qwk or kee-wik, kee-wik. There was a splash of orange on the front edge of their wings and bright yellow on their cheeks and crown.

At dawn, and especially at dusk, there were the squawks and swoops of flocks composed of pairs or trios. The latter were probably parents with a juvenile. These birds were returning from the hunt for food to roost in coconut palms and share the day's news in bird talk.

There was a coconut palm near my second-floor window, so an avian alarm clock sounded from what I later identified as Orange-winged Amazons. Months later, I would have an even greater wake-up call—one of my life's epiphanies—and it too would involve birds.

Orange-winged Amazons

Chapter Three

Hinterland Adventures

I'd arrived in Guyana in early spring, less than a month from the Easter long weekend of four days. Barely grounded in my home and work life, it was now holiday time. Caroline and I both decided to head south into the hinterland, which isn't a negative term in Guyana.

Caroline said, "I'm going by road overnight with friends. I want to attend the Lethem rodeo. It's dry savannah time and cattle country. They say, 'All the cowboys are Indians'—that is, Amerindians." She'd be in Region 9 at a border town with Brazil wrapping around Guyana on its southwestern and southern sectors.

I replied, "Hmm…for me, it's not broncs but birds. This place is a birding bonanza. I've heard of a tour company that'll arrange an Indigenous ecotour in the North Rupununi northeast of Lethem up in Region 9. No bone-rattling roads for me. I'm taking a hint from the birds and flying." I knew it would be expensive, but I'd brought extra funds from Canada specifically for such outings, something I knew that some of my fellow volunteers, including Caroline, might not be able to afford.

I held no illusions about my birding credentials, which were relatively short and modest—a few years in India and under a decade in BC. I didn't use birding apps to learn the finer points of bird calls. I had no life list of birds seen as do truly avid birders. I had arrived in Guyana with my old, palm-size digital camera, binoculars with minimal range, and the wrong birding book. Not a stellar start. One of my goals was simply to use birding to give focus for my walkabouts and have birds as bridges connecting me with the natural world of Guyana.

Kiskadee

Neighbours had helped me identify pairs of birds that were bright yellow, black, and white. They flitted around my balcony daily and were called Kiskadees, though whether Great or Lesser I couldn't distinguish.

Caroline and I packed small bags and headed south. I reported to Ogle, the small airport near the coast, and flew in a small, dual-prop plane to Annai, a town in the middle of the country at the northern border of Region 9. This large area of southwest Guyana was the southern savannah of the country that also flooded in the rainy seasons. There were ten regions in all with half strung along the coastal area and numbers starting in the northwest. Georgetown was in Region 4.

My daypack had my birding equipment and my carry-on bag held everything else and couldn't exceed twenty pounds. These were small planes with minimal luggage capacity and stringent weight restrictions. I also stepped on a scale so my body weight could be noted. Such were the preparations for human flight.

Georgetown homes and agricultural land

Less than a month earlier, I'd arrived in the country on a red-eye flight from Toronto. I'd gazed at dawn brightening the rainforest canopy and had glimpses of Georgetown as we'd veered south to the international airport.

Now I enjoyed a panoramic view of the Georgetown grid stretching along the Atlantic coast. The Demerara River, with freighters anchored, was its western boundary. I studied the cityscape and miles of sugarcane fields with their grid system laid out to the east and the south. Many fields were fallow. Sugar beets grown in temperate zones were more profitable and less labour-intensive than cane, which grows only in tropical or subtropical conditions. I noted how colonial settlers used canals and roads to mark boundaries. All were executed with hand labour by slaves or indentured workers under the blazing sun.

On my initial flight into the country, I'd seen the thick blanket of rainforest to the west of the city. Now I studied it again with even greater interest as it reappeared when we winged our way southward. Serpentine paths of silver and others of reddish-brown threaded through the forest. The silver streaks were likely Guyana's glistening rivers that tumbled down from the mighty Amazon to the Atlantic. Silver threads appeared occasionally and were probably creeks flowing from the rivers. The reddish-brown pathways were likely the laterite dirt roads that wound through the vastness of a country that retains eighty percent of its rainforest.

I imagined the glitter of Guyana's gold and diamonds clawed from the treasure chest of its rock and soil. My mind's ear heard the crack of a massive hardwood tree crashing to the forest floor with the whirr of a logger's chainsaw. I sensed the fear of the long-legged agouti darting through the forest only to be caught in a trapper's snare. I imagined the high-pitched chirp of a tropical songbird tangled in a net and destined for distant travel as part of the illegal bird trade. I shook my head and reminded myself that I was on an ecotourism excursion. For the next few days, I'd be experiencing life as free as a proverbial bird.

Gradually, the rainforest thinned and gave way to grassland bounded by mountains in the distance. My heart raced with anticipation as I studied the changing landscape and was amazed at such diversity in just over an hour's flight. All four ecosystems—coastal floodplains, rainforests, savannahs, and mountains—were on display. The silhouette of the plane appeared below like a dark bird gliding southward.

When the plane eased onto a small runway in the dusty savannah and bumped to a stop, I hoisted my gear and climbed down steep metal steps. I was greeted with a lone vehicle, a pickup truck, and a driver with the bronze skin of an Indigenous South American. Stepping forward with a smile and taking my carry-on bag, he said, "I'm your ride to Iwokrama, ma'am" tipping the brim of his khaki baseball cap.

Dust clouds swirled behind as we lurched over the dirt road between potholes heading further into Amerindian—now more commonly called Indigenous—territory. "We all have phds here in the Rupununi," said my driver with a grin. "We're pothole dodgers." I then heard this line from every driver whenever I travelled in the southern interior. I continued to chuckle while keeping limber in body and spirit.

We were in the centre of the Guiana Shield, one of the oldest rock formations on the planet. For two days, I would be at the Iwokrama Centre for Rainforest Conservation and Development, a nationally protected area. The Canadian government via its Canadian International Development Agency, or CIDA, had provided approximately a million dollars to the Commonwealth for conservation efforts to be undertaken by the government of Guyana. Several other governments and organizations also contributed. Now Iwokrama was nestled deep in one of the few remaining intact tropical rainforests in the world.

Arriving at the compound constructed in a cleared area of the rainforest, I was greeted by a beautiful young Indigenous woman with a broad smile. "Welcome. I'm Marcy, your guide. Let me take you to your cabin." A small wooden building crafted with Guyana's exquisite timber was a simple and welcoming space with the refreshing smell of raw wood. "When you're ready, we can have a short walk on a nearby path through the rainforest before dinner."

When we met, Marcy pointed out a black bird with a touch of white on its wing and a bright red beak. As it hopped around the compound, Marcy said, "Black Nunbird." I nodded at the apt name and jotted in my pocket-size notebook. She not only identified birds for me but also shared the names and attributes of many trees and plants of the rainforest.

I learned that she was trained as a tour guide at the Bina Hill Institute Youth Learning Centre here in the North Rupununi. I tucked this piece of information into a safe corner of my memory bank never guessing that I would withdraw it as a significant element of my later work in the interior.

On our initial walk, we'd experienced what the region and season were known for, a downpour, and returned to the compound wet and laughing. Gazing to the west, I saw Iwokrama bordered by the Pakaraima Mountains glowing in what photographers and filmmakers called the golden hour before sunset.

After dinner, we took a boat ride in the dark on the nearby Essequibo River. Marcy aimed a flashlight at the riverine bushes, and I saw the glistening eyes of birds roosting. I wondered what they thought of the eye of our big light and the sound of the hunting purr of our engine.

In the morning, after a night's rest in my snug little cabin, I savoured the pastel hour, the delicate time of light before the appearance of the sun. Soon its rays brightened the highlands scattered to the east into Suriname. Iwokrama's ecosystem was also where Guianan and Amazonian flora and fauna met. I learned that the abundance of life included over four hundred kinds of fish, ninety varieties of bats, and over five hundred native species of birds. Megafauna were also present, such as the Giant Anteater, Jaguar, Puma, and the Giant River Otter. I wondered if I would see any of them. In addition, Iwokrama was a global hotspot for a wide range of tropical plants.

I was in a region akin to Eden here in South America but also having a tantrum over technology. My equipment was so inadequate for even seeing, much less photographing, the magnificent birds of Guyana. Birds in the high canopy and those far away were beyond my gear's capacity. I consoled myself that everybody starts somewhere when upgrades are due: in this case, overdue. So, I jotted names and descriptions that Marcy gave me and later studied the *Birds of Northern South America*, which weighed as much as a standard Bible. Yes, I was travelling with the best birding book for the area. How had

I snagged a copy for the trip? It was synchronicity, an encounter in Georgetown the week before my trip.

I had been in Queenstown, a prosperous section of Georgetown, and cramming the impossible into one photo frame to make a point about contrast. On the left was a dilapidated little Georgetown house. On the right was an all-glass, multistorey, cylindrical office building. In the background, between the two structures, was a wind tower and a dead tree with a big bird of prey roosting on top. I was going for smooshing the grubby and gaunt old with the nifty new. The middle ground was dead nature and a bird. I knew this shot wasn't going to win any awards, but I did like the story that it told.

Standing in the middle of this quiet residential street aiming my camera, I heard a voice from behind. "Hello, may I help you?" came a question with a plummy British accent. There stood a pleasant-looking, middle-aged chap on the sidewalk in front of a well-kept classic Georgetown home. He was a contract maritime engineer employed internationally with Georgetown his home for decades. "Do come in for a cold drink," said Peter.

We talked about my photography and his vocation as well as his avocation, painting. While we sipped juice, he identified birds flitting around the trees and shrubs that filled his yard. Since I'd just booked my trip into the hinterland, I bemoaned my lack of an adequate birding book. Austin's Book Services was the city's and the country's only general bookstore. It didn't carry it.

"Come with me. Our library might just contain what you need," said Peter. "My wife loves novels, so all the paperbacks are hers, but I do have a few books on the natural history of Guyana." Entering the downstairs library, I was greeted with a wall of shelves filled with books. Peter plucked out a volume. "Ah, here's the Restall. The plates are wonderful." He handed me the book and my eyes grew wide as I leafed through exquisite drawings of birds that displayed every colour on the spectrum.

"I don't normally loan my books, but I'll make an exception for you, if you promise its safe return and recounting of your adventures in the North Rupununi." Done deal. The book gave me visual and descriptive elements to start my Guyanese birding career. It also constituted three pounds of the precious twenty pounds allotted for my carry-on bag.

Back in Iwokrama, on day two of my hinterland adventure, we travelled up the Essequibo River in a small aluminum boat and spotted various birds at a distance. Marcy supplied names. I looked and jotted. We also followed a watery pathway off the river and tromped through the rainforest encountering more species.

At this point, names and calls were a blur of input that I decided to sort out later. Immersion in the region was enough for the present as I observed massive trees such as the mora and trunks encircled with gnarly growth given the beguiling name of monkey vine.

"Here's the wallaba tree," said Marcy tapping the trunk. "Good hardwood with an oily sap that fights insects and decay."

"What's it used for?"

"It's good wood for shingles and poles. It's also good for flooring and fence posts."

"What's this tree?" I asked stroking a nearby trunk and relishing its grainy texture.

"Wamara. You might know it as rosewood. Very solid and expensive. Used mostly for inside work and fine furniture in city buildings."

We climbed nearly three hundred metres over rock outcroppings and slippery footpaths to the top of Turtle Mountain to view the magnificent Essequibo in the distance. It was the largest river in Guyana and the fourth largest in South America. The panoramic view literally took my breath away—a peak experience in both senses.

When descending and threading our way through the forest and outcroppings, we met a group of American birders from Iwokrama. "You all were up to the top of the mountain?" asked one birder.

"Yes, great view of the Essequibo," I said.

"We'll take your word for it," said another person. "We're turning back here. No rock climbing for us." I smiled, nodded, and felt admirably accomplished as Marcy and I continued our downward march.

During the boat ride back to the lodge, I spotted something pink and grey in the river and thought it must be a dead fish, belly up. However, Marcy told our boatman, James, "Turn back!" We circled and I saw something swimming, not floating, midriver.

Marcy extended an oar as James eased toward the creature. "Three-toed Sloth," she said with quiet excitement. "Don't let it touch you or it'll grab on and never let go." Slowly she drew the oar back and brought the animal, with its calm baby face, to the boat. It clung to the side, and we studied its massive, curved claws.

James motored slowly to the far shore. As we bumped into the bank, the sloth looked at the drooping branches and s-l-o-w-l-y reached up to latch onto one while easing its way upward.

I was amazed at its calmness and purposeful movements. Marcy and I wondered aloud why it was swimming midriver. I said, "Maybe it's seeking better food or even a relationship."

Three-toed Sloth

James spoke for the first time. "Or meyb' he's trying to get away from a relationship." Marcy and I turned and stared at him before bursting out laughing.

"Good point, James," I said. "Maybe love life gone bad."

That evening, I met the birding group from the mountain. They were from Montana and curious as to my solo presence at Iwokrama. We exchanged the usual questions about where we were from and what we had seen. After dinner, they all strapped on headlamps, powered by batteries, and prepared to compare bird sightings and who was ahead in life lists.

First, they graciously asked me about my best sighting of the day, so I shared my grand story of the Three-toed Sloth. Then I settled myself nearby and sipped award-winning Guyanese El Dorado rum and just let the bird names and final tallies fly by.

My Easter weekend booking also included two days at Surama Eco-Lodge, the country's first of such ventures owned and operated by Indigenous people. This facility was created by the Macushi of the nearby village of Surama.

Marcy and driver Colin took me from Iwokrama to Surama on the same bad road. There was no other. It was now even more treacherous with its surface further destroyed by recent rain. Traffic navigated dirt ruts with difficulty in the best of times. Now all vehicles had ground to a halt. We watched while a truck tried to pull another vehicle, top-heavy with a crane, back onto the road. The truck in trouble was off the road at a curious angle. I said, "I'm concerned that either the axel or frame of the disabled vehicle will crack, the chain will break, or the towing truck will be damaged."

"We'll see," said Marcy with Colin standing next to her, arms crossed against his broad chest. There we stood in the middle of the road with a couple dozen other spectators.

I was wrong. Wheels spun. Dirt flew. The cable strained, and the truck with the big crane lurched back onto the road. Onlookers climbed back into their vehicles and traffic flowed onward. "Yup, just another day on the road," said Colin. "Breakdown and rescue."

At a small, shallow creek running through a culvert under the road, Colin pulled over and told us that he had once stopped in just this spot to do a little fishing. "I cast rapidly the Macushi way, hand over hand, with just a baited and weighted line. Suddenly, an anaconda reared up from the shallows to nearly my shoulder. It grabbed for me but missed my arm because my hands were moving so fast. I jumped away and lived to tell the story."

An anaconda's teeth are angled back toward its throat like a barracuda's. If it had caught his arm, it would have yanked him off balance into the creek and drowned him before having him for lunch. The snake had been maybe four metres long. Shallow waters like this were an anaconda's favourite place. "Good thing I fish like a Macushi. I'm the man who got away," said Colin turning back to the truck. I'd peered over the bank and saw the bottom of the creek, which looked more like a ditch to me. Despite the heat of the tropics, a shiver rippled through my body.

As we lurched onward to Surama, I kept my body loose letting it go where the jerking motion took it hoping to avoid later muscle pain. When Colin stopped by a path into the forest, Marcy stepped out and said, "I hope we can see our famous Guianan Cock-of-the-Rock."

We hiked up to an outcropping of immense rocks. Marcy pointed high up to the boulders where a brown female was nesting in a crevasse. We stayed far away from the site and walked slowly, so that we wouldn't disturb her. Alas, even as we scrambled up and around various other massive boulders, we didn't see the show bird of the species, the brilliant, orange-crested male.

Surama Eco-Lodge was much smaller than Iwokrama and had buildings fashioned in Indigenous benab style, circular and wooden with cone-shaped, thatched roofs. A larger version of this benab served as a dining hall and kitchen on the ground floor with a meeting area upstairs.

Staff welcomed me and I was introduced to my personal guide, Milner, an older Macushi of dark complexion, sturdy build, and a ready smile. Soon we set off exploring the surrounding savannah with Milner naming birds that flew past or whose distinctive calls he identified. I watched, listened, and jotted names as per usual. We also headed into the nearby rainforest where I saw the Capuchinbird with its bald head and throat puffing out and emitting sounds like a mooing cow. The Screaming Piha then made its presence felt. It was aptly named for its startling cry, one of seven different versions according to Milner. This bird was sounding off like a wolf whistle today.

The Spix's Guan sported a distinctive red neck wattle and, though a large bird, rarely remained on the ground. I saw it swoop past over the savannah and into the rainforest as Milner called out its name. When we slipped into a small grove, he pointed out the Great Potoo, which looked like a lump on a branch that was perfect camouflage.

Yellow-rumped Caciques built dozens of nests like the drooping, woven ones that orioles make. These nests were hanging in the big tree right next to the lodge's dining area. Caciques kept up a constant flow of chatter and flitted about giving me no hope that I could capture a clear photo of any of them. Only the Great Potoo had been accommodating enough to let me take a picture. I envisioned myself telling friends, "See the bird? No? It's the bump on the branch."

Another American birding group was at Surama. We chatted over dinner of savoury Guyanese cuisine of Cookup, local vegetables, and tropical fruit. Again, there were spotting scopes and cameras with long telephoto lenses everywhere. The owners were gracious about sharing their experiences of birding in paradise. They also let me attend the birders' nightly ritual of strapping on headlamps for a tally of data. I sat to the side sipping my rum while thumbing through Peter's birding book and studying details of my day's experiences. It was a wonderful day, but the night wasn't at all pleasant.

One big mistake. I hadn't asked enough questions about my accommodations. The charming little Indigenous guest buildings were full of Americans, so I was assigned to a nondescript building at the edge of the compound. It was comfortable enough with a double bed and mosquito netting plus an adjacent bathroom. There was ample ventilation with a window about four feet square with two wooden shutters flung wide open but no screen or grill. I could see the savannah and the rainforest at the perimeter of the site.

What if a jaguar leaped through the window at night? It didn't help that a lizard high up on the wall of my room was devouring a huge dragonfly. I tossed and turned. I aimed my flashlight a couple of times at the late-night dinner scene. The dragonfly was getting smaller, and the lizard was getting bigger. Ah, well, just the way of the natural world. It was late. Guests and staff were asleep. I finally stopped tossing and let caution prevail. I closed the shutters.

Bad choice. The room got stuffy, and I awoke sweating. Just before dawn, I made a second bad decision. I took myself up to the second floor of the big benab where I'd seen hammocks hanging. It was much cooler, and I fell asleep forgetting that insects were most active not only at dusk but also before dawn. I awakened with itchy blotches on my lower abdomen and thighs. I felt too stupid to mention the situation to anyone, doubtless another in a series of mistakes.

After breakfast, my curiosity returned, and I got clear pictures of easy photographic prey on the grounds at the eco-lodge. The Black Vulture and Tropical Mockingbird were both sitting quietly on fence posts. Despite my inadequate equipment, along with the distraction of some scratching, my prize photo was a clear image of a Savannah Hawk high on a branch near the lodge.

Milner suggested a tour of the village, which I saw as a higgledy-piggledy array of scattered cement block homes and civic buildings, such as the school and health centre. There were no signs of Indigenous buildings. What I did enjoy was the arid scent of the grasslands.

We continued our hike through the rainforest to the Burro-Burro River, which would maybe provide more bird sightings. I did get a fuzzy photo of the Red-throated Caracara and was also nearly brained by a coconut. "Milner, that monkey way up there just threw a coconut and then peered over the branch to see if it got me!" I hollered when a coconut landed at my feet, and I felt my heart racing.

"Yeh, that's what they do," said Milner with a grin. "Good thing it missed." I now saw value in the colonial pith helmet instead of my floppy brimmed cotton hat.

When we reached the river, Milner said, "It's running too fast to take a boat out." We stood high on the bank, and I looked down at two men and a boy in a dugout canoe casting a net that flew out with the grace of a piece of weighted gossamer lace. The fishermen were at least ten metres below us. They knew how to handle a boat in these conditions and probably needed fish for the family's dinner.

"Come the really heavy rainy season, the river will soon be up here," said Milner, tapping my shoulder. Oh, the power of the Amazon rushing into lesser rivers and creeks that would roar onward to the Atlantic.

The author and Milner in Surama

By the time I flew out of the North Rupununi, I was stuffed with bird sightings and sounds, and entranced by life in the interior. When we winged northward from the Annai airstrip late in the day in our mechanized bird, there was another opportunity to study the country's geography. The flight schedule meant the golden hour gilded my view of the anchored freighters to the west on the wide Demerara. I took a deep breath and realized a whole new world had revealed itself to me in a mere four days.

Back in our Georgetown apartment, Caroline and I shared experiences. "The rough ride to Lethem and back was an adventure in itself," said Caroline, "but it was worth it. What a great rodeo! South American style with Indigenous people riding barefoot in stirrups."

"My scariest moment was the monkey that nearly creamed me with a coconut," I said. My other tales consisted of the birding treks, rough roads, the sheer beauty of the flights over the rainforest and savannah, and the relaxed manner and good humour of the Indigenous people.

"The best part," said Caroline, "was just time with my Guyanese friends and a chance to meet Indigenous people at the rodeo."

"For me, my best times were split between the people I met and the birds that I saw and heard. Oh, and sharing a boat ride with a sloth. My guide asked me to send the photo. It was her first experience of a sloth swimming."

With holidays over, it was back to city life. Caroline needed to wrap up her assignment. She was rushing to finish and deliver her report, say goodbye to numerous friends, and make final decisions about what to pack and what to pitch. I told her to get on with her day. "My farewell gift to you is hanging out all your wet laundry, including your undies. I'll also take care of the stuff to be pitched after you leave."

"You're the best roomie ever!" said Caroline as she grabbed her bag and headed out the door for last-minute tasks. I smiled a goodbye and then went back to scratching my belly. Darn those bug bites!

Chapter Four

Through the Soles of My Sandals

Scratch, scratch. The itching got worse on my belly and thighs. Why hadn't I remembered more about life in other Caribbean situations? I just didn't connect the savannah of the North Rupununi with previous sun, sea, and sand places that I'd experienced. I studied the blotchy red bumps with little pustules on top. I was definitely not in bikini-mode but knew that help was available.

During Cuso's initial week of in-country training, we'd been introduced to a local doctor who specialized in tropical medicine. Feeling invaded, I called for an appointment. The doctor was visiting outlying clinics, but I could meet his son, a medical student nearing graduation. Better than nothing.

The faded shingle tacked to the front wall declared the doctor's name and looked even less reassuring than when we trainees had visited three weeks prior. I dodged the puddle and dog poop and entered the reception area. A large lad with dark, wavy hair and kind eyes greeted me in a space that looked just as I remembered it, the first stop in a warehouse.

"Good day. My name is Dwayne." I consoled myself that at least he was bound to know more about what plagued me than I did. I scratched my navel and hoped the itch wasn't some tropical weevil in burrowing mode. "For an examination, we should have a lady attendant present," said Dwayne with reddening cheeks.

"I'm desperate with all these Rupununi blotches. Do I look like somebody who can't take care of myself if I don't like the situation?"

The good fellow turned a deeper shade of red and led me into an examining room with splotchy whitewash on walls that reached only three-quarters of the way to the ceiling. As I hopped up onto the examining table, I looked over into what resembled a long-forgotten warehouse filled with dusty, indescribable objects.

"Do you have a sample area that I can examine?"

"I can do belly, thigh, or calf."

"Calf," squeaked this sweet young man.

"Belly is better, or worse, as there may be infection." I whipped up my blouse and lowered my slacks with an elastic waistband. Then I rolled down my undies enough to expose my postmenopausal flesh with the raspberry-coloured marks the size of thumb prints.

"Hmm," he said as he regained his composure and gathered interest in my mottled blotches. He snapped on a second latex glove and said, "No streaks, so no infection. Any pain?"

"Nope. Just don't like what I'm seeing and feeling." Now my rookie medical man was getting more interested in the various spots elsewhere on my cushion-like belly and the new manifestation on my calf.

"All slightly liquid-filled. Probably bug bites but I'll check with the doctor." Yes, bug bites. He agreed with my diagnosis.

I was the only patient with others apparently aware that Dr. Dad was unavailable. I waited for the results of the phone call and gently rubbed a couple of itchy spots on my thigh. I looked around and decided that even a warehouse office or supply room would be better equipped. Everything here looked and smelled like a thrift store reject. I then readjusted my thinking and decided maybe money for office décor was used to fund trips to clinics in other areas.

Finally, my now more confident examiner stepped out of the back room with a container of pills and a tube of cream. "Take this medication for a week and use the cortisone cream daily," he said handing over my treatment supplies and an invoice for a modest sum.

"Do call in two days to let us know how you're doing," he said with a smile of accomplishment.

"Much appreciated. Oh, and you might want to deal with the dog poop out front. Bad for business."

Later, I learned various names for the bug, none of which Dwayne used: sand fly, biting midge, no-see-um. There were no-see-ums in the Bahamas. The pesky little insects liked sandy soil, but my previous encounters with them had been on beaches. Then I remembered that Surama Eco-Lodge had sandy soil. That explained the insect attack during my ill-chosen morning move to the hammock. No-see-ums can get through multiple layers of clothing and always head for the juiciest parts. I settled on sand fly to name the source of my Surama misadventure.

With the aid of the tablets and cream, I was soon back to full health and bikini ready. However, no beaches in Guyana, just sand mixed with gravel at the edge of a coffee-with-cream Atlantic.

With Caroline gone and my work on strategic planning coming along, the delight of birding in the interior gave me increased interest and confidence in identifying birds in the city. My most common visitors were pairs of kiskadees that flitted around daily with their black, white, and bright yellow plumage. Much of their shrill kis-ka-dee calling was pairs keeping track of each other. My birding book identified them as the Great Kiskadee and the Lesser Kiskadee, smaller in body and with a long, thin bill. Unless I saw them together, I couldn't distinguish them and simply noted them as kiskadee. Such was the level of my bird identification skill.

I had fulfilled my promise and returned Peter's book after the North Rupununi visit while sharing highlights of the trip. I then ordered a copy of Restall's book online through the ubiquitous Amazon.com and paid the customs duty. The book helped identify even more birds that I met daily. The Striated Heron was a common bird near the city's grid of canals and ditches that guided rainy season downpours out of the city to the ocean. I called it the no-neck bird as it was always hunkered down by water's edge with a slackened neck seeking prey.

The Little Egret, tall and slender with white feathers, was also a common sight. Nonbreeding birds sported dark gray beaks and legs with bright yellow feet. During breeding season, their feet were red. Could I keep all these features straight without referring to my photos and the birding book? No. Never.

I honoured birdwatching, as in regular birding surveys, as one way of gauging the health of the environment. It was easier and more pleasant than monitoring, for example, earthworms. However, I wasn't devoted enough to get anywhere near the obsessive level of the UK's Mad Hatter of birdwatching. If a rare bird was spotted, the eager birder—nicknamed a twitcher—would dash off. Even a glimpse of the bird would bring great satisfaction and its name would be added to the birder's life list of sightings. This wasn't me.

Vanessa and local girls in the wetlands

Vanessa, my Cuso program manager, had noted my interest in birding. She was a stately, wise woman of Afro-Guyanese heritage with an ability to burst into full-throated, uplifting laughter even when we were faced with difficult situations. I enjoyed working under her direction and respected her handling of Cuso operations.

There was an incident much later in my Cuso career in Indigenous territories when this adventuresome person even accepted a questionable ride wearing white pants. It was a dugout canoe at low tide and produced predictable results.

What was Cuso International? It began at a time when the Western world had recovered enough from the Second World War to become interested in international development in what was initially called the Third World. Western countries considered themselves the First World and the Communist USSR was the implied Second World during the Cold War.

In 1961, a consortium of older NGOs, which started in the 1950s, came together to form the Canadian University Service Overseas, or CUSO. This new NGO recruited volunteers for two years to engage in aid work abroad. The US established a similar organization, the Peace Corps, in the same year.

By 1981, Cuso International simply became a brand name with only the first letter capitalized and no longer an acronym. The NGO wanted a broader base for recruitment where citizens of all ages could become involved for varying periods of time. Types of involvement expanded for assignments in what was now called the Global South.

Guyana had been involved with Cuso since 1962. The continuing call for volunteers to fill specific placement requirements and then finding suitable candidates was an ongoing and challenging process. Volunteers arrived and departed at various times. This meant that the initial week of in-country orientation was on an ad hoc basis involving staff, guest presenters, and various current volunteers.

At one point, an internal issue at VYC got in the way of my taking the next step, which was to conduct a staff meeting for input. With my work on the strategic plan paused, Vanessa redirected my efforts until the matter was settled. "You walk the city regularly. Can you share some of your favourite places and encourage new volunteers to explore?"

"Sure," I said thinking about my regular forays into the city. "I can prepare a walking guide. It can be a variation of the blog that I post online." I was happy to help because I found the heart of Georgetown one of the easiest cities to explore of any that I'd experienced in the Caribbean. It was a relatively small mixture of urban downtown and residential life that captivated me in my daylight walkabouts in select areas.

"Good," said Vanessa. "A guide based on your recent experiences might give new volunteers confidence in exploring Georgetown and enjoying Guyanese life more quickly."

The guide was easy to construct using elements of my blog, *Kindred in Guyana.* I also expanded the guide as I conjured responses to common questions about Georgetown and added photos with a few chatty comments. I didn't mind taking on the role of a tour guide if it would help improve Cuso's overall effectiveness.

Demerara louvres

"*What are the top things to do?* Get the city's tourist map and start walking. Savour the classic clapboard homes with intricate wooden fretwork and the Demerara louvres that provide shade and breeze. Note the good old bones of Georgetown houses, though many are now decrepit. Enjoy the vegetation everywhere that celebrates tropical life. Chat with the locals. For a glimpse into the lives of the nine tribes of

Indigenous people of the region, the Walter Roth Museum is worth a visit to view artifacts of Amerindian life. Visit the markets and plunge into the bustle and the abundance of Guyana's agricultural produce.

"*How should I get around?* The city is relatively small and can be walked east to west from Sheriff Street to Water Street in an hour and north to south from the seawall to Brickdam Street in about the same time. I recommend learning the soul of the city through the soles of your sandals or shoes. Explore various neighbourhoods and downtown areas in the daytime. For me, it's using what I call my see legs for strolling and photography. People are friendly and helpful and there's much to enjoy in Georgetown's natural and human-made environment."

I also included practical advice about getting around. Transportation was a key issue as we navigated our way about the city for work and pleasure. If a minibus travelled at a reasonable speed and lacked a frills-n-thrills paint job, that probably meant a crew without buccaneer traits. A minibus only cost GYD60 or thirty cents Canadian, and a taxi was GYD400 or two dollars Canadian.

I could recommend minibus travel since I'd overcome my own fear of entrusting my life to possible madmen. The day had come when I'd decided to tackle what I considered a transportation improvement project that related to terror on the tarmac. Drivers were rightly reputed to be maniacal, especially out of the city on the open roads between settlements. A relative of my landlady had lost a thumb in a minibus rollover and now lived with a toe stitched in place of the missing digit. Vanessa had encouraged me to try a bus coming from the East Coast area with a pickup point a block from the Cuso office.

I'd figured that once drivers reached the city, they couldn't gain a full head of steam that could lead to dismemberment or death. I'd try a short trip applying the so-called carrot to address sullen drivers, surly touts or conductors, plus loud music and reckless driving. My first effort was taking a minibus from near the seawall and aiming for a common downtown destination. I waited in the dust by the roadside with traffic zooming by. A minibus veered to the side lane and screeched to a stop in front of me.

It didn't have the dreaded wild paint job of tiger stripes or shooting stars, so I might survive the trip. The conductor slid the side door open and jumped out. I leaped in and was scrunched between him and a woman clutching her large handbag as though it was about to escape.

The conductor slammed the door and the bus roared on. I pulled out a map of downtown and leaned against the fellow, a muscular young man with a handsome profile and fierce frown. "Where do I get off for the library?" He looked at me sideways and glanced at the map. I soon realized that he couldn't read a map as I pointed to the location of the library.

Jazzy paint job signals the ride to come

"I'll tell you where to get down," he said, again looking straight ahead. When we neared the spot, the conductor cued the driver with a curt knock on the side window, then slid the door open and jumped out.

"Thanks, you've been a good teacher," I said as I handed him double the fare. He started making change, but I waved it aside. "I pay double for a safe ride and, driver, thanks for the good music." The driver turned and grinned and the conductor gave me half a smile. I was gushing, but it worked.

The conductor then pointed and said, "There's the street that'll take you where you wanna go. Now be careful, ma'am."

"Thanks, I will," I said as I headed in the prescribed direction, and the bus roared away. I continued the practice of occasional minibus rides with doubled fares and found that responses included more smiles and startled thanks. Sometimes I was assisted as I exited the vehicle, even helped with handling my heavy market bag if it was Saturday. Carrot diplomacy worked.

The issue of safety continued looming large with Cuso headquarters in Ottawa even sending a trainer to host a day-long conference on security. Independence in 1966, along with interference by the US CIA because of the new country's socialist leanings, had heightened racial and ethnic discord between Afro-Guyanese and Indo-Guyanese. These tensions continued to affect the country's ability to deal with not only its political but also its economic and social challenges.

An estimated eighty percent of the country's population of 780,000 lived in and around Georgetown. The Guyanese diaspora were scattered all over the world, especially in English-speaking countries. They had left years or even decades earlier in fear, anger, disgust, hope of a better life, or any number of other reasons. It was estimated that over a million people of Guyanese ancestry had left the country since independence. The number of those born matched the number of those who continued to depart. Guyana was a no-growth country.

My experience, on a day-to-day basis during daylight hours, was that Georgetown was just another busy city with people who hustled around taking care of business. The seawall to the north was relatively safe but only in the daytime and in the company of others. Homes and businesses were often heavily barricaded with fences, grills on windows and doors, and security systems. This was a better situation than I'd experienced in other Caribbean countries. My first Cuso experience forty years prior was a time when many homes in Kingston, Jamaica had what were called rape gates between the common living spaces and the bedrooms.

Present conditions are often rooted deep in the past. I started reading colonial history more deeply looking for answers. The name Guyana was an Amerindian word for "land of many waters." In 1499, Alonso de Ojeda's expedition from Spain found the mouth of the

Essequibo River but didn't settle the area. The British did further exploration during the reign of Queen Elizabeth I in the late-sixteenth century. She sent one of her favourites, Sir Walter Raleigh, to assess this enticing land of possibility. He wrote a book entitled *The Discoverie of the Large, Rich and Bewtiful Empyre of Guiana.* Raleigh boasted of El Dorado, "a city of gold," to woo other adventurers. The infamous Age of Exploration and exploitation was underway in this new and promising land. I too was coming for exploration but also to render practical assistance—not a consideration of many early visitors who quested for wealth or the saving of souls.

The Spanish, Portuguese, French, Dutch, Danish, and British all jockeyed for power in the New World. The British slave trade from Africa started in the mid-sixteenth century and ended early in the nineteenth century. The peak years for the slave trade in the British West Indies were from the 1700s to the 1830s when it was finally abolished in the Caribbean. The so-called apprenticeship period in the colonies with freed slaves paid low or no wages ended later in the same decade.

Then began another chapter of Guyana's labour history, shared with Trinidad and Tobago and other islands to the north. India was part of the British Empire, so East Indians were brought to these colonies as indentured labourers for a set period. They fared only slightly better than slaves because they were allowed to retain more of their languages, religious beliefs, and overall culture. All these aspects of life had been beaten out of slaves or driven underground in the centuries when they were forced to build colonial prosperity. The Europeans, including the Portuguese from Madeira, the Chinese, and the Brazilians in the southern part of Guyana, also laboured to develop the country into what it is today.

I've always been intrigued by the concept of taproot. The dominant root of certain plants, such as carrots, that embeds them deep into the earth is the taproot. This organic metaphor describes people's often strong attachment to their homeland and sometimes provides insights into the way contemporary lives are conducted.

In Guyana, the taproots of the two major groups of those transported, Afro-Guyanese and Indo-Guyanese, are fiercely protected in various cultural practices and political parties. Neither group knows exactly where their roots were in Africa or India—what tribe, what state—but they are proud of their respective heritages. Despite hundreds of years in the New World, the element of taproot remains a significant feature of Guyanese life. Those with the deepest taproot are the nine tribes of the Indigenous people. Guyanese celebrations reflect the pride of all these segments of its society.

Another aspect of taproot is the design and construction practices of the country's past. Guyana, as part of the Caribbean world, has no Mayan pyramids. There's no Machu Picchu. Historic architecture in Guyana only dates to a few eighteenth-century Dutch buildings and Georgetown filled with an array of British colonial buildings, fashioned for the tropics, dating from the nineteenth and twentieth centuries. Some ancient Indigenous design elements exist, but the original buildings have long since rotted or burned. Wood, bamboo, and thatch don't last in tropical conditions. Then, of course, there's the ubiquitous modern architecture of the West also in Guyana. Buildings have their own stories to tell.

Chapter Five

Life on the Coastal Floodplains

I strolled by a classic clapboard home in fine repair with handmade wooden fretwork or cutwork at the eaves and a sparkling exterior in pale yellow with white trim. Amid cascading bougainvillea blossoms near the veranda, I noticed an elderly homeowner clipping dead branches. "Your flowering bushes are wonderful! I so enjoy that orange variety you're tending."

He paused and straightened up with his clippers at rest. "Why thank you, ma'am. My wife loves flowers but can't do gardening or get around much anymore, so I keep them in nice shape. She likes to look out the window at them. It makes a happier day for her." He then reached up to snap a dead branch.

"Thank you. You've also made a happier day for me too." I waved farewell and he nodded and returned to his yardwork.

Just as birding sensitized me to the country's natural world, buildings, especially homes, and opportunities to talk with people gave me insight into ways of living in the built environment, whether by choice or necessity.

This modest and stately home was part of Guyana's architectural heritage that dated from the early-nineteenth century. The jockeying for possession between the Dutch and English colonies had finally been settled. The British stayed and called the area British Guiana, which became the only English-speaking country in South America. The Dutch moved to similar territory to the east and called it Dutch Guiana and then Suriname.

The early Dutch colonists had established plantations along riverbanks, but the British preferred the Atlantic coast. This was the coastal floodplains—marshland—and starting in 1855, prison labour was used in building what became a seawall running for 280 miles. The capital city, Georgetown, was named for Britain's King George III. He was the same so-called mad King George at the time of the American Revolution.

Koker sluice gate on the East Coast

Both the city and the plantations were laid out in a grid pattern with canals and *kokers*, the Dutch term for gravity-operated sluice gates. At low tide, the system provided drainage to the ocean. This made the coastal lowlands habitable and agriculture possible even after the rainy season. However, Guyana has always had challenges maintaining this initial infrastructure.

I observed some of the country's earliest Dutch colonial architecture on a day trip to Fort Island, which is south on the Demerara River. An eighteenth-century brick church remains a solid structure with hardwood doors, heavy wooden shutters, and well-crafted wrought iron hinges and clasps. Nearby, remnants of a fort in stone and brick were a reminder of the battles between colonial powers. Fort Island was a testament to good design, capable craftsmanship, and diligent maintenance.

Colonial tropical architecture dominated Georgetown for the next century and a half. The two-storey Georgian houses with pitched roofs—two sides sloping down from a central ridge—were common as town houses and perhaps businesses for wealthier citizens.

How to keep cool was always a concern for settlers. The early colonists laid out the city with wide streets, especially those running north to south, to allow the flow of cool air from the Atlantic. A distinctive feature of this architecture was the Demerara shutter. This louvred frame of slatted panels hinged at the top was held ajar with a pole or long hook at the bottom. On more expensive homes, there were often ornate, perforated triangular side panels for greater privacy without blocking breezes from the Atlantic. A Guyanese friend told me, "Before air conditioning, the wide ledge at the bottom held a block of ice. When I was a little boy, icemen came regularly to deliver new blocks."

Jalousie wall inserts were cheaper and were made of slatted pine panels built into some of the outer walls between the studs, dimming sunlight and providing ventilation. Later, screening behind the panels blocked insects. Sash windows, with vertically sliding glass panes, were often whitewashed with thin paint to decrease heat and glare.

Verandas provided shaded social space and sometimes ran the full length of one or two exterior walls. If enclosed later with jalousies and sash windows, they were called galleries and provided more private living space. Skilled carpenters provided carved pine trim on eaves and porches, verandas and galleries. This was called fretwork, cutwork, or carpenter gothic. It was as delightful as any Victorian maker of lace crafting delicate cuffs or collars for clothing.

Settlers from Europe knew that the mighty Atlantic had to be kept in check if they were to colonize this fragile area where river and ocean waters mixed. Guyana's coastal plains are now approximately twenty-five percent shielded by the centuries-old seawall. Mangroves, the small trees and shrubs that thrive in the ebb and flow of tides, protect sixty percent of the coastline. Natural sandbars provide a buffer for the final fifteen percent.

Now all barriers are under stress with oceans rising. The seawall—five to six feet high—is weakened by sheer age despite fix-up patches of stone and concrete. The mangroves can't migrate inland because of coastal development. The sandbars are eroded or overrun by the higher ocean.

Flood protection had been provided by building some homes anywhere from eight to fourteen feet above ground level. Initially, this was done with brick pillars from repurposed bricks used as ships' ballast. Later, locally made bricks were used. Now it was concrete blocks or poured cement pillars. Sometimes the columns were sturdy wooden posts. The height also provided more breeze and distance from the damp ground that breeds mosquitoes.

Buildings, whether maintained or derelict, were blessed with the flora of the region that made even modest places look spectacular. Palms of many species filled the city with their textured trunks and lush foliage. Crotons showed off dark green leaves flashing various striped combinations of pink, red, orange, or yellow. Flamboyant trees provided a brilliant display of vivid red-orange flowers. The gossamer-blossomed bougainvillea sprouted everywhere with stunning variations of colour, the orange my favourite.

I meandered through neighbourhoods and enjoyed houses that displayed thoughtful evolution in design. A tiny pink home was the first that I photographed on my initial stroll. It was a tidy summation in perfect trim of some of the best features of Georgetown working class houses. It had started out as a simple house that rested on concrete pillars with a rectangular footprint and a standard pitched roof.

The front porch was later enclosed with windows that created a habitable gallery. Three extensions had been added at the rear of the house. The first two were enclosed and the last was a porch with latticework screening at the back. Under that porch was an area enclosed with concrete block. I guessed that it was for storage because there were no windows, and it probably would be emptied if flooding occurred.

The little pink house

Though the house was obviously built in stages, the pink paint united the overall structure. White trim harmonized each of the varied window styles. The overall effect was of a house that had evolved as need arose and money was available.

On one of my residential walkabouts, I turned onto a new street and saw a tall, narrow house squeezed onto a small lot. It was very close to an imposing commercial building on the corner. There was a steep, red-carpeted stairway leading up to a bright red front door. It almost looked like a single-wide manufactured home of North American design hoisted up on sturdy concrete pillars. The overall effect was of a snug building whose owners had cleverly used a scrap of land to make a home.

Several classic homes in Georgetown, whether inhabited or derelict, had a square tower at one corner of the front with windows on each side. Originally, I thought this might be a feature of a rural plantation owner's home as a lookout over fields. Later, I discovered that I was only partially right. A lookout tower was also a common design element of an urban home so that owners of ships could watch river traffic on the Demerara.

On one excursion, I spotted the framework of an old house with the watch tower. The house was an empty shell with no roof, floors, windows, or doors. This well-proportioned dwelling was down to its structural bare bones and taken over with vines and weeds, mold and dry rot. When human beings vacate, scavengers arrive, and nature returns.

I continued searching for ways to experience life beyond the busyness of Georgetown. A couple of months into my assignment, I heard about a rustic resort just an hour south of the city. Minibuses serviced the route, but I knew that the freedom of the open road would unleash terrifying driving. I booked a weekend visit with a taxi ride figuring that the fare would be a lifesaving investment.

The resort was a homemade oasis in an area that was originally rainforest. Colonial work crews had cleared the land for plantations. Now everything was scrub brush with a rutted dirt road that led to this eccentric gathering place. The dining area was roofed, but there were no walls. Central seating was around a massive, cobbled together high table with splashes of bright colour and an array of high benches and stools.

Guests were invited to perch, share in the group conversation, and savour homemade food and wine. Wooden benches and lounge chairs of repurposed tires sliced, reconfigured, and painted bright yellow were around the edge of the gathering area. The whole place had the comfort level of a beloved old slipper. People could relax and lime and gaff—gather and gab—in traditional Guyanese fashion.

Tucked into the nearby scrub forest was a cluster of whimsical, two-storey cabins. They were elevated three steps high on four-by-four wooden posts. Wooden walls were chest-high with wrap-around screening above providing ventilation and protection from insects. Corrugated metal roofs and awnings on the lower storey provided rain protection. Each cabin was equipped with a double bed with mosquito netting plus a nightstand. The simplicity of the place appealed to the backpacker in me.

Another feature of this rustic resort showed Guyanese ingenuity in the face of reality. Despite its Caribbean culture, Guyana has an unattractive, unwelcoming Atlantic coastline. Without the beauty of the Caribbean islands dotting a turquoise sea, the Guyanese divert some of their rivers and creeks making shallow ponds as swimming holes in outlying areas. These were called blackwater ponds.

A boardwalk from the gathering area led to the pond and widened to a deck with wooden benches and lounge chairs. A canopy was rigged with inviting hammocks slung between posts. Wide wooden steps led down into the small pond.

I slipped into the welcoming water warmed by the sun. I paddled around with the embrace of palm trees and other tropical vegetation at water's edge. My toes delighted in the squishy, fallen leaves when I stood up in water reaching my shoulders. When I finally climbed partly back up the steps, I was aghast to see my submerged feet and legs bright reddish orange underwater.

A Guyanese fellow bather laughed and said, "Don't worry, you're not stained. It's the tannins from the decayed leaves in the water. Quite medicinal, they say."

I giggled with relief. "Very glad to hear it. I thought maybe I'd acquired some new tropical disease." An oddity of this reconfiguring of the natural flow of water and the marination of tropical vegetation was that skin, light or dark, glowed the same reddish orange when dipped even six inches below the surface.

Now cooled, I ambled back to the gathering area for vegetarian Cookup in a calabash bowl, which is the hard shell of a plant also called a bottle gourd. I accepted a sample of homemade wine when the host handed me a small glass and said, "Here, try this."

I sipped gingerly. "Interesting. What's it made of?"

"Aubergine," he said with sleepy eyes.

"Eggplant! As good as a grape," I said and extended my glass for a refill.

In this minimalist resort of quirky design and construction, I studied and photographed a pair of caged Blue-and-yellow Macaws, or parrots, who roosted as true lovebirds. This was my first close look at some of Guyana's iconic great birds. I noted their bright yellow breasts and dark blue feathers on their back and wings. Their tails were a mixture of the two colours, and a splash of green capped their heads. The faces of the macaws were white with distinct black lines, and they also sported black throats and beaks. Lovely great birds.

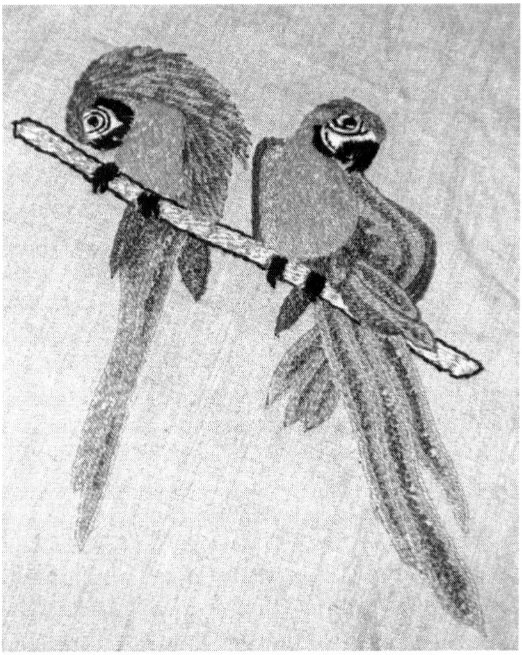

Embroidered macaws

I photographed the pair's various poses with a distinct purpose in mind—embroidery. Just as my walkabouts helped me learn a place through my feet, handwork helped me record and absorb a place through my hands.

While I was still in Canada before my departure, I'd rummaged through my interest inventory for at least one pleasant handcraft that I already knew. Fibre arts were always my go-to relief from reading and wordsmithing and could provide hands-on activity for what Cuso said might be many evenings at home alone.

I opted for embroidery, something my mother had taught me. She was born in a sod house on the Saskatchewan prairies. When she was a little girl, her mother taught her to use a cork-lined metal hoop with a spring adjustment to do embroidery. When I was preparing for

Guyana, I'd found a similar hoop in an antique store in a neighbouring community. I also stocked up with an array of embroidery floss and thought of imagined projects as thread therapy. Handwork would ease the strain of headwork.

What to embroider? I'd also thought about that while back in Canada. When observing the pair of macaws, I'd decided to stitch them onto a precut vest front in raw linen that I'd brought. I used my favourite photo of these macaws to immortalize them on this panel. My enjoyment of embroidery, one of women's devalued handcrafts and a word often used with a sneer by non-handcrafters, especially men, kept me occupied for hours.

Embroidered travel vest

I'd also packed my now-faded old denim birding vest that was made in India. It had numerous pockets that were useful during my outings. Early in my posting, I'd noted the two-inch-by-two-inch checkerboard pattern stitched on the back of this cherished garment. Living in Georgetown at home most evenings, I'd decided on tiny embroidery efforts on that grid. I'd started with a Guyanese flower here and a bird there. I then added more local flowers, birds, and animals. With my bird sightings increasing, I gave the Hoatzin central placement on the vest. It was Guyana's multi-hued national bird whose wildly plumed head looked as though its beak had been stuck into an electrical socket.

With birding and fibre arts the staples in my life while off duty in Guyana, buildings continued to charm as well as sadden me. Architectural evolution is inevitable. The country's traditional building materials such as wood, stone, and brick were becoming less abundant. Glass, concrete, and steel have dominated architecture globally, especially after the Second World War. Buildings from the 1950s onward in Guyana demonstrated that the technology and mastery of concrete construction was still in its infancy. Finishes were often discoloured and flaking despite attempts at maintenance. Commercial buildings also shared the cookie-cutter look of modernity. Vernacular or local architecture with Guyanese materials wasn't dominant. Modern buildings had little or no link to place.

Much modern construction in Georgetown disregarded over two centuries of thoughtful design for the climate and culture. Windows of many modern buildings were fixed casements, not openable. That meant air conditioning, the costliest item in building operations, was required. The siting of many buildings with huge windows ignored the effect of the sun and the natural flow of ocean breezes. Popular flat roofs increased interior temperatures and tended to leak during the rainy season.

I was further saddened by Guyana's far too many inhabited shacks. Unpainted siding and drooping shutters were common on wobbly structures. Rotting staircases with missing boards and broken handrails were often the only way to get to traditional homes raised above ground level. In some neighbourhoods, it appeared that every other house was destined to crumble with the next bout of torrential rain or slamming of a door.

Current domestic and civic architecture ranged from top shape to toppling. Buildings were often framed with solid local hardwood such as greenheart. Cladding and wall partitions were built of cheaper, lighter pine from North America, and prone to rot and insect invasion. Styles for large public buildings, such as churches and civic institutions, included a wild array of Gothic, Tudor, Romanesque, and Italian Renaissance design.

City Hall had been constructed in the late nineteenth century with the Victorian zest for excess in cobbling together design elements. It was in sad condition with little motivation or money for repair and maintenance. A half-hearted call for bids on restoration quoted one contractor who said, "Ninety percent of the wood could be reused for repair."

Ha! There's a technical term called metal fatigue, which makes some metal judged as worn out and unusable for other projects that require strength. There's also something equivalent in wood that we should call wood fatigue. I took photographs of the dry rot, insect damage, lack of paint, and sheer disintegration of this grand old hulk. It was probably best served by demolition if new timber and other critical elements of construction weren't going to be used by competent contractors.

My greatest sadness came from knowing that all this wreckage of residential and civic structures didn't have to happen. Decades of political, economic, and social turmoil had caused and still causes citizens to abandon Guyana and let the infrastructure, buildings, and vibrancy of Guyanese life crumble.

When I nudged myself out of despondent thoughts about Guyana's architectural history, I remembered there was another distinct method of building that I wasn't seeing. Classic Indigenous homes of wood, bamboo, palm thatching, and sometimes local brick existed in villages. I was missing examples of heritage architecture from the Amerindian tradition.

Meanwhile, an opportunity to study current residential architecture of the country was announced in the newspapers as a Housing Expo. I arranged for my favourite taximan, Linton, to collect me so that the two of us could attend the government's weekend exhibition of affordable housing. I told him, "I'll need a half day of your time and will pay what you'd expect to earn. We'll be heading to the old cane plantation area."

When he arrived, I climbed into the front seat and said, "On to Perseverance!"

"Right away," said Linton who was a cheerful and solidly built Afro-Guyanese and one of Cuso's favourite drivers. I loved his hearty laugh and willingness to talk about some of the nuts and bolts of everyday Guyanese life.

"How's your Cookup coming?" he asked.

"Better with each batch. And how's your daughter liking school?"

"She's doing well and really likes her teacher this year."

Continuing our conversation about this-n-that, we followed the main road south through thickly populated areas and on to Georgetown's industrial sector with factories, warehouses, and dockyards. We turned at a road leading toward now defunct sugar plantations.

Fanciful names abounded in Guyana from the days when colonial settlements thrived. I remembered names from other trips outside the city: Hope and Success, Land of Promise, Try Best, Bounty Hall, and Health Field. All spoke of the dreams of past plantation owners. Now so many of these sites all over Guyana were fallow or sprouted scattered concrete houses in various stages of construction.

When we approached an elaborate archway with a big sign saying Housing Expo, I noted a pair of houses nearby that weren't part of the exhibit. Each characterized a response to climate change. I imagined that the single-storey house on a concrete pad, called slab-on-grade in construction parlance, was the home of climate change deniers. Next to it was the home of believers in climate change, with concrete piers that lifted the home's living area roughly four metres above ground level. "That's what I call a pantlegs-up house," I said as Linton looked at me with a question in his eyes.

"You mean if there's a flood?" he asked. I nodded and Linton took a few steps closer to the house. "Those high houses make good sense," he said. "In 2005, I lived outside Georgetown on the East Coast beyond the old seawall. It was rainy season and the canals in the fields were flooded. The *kokers* wouldn't work at high tide." Linton was nearly six feet tall, and he pointed to his chest. "The water was up to here on me." I looked at him in amazement. Here was an example of what I'd heard about failure of those kokers and how precarious life was on the coastal floodplains.

As we walked on into the exhibit area, I thought the government was doing well in creating space for private developers to showcase their ideas for homes. Contractors had built several models, single-family houses and duplexes, with some in both wood and concrete. They were placed side by side for people to visit and compare. We evaluated the merits of everything we visited. One pair of modest houses high up on pillars with traditional pitched roofs and their own little covered entrance turned out to be our mutual favourite.

"Linton, why do you like this house?"

"The wood one is friendlier. And it's bigger with the wood on the outside of the frame of two-by-fours."

"Yup, I like the wood one for exactly for the same reasons."

While we strolled through the exhibit, I told Linton some details about concrete. "Making cement creates nearly eight percent of CO_2 emissions globally. This makes concrete second only to all fossil fuels like coal, gas, and oil for emissions. And it can't be reused."

"What about all the junked concrete we see around?" asked Linton. "We use some of it to fix the seawall."

I laid on some more facts while we strolled through the exhibit. "Waste concrete is as much as a quarter of landfill materials. It can only be used like you said: rough fill. If you add up all the carbon emissions from getting materials for concrete and add the manufacturing, transportation, construction, emissions from the buildings, and then maybe disposal of everything eventually as junk, buildings create more than a third of CO_2 emissions globally." At that point, we both stopped walking and looked around at all the concrete in the buildings on display.

Linton looked at me and said, "All those big houses we saw getting built in the old cane fields when we drove here, they're all concrete." I nodded and we continued walking.

The Perseverance area also displayed the last government's housing scheme, which was hundreds of tract homes on long stretches of straight streets. All were small, one-storey, slab-on-grade look-alikes.

Most were empty. From a distance, I guessed them to be made of concrete blocks with a stucco overlay.

Linton said, "Too expensive and built bad. People won't buy them."

I also noted that the location was miles from anywhere and demanded gas-operated vehicles for everything such as school, work, shopping, and recreation. That meant people were left to rely on their own vehicles, taxis, or madcap minibus rides.

With rows of empty houses, the current government had declared itself out of the housing business. These new models were designed and to be built by private developers. I couldn't determine at the time how the Housing Expo scheme was going to proceed. Would Guyana be any more successful in housing its citizens than any of the other countries in both the Global South and the Global North?

When Linton dropped me off at home, I switched off thinking about the Housing Expo and made my shopping list for Saturday. There was comfort food, but there was also just comfort in marketing for food. I found more stress relief in the latter. I was now chatting with vendors more freely and gathering information and cooking tips.

"Can you give me a papaya for eating now and show me a good pineapple for eating later this week?" I asked one vendor.

"Here's the papaya you want. Press here on the pineapple. Hard, yes? It'll be soft and tender come the end of the week, just when you want its sweetness," said a smiling market lady with a flowered blouse, plaid skirt, and an apron with polka dots.

Soon my sturdy bag held provisions with comforting scents. A cucumber rested next to an aubergine along with eddo root, onions, fresh mangoes, and other luscious produce. The kaleidoscopic colours and distinct fragrances gave promise of a week of tasty eating.

For my usual Saturday treat, I lugged my marketing treasures a block away to House of Flavours and chatted with Captain. I ordered a large calabash bowl filled with my usual order of his steaming Rastafarian vegetarian ital food. I knew that in Rastafari vocabulary, the word ital came from the English word "vital" with the "v" removed. Ital meant the unity of the speaker, the I, with the natural world. Ital food was to increase liveliness. I also knew this plant-based diet had been influenced by observance of the food habits of Indian indentured labourers in Jamaica where Rastafarianism began.

I inhaled the siren scent of today's half dozen curry sauces. "Good as ever, Captain." Each stainless steel container shared its pizzazz with scents of cumin and coriander, cloves and garlic, and other spices that set my nostrils aquiver. Captain spread a dollop of each curry onto a bed of steaming rice and returned my calabash bowl.

"How's Caroline?"

"Fine. She's finished training and has a new assignment in Zambia. And I'm practising those cooking tips you taught her that she shared with me."

"Some dahl on the side?" he asked with a twinkle in his eye.

"Sure," I said, and he added a sauce of red lentils with garlic and ginger root to my curry potpourri.

"Happy to please," said Captain with a grin.

I sat and cradled the bowl in both hands raising it to my nose and inhaled the pungent aroma. Yum. I dipped my spoon into the aubergine and tomato curry with the strong scent of cloves and let the sauce flow over my tongue while my eyelids drooped to half-closed in satisfaction. Then I tucked my spoon into the rice and munched chopped bora with a hint of cinnamon for another flavoursome mouthful.

I watched men with long natty dreadlocks chat with Captain and order similar meals. We all sat at flimsy aluminum tables with matching chairs and stared at the featured film *de jour*. Besides his ital food, Captain sold DVD action films.

I savoured each morsel, returned my calabash bowl with my usual "Till next week" and hefted my market bag. Now to work my way through the crowds on Regent Street to reach the minibus stop.

Then I heard a woman's voice ordering a bowl of the same Rasta ital fare that I'd ordered. I pivoted and saw a tall young woman with golden brown complexion and short Rasta dreadlocks. When she settled herself at a nearby table with her calabash bowl, I paused and then—out of character—said, "Excuse me, I'm living here in Guyana. I'm just curious. I can't place your accent."

She looked up with her spoon in hand and said, "Oh, I'm a visitor from Vancouver in Canada."

"BC! I'm from Penticton," I declared. Then, again acting out of character, I asked, "May I join you for a moment?"

"Please, have a seat," she said and motioned to a nearby chair. Captain glanced our way with interest as he filled another customer's order. Serendipity was underway.

I learned that she was visiting Guyana for the first time. She was on holiday with her father, aunt, and uncle who were all born and raised in Guyana. Lydia's relatives were part of the diaspora. "I've heard stories about this place all my life, and now I'm experiencing it for myself." She spoke with a smile of pure joy.

When we continued sharing backgrounds, she said, "It's Guyana's agriculture that really interests me. I've worked in urban agriculture in Vancouver and been a wwoofer in Hawaii for a couple of months."

"I know about wwoofers but always forget the full name," I said as I tapped the table.

"World Wide Opportunities on Organic Farms," Lydia replied. "I really want to work more in organic tropical agriculture."

"That's it. I know a former wwoofer from Germany at our city's farmers' market. What a great opportunity to gain basic skills," I said as I eyed her and conjured a plan.

Sometimes part of one's placement assignment is detecting need for a person with another skill set. I told Lydia how I'd come to be in Georgetown and described the range of current Cuso assignments in Guyana. Lydia listened with attention while savouring her lunch.

Finally, I asked, "Would you like to meet our program manager before you leave tomorrow?"

"Sure," she said with another beautiful, relaxed smile.

The next day we met at the Cuso office, and I introduced her to Vanessa, who was anticipating her visit. Later, curiosity brought me back to the office to learn the outcome. Vanessa said that everything went well and thanked me for connecting us. "More knowledge of organic agricultural practices could be a real plus here in Guyana."

“I know we’re pressed for adequate staff support at times. Would you like me to draft a formal placement description for this position? It could be titled ‘Organic Tropical Agriculture Development Advisor.’”

Vanessa smiled and leaned forward outlining a course of action. “We’ll send it to our other agricultural volunteers here for comment before it goes on to the regional office in Jamaica and then on to Ottawa.” I nodded. Vanessa nodded. A plan was underway.

Over the next couple of weeks, after Vanessa and I had worked with other volunteers to polish the initial draft, the document made its way through the local ranks and to headquarters where it was approved. I was ecstatic that Cuso accepted the concept so promptly. This was partnership development writ large.

Meanwhile, as this process was unfolding, Lydia had returned to Canada and was boosting her preparedness for such an assignment by spending months in Costa Rica engaging in more study of organic tropical agriculture and soil restoration. She had then applied to Cuso, was accepted for placement in Guyana, and would arrive exactly a year from our initial meeting. Her dream would be coming true when she returned to her taproot.

Chapter Six

Raging Fires Everywhere

Guyana has a rich agricultural history as a country five degrees north of the Equator with an average temperature of 27.5° C or 81.5° F. It averages 231 centimetres or nearly 91 inches of rainfall annually. Because of varied terrain, rainy seasons occur at different times and locations. The summer rainy season on the coast, producing half the annual rainfall, is roughly May through July. The coastal area also receives a winter rain from November through January. Inland, the rainy season is from April into September. However, with climate change, these times are becoming more unpredictable.

The summer rainy season in Georgetown is characterized by sudden, short downpours and then clear blue skies and sunny weather. I always carried an umbrella, even on cloudless days. With water pooling in the rainy season, the chance of malaria increases. The city would spray at night for mosquitoes, which continued to be troublesome—both the insects and thoughts about the spraying of DDT.

I used Indigenous crabwood oil with its pleasant, woody smell as a mosquito repellant. The oil comes from the seeds of the crabwood tree, *Carapa guinanensis*, a member of the mahogany family. It's part of the rainforest canopy along rivers, in seasonally flooded or swampy locations, or in low hills of the hinterland savannahs. I also took an antimalarial tablet weekly as required by Cuso.

Rain or shine, I still tromped around various neighbourhoods. During one of my early morning strolls, I scanned the tall grass of a nearby field and spied Limpkins. These tall, brown birds with long necks foraged in fields and soared to treetops like raptors—birds of prey—scanning for their next meal.

"Enjoy birding?" A tall, well-built young man was across the dirt lane and leaning on his yard's concrete wall with his strong forearms crossed.

"Yes, indeed," I replied strolling over for a chat. He identified himself as a miner working the gold mines in the Rupununi area. I soon cut to the question that I'd wondered about ever since I learned the history of Guyana's rich deposits of gold and diamonds. "Do you use mercury when you dig for gold?"

"Yes," he said with a diminishing smile. "We use mercury because it's cheaper. We know we shouldn't, but it's a matter of money." I had asked knowing the toxicity of this method. A thimbleful of mercury could poison a large body of water. During my childhood in the 1950s, the new Metropolitan Beach facility on the shore of Lake St. Clair near Detroit had been closed because of the toxic condition of the water. It was caused by mercury and other industrial wastes spewing out of auto plants in the so-called Motor City. I wondered what mercury was doing to the soil and water—and the vegetation and wildlife—of Guyana's interior. What was mercury doing to this man's body?

He suddenly switched topics and said, "I've eaten nothing but plant-based foods since I was a teenager. I'm twenty-nine and healthy these fifteen years."

Imagine, a vegan miner. He used a term I'd only really registered recently. When I heard another bird call and turned to the grasslands, he said with a chuckle, "Back to your birding."

"I do enjoy them as a puzzle to be solved," I said as I hoisted my binoculars, and he headed back to his house.

Whenever I walked through the neighbourhoods early in the day, I would offer the common greeting—Mornin', mornin'—to people when I passed. Some folks replied in kind, some nodded or smiled, and some ignored the exchange. Whatever the response, it felt good to be part of the neighbourhood, even if just for a leisurely stroll seeking birds.

Back at home, I continued reading, cooking, and cataloguing Guyanese life in embroidery on my vests. I got better at my Guyanese Cookup and tinkered with new combinations of ingredients. I'd try sweet potato instead of regular spuds. Sometimes I used other local root vegetables besides eddo such as dasheen, which I'd used in Jamaica. I was becoming a good enough cook in my own way.

One beneficiary of my cooking efforts was Robert, an old homeless fellow with muddled mind who slept in a shed in the family compound. He had wooly grey hair and the bone structure of what must have been a handsome young man. He swept around our yard and did other simple tasks for neighbours to earn a little money, always carrying the traditional cutlass. Sometimes he came up the back steps to my kitchen gate with the same request, "Got bread?"

My standard reply was, "No, I don't keep bread. How about some of my Cookup?" His suspicious look decreased as the weeks rolled on and he'd say okay more readily. My curry efforts in Cookup must have been getting better, or maybe he was getting hungrier and less discriminating. I also passed along newspapers. I didn't know if he could read, but at least the pictures might have interested him. I asked Miss Lam, my congenial and helpful landlady, "What's Robert's story?"

"I don't know," she said. "He doesn't know his full name or birthdate or any of his history, so I can't help get him any government benefits. But we give him shelter and some food and drink. Neighbours help with odd jobs. He likes my coffee and often hollers up the steps, 'Coffee!' and I oblige. It's the least we can do for him." When I shared my food from time to time, I figured that it was my contribution to this informal community support of those in need.

Going about my daily life with chance encounters and repeated interactions with people such as Robert, I continued reading and thinking about my place as a representative of the Western world in a colonized country. Was international development just another strategy for creating a global culture with all the bells and whistles of Western economic, political, and social structures? Did we, the colonizers and the colonized, have space in our thinking for fragments of Indigenous practices? These might be remnants of Earth wisdom. Thoughts swirled and I always ended up with more questions than answers.

I struggled with new ways to see, understand, and conjure approaches in helping VYC develop a stronger presence in Guyanese society. With the eventual resolution of their internal difficulties, I was able to host a staff meeting and gather critical input for continuing work on the organization's new strategic plan. Goldie agreed with one key recommendation that I made. Since the organization's work had to follow the flow of funding, I suggested just a two-year strategic plan and a scaffolding arrangement that could be readily updated in-house as needed.

Volunteer Youth Corps staff meeting

I also reflected on the contrast between Cuso of the last quarter of the twentieth century and the first quarter of the twenty-first century. In Jamaica, our small cadre of Cuso volunteers were traditional Canadian settler stock. Translation: white and middle-class. The organization's operations and expectations had evolved with emphasis on recruiting older, experienced people with a greater variety of occupational and ethnic backgrounds. In the 1970s, volunteers were mostly teachers, librarians, and community developers in Jamaica.

Now volunteers with expertise in business management were in high demand in helping government ministries and NGOs upgrade performance. Educators were recruited to share best practices in curriculum, methodology, and online skills. Our backgrounds also included areas of leadership studies, business development, youth entrepreneurship, and agricultural practices and marketing. My work focused heavily on Gender Equality and Social Inclusion or GESI.

There were fewer than ten volunteers in Guyana when I first arrived, with Caroline providing the other bookend to the ages and generations represented. We brought our formal education and work experience in the Global North plus often experience from other Caribbean countries, Europe, Africa, the Middle East, India, and elsewhere in South America. Today's Cuso was providing greater breadth and depth of experience than my involvement four decades prior.

Cuso also offered several ways of volunteering. Over the course of my service, three volunteers were South-to-South recruits from Jamaica, Uganda, and Uruguay. Another three volunteers were part of the diaspora returning to assist their homeland. Cuso's International Youth Interns Program provided recent graduates experience in development, which was how Caroline had served.

I continued to poke around Georgetown for ways to engage with more people and increase my understanding and enjoyment of the country. A Cuso colleague, who had arrived earlier, suggested that I check out the local chapter of InterNations. The first meeting that I attended was at Cara Lodge, one of the city's treasured hotels created with the clever bridging of two classic Georgetown residences. We met in the lodge's courtyard with massive palms in the centre. A tasteful arrangement of other tropical vegetation around the periphery bordered an array of dining tables with cushioned chairs. The venue allowed locals and expats to mingle freely for drinks and a meal.

While circulating, I met a dynamic British woman with abundant curly blond hair who spoke loudly of Adel's Rainforest Resort and Shell Beach where turtles were nesting in an area up the northwest coast. I accepted one of the information sheets that she thrust forward as she described the magic of a beach where as many as four species of turtles come to lay eggs. I said, "I've just heard the area is closed due to flooding from heavy rains."

The woman halted her pitch, blinked, and said, "I'll have to check that," and dashed onward to speak to others about this place called Adel's. This was a less than auspicious beginning of a relationship where the two of us would become two peas in an ecotourism pod within a few months.

My base of operations was working from my pleasant little apartment with forays out to VYC and the Cuso office. I was still connected to the greater world, especially my home in British Columbia, with the umbilical cord of the Internet. Disturbing news had begun to arrive. Penticton was experiencing severe flooding with rushing rivers carrying rapid snowmelt down into bordering lakes to the north and south. Also, over two hundred and fifty wildfires were blazing in BC. Some fires were the result of heavy spring rains that had produced abundant growth that was now dry and acting as kindling. Lightning was often the match. Other blazes were caused by smoldering campfires and discarded cigarettes. I wondered if flood or fire might affect my home but let concerns fade as there was nothing I could do.

Suddenly, more news arrived. On what should have been a quiet Sunday, the phone rang. It was Vanessa. "How are you doing today? Are you at home?"

"I'm fine here in my apartment. What's up?"

"There's a situation underway and we've received word from the Canadian High Commission to alert all volunteers. There's rioting at the prison in Georgetown and the facility is on fire. We're asked to take extra precautions for volunteer safety."

After a startled pause, I said, "I appreciate the information. I'm here in the family compound and feel quite safe. I'll stay put and speak with them."

"We're asking volunteers to maintain their schedule of work and visits to the office and essential outings such as marketing, if possible. We're also asking everyone to remain alert and based at home after dark until the situation is stabilized. I'll let you know whether we'll be meeting at the office tomorrow as soon as I contact regional headquarters in Jamaica."

When our brief conversation ended, I went to the balcony and saw smoke to the west. I ran my fingers over the table and saw grey ash. A family member was on the nearby landing of the staircase at the back of their home.

"Have you heard about the prison riot and burning?" I asked.

"Yes," he said with an odd smile, which I didn't know how to interpret.

"I've just had a call from my program manager. We're asked to remain close to home but continue with our work routine. I told her that I feel very safe here with you and your family," I said as I brushed ash from the railing.

"Yes, you'll be fine."

"By the way, how far are we from the prison?"

"Oh, it's way the other side of the city—about two kilometres. We'll be fine here." Two kilometres. I guessed this was considered far away in Georgetown.

The country's central prison was built in the late nineteenth century by the British. A thousand prisoners were squeezed into a facility designed for three to four hundred. Such kindling of discontent doubtless helped ignite the riot and fire. The facility was mostly wood with some newer concrete buildings. Amazingly, there was minimal loss of life, and few injuries were reported. Prisoners who didn't escape were still eager to leave and were herded into cattle lorries and buses and taken elsewhere. Many, imprisoned for minor offences, were soon released outright.

Eight prisoners, including one mass murderer, who was considered the ringleader of the riot, were still at large. They were believed to be heading south through now fallow and swampy cane fields and over canals into the hinterland. They were probably heading to Suriname or Brazil. Local and national authorities were doing their best to deal with the situation on a scale never experienced in the country's long history.

The following couple of weeks ground on slowly. The media reported that the mass murderer and his small band had hijacked a car and forced a young father to drive them south before abandoning the vehicle. I imagined the ensuing scene from a news report.

"Let's just kill him," said one of the prisoners.

"Please, no!" said the young man. "My wife just had a baby—our first."

The mass murderer looked at him for a long minute and said, "Get out and run north. Don't look back." The young man—who had lost his sandals somewhere during the hijacking—ran. With bloody feet and in tears, he had arrived at a settlement at the edge of the city and told his story.

I swept my balcony as ash kept falling and thought about all this trauma and drama. Prisoners, all in plain clothes because there was no money for uniforms, were taken to other confined spaces in the coastal area. One group was herded into a fenced cow pasture. When some in the group, not Indo-Guyanese, slaughtered a cow and roasted strips of meat, there was an uproar from the Indo-Guyanese prisoners and community with more rioting. When some prisoners escaped from the pasture and were caught, their attorney declared that they couldn't be charged with escape from prison—only from a cow pasture. Ah, the finer points of judicial debate.

With turmoil in BC and Guyana swirling around me, a friend in Michigan posted information online that sparked another bout of comparison. The article reflected on the racial causes of the Detroit riots in June of 1967—exactly fifty years prior.

I was raised in Warren, Michigan, which was a suburb eleven miles north of downtown Detroit. Three days before the riots, I had flown to my first overseas posting in the US Virgin Islands. Elements of social unrest that I sensed growing up in the manufacturing mecca of America had culminated in that episode of rioting and burning. The Detroit riots and now the situation in Georgetown bookended the half-century span of my involvement with international development. Even at the time of the Detroit riots, I had realized the irony of going to set up preschools and community health centres in a place that was home to former slaves when there were also African Americans with a history of slavery rioting near my home community.

With memories rolling themselves farther back in time, I realized that I had witnessed racism as a preschooler. In the post Second World War era, my parents and I had arrived in Detroit with Dad seeking work in the auto industry. A scene played out again in graphic detail as a mental slideshow.

A man was writhing on the sidewalk with his face shielded from the concrete by his felt hat. He moved his head from side to side, his face creased with pain.

"Mom, we need to stop. He's hurt," I said with concern.

"Someone will come to help him," said Mother tugging my hand.

We stepped by him with Mother keeping me as far from him as she could on a crowded sidewalk. I remembered his brown suit and black skin. Black skin was new to me. Why was nobody stopping?

I looked back and saw him glance at me with his mouth twisted in pain, but he made no sound. Soon the swirl of pedestrian traffic blocked my view of him. I still remember the look of pain and the sound of his silence. I fast-forwarded to the present and embroidered another motif onto the back of my birding vest. I stitched red, orange, and yellow flames of unrest.

Despite my years in other international settings, this posting in Guyana was proving quite the challenge. I thought I was handling my assignment well enough. My cotton slacks with elastic waistbands were telling another story. They were slipping down to my hips. I decided that it must be the heat and humidity of the tropics that was causing the elastic to deteriorate. I traipsed around Regent Street and found new elastic and replaced all the waistbands. The pants still slipped with the hems dragging in the dust.

Colleague Andrea then took charge. She'd known me since our training in Ottawa. Andrea was an Uruguayan-born fashionista in high heels who'd come to Guyana equipped with a scale. "Come home with me. I'm weighing you," she said as she dragged me off to hers and her husband Claude's apartment across from the Cuso office. "What did you weigh in Canada?"

"Uh," and I mumbled something. "I really don't keep close track."

"Look here," said Andrea pointing to the numbers between my feet.

"I was raised in the US and don't do metric well," I said with a slight whine.

Andrea grabbed her smart phone and computed in pounds. "No wonder you're losing your pants! You've lost twenty pounds, silly."

How did I miss that? "Hmm. Maybe Cuso should advertise volunteering as a weight-loss program," I quipped as Andrea frowned. It took return to Canada, as scheduled, a few weeks later, and a full medical examination to determine what I'd obviously overlooked about my Guyanese experience.

Since we were still on high alert from the prison situation, several of us decided that the National Park was our best bet for safe and comfortable space to rendezvous for Sunday morning walks. It was a well-used space for residents of all ages and located just south of the seawall with an ocean breeze. People ran or walked the circuit from early morning until late in the day. Football matches were always underway in various locations with shouts of spirited competition.

I would stroll with either Andrea or friend Jan from the Canadian High Commission. Sometimes we would rendezvous as a trio to swap news and stories. Egrets and hawks eyed us from leafy perches, while I eyed them and took photos.

When Jan and I were walking the circuit one morning, we realized that we could both request and synchronize just enough leave time for one more journey to the hinterland before my assignment ended. One of my Cuso colleagues had told Jan that her time at Rewa Eco-lodge, the most remote of the Indigenous facilities in the North Rupununi, was extraordinary. It would be travel by air, a short road trip over the dusty savannah, and then a long boat ride on rivers still high from the prolonged rainy season of late summer.

Jan said, "I have to serve as next in command before the arrival of the new High Commissioner. Let's see how many days I can be away and what you can arrange." Since we were both experienced travellers and organizers, we split the arrangements once we settled on the five days that we could both be out of Georgetown.

Jan volunteered to arrange transportation. "I'll handle flight arrangements if you'll take charge of accommodations and daily outings." This sounded straightforward, but each of us experienced our challenges. Guyana was struggling to establish the well-coordinated tourism operations pioneered by other Caribbean countries. Guyana lacked the welcoming sand and turquoise waters of its island neighbours, but it did have an exquisite natural world. The challenge was the costly flights into the interior and the need for accommodations and outings to satisfy tourists.

With preparations eventually hammered out, Jan and I finally departed on the designated day. We savoured the flight, endured the bumps and ruts of road travel, and anticipated the river passage. Two Indigenous men, Ken and Winston, greeted us riverside and we climbed into a boat bound for Rewa.

A Ringed Kingfisher with its pronounced bill, crested head, white collar, and rufous breast was our scout. It veered left and right repeatedly while keeping well ahead of the bow of our boat before zooming into the surrounding vegetation.

We spotted the Channel-billed Toucan with its distinctive large black bill jazzed up with patches of red, yellow, and blue. Perched high in massive trees beyond the thick riverine growth, this bird of aerodynamic impossibility regarded us with moderate interest. I imagined the bird's perspective of us in an aluminum boat as calmly noting us as just more creatures floating by in those shiny hollow logs.

Jan wasn't an avid birder but willing to humour me and loved just being on the water. She hoped to see some of the iconic big animals such as the giant river otters, tapirs, capuchin monkeys, jaguars, and giant anteaters. We saw plenty of birds but learned that the big animals had retreated to the drier savannahs away from the flooded riverine areas.

Rewa Eco-lodge was situated at the confluence of two major rivers, the Rewa and the Rupununi. Comfortable cabins were lined up beyond the Indigenous benabs. A large version of a benab served as the kitchen and dining area. The office was housed in a smaller structure, which was square built with a ridge pole and thatch roof.

Channel-billed Toucan

Thatch craft was everywhere. As Jan and I swung in hammocks on our front veranda in uber-tourist manner, we studied, from the underside, the awe-inspiring intricacy of thatch roofs woven in a variety of patterns.

Our hosts were members of the Macushi tribe and at ease in welcoming guests to a facility where their village provided goods and services. Vegetables and fruits were harvested from nearby Rewa village, and the rivers supplied fresh fish. Their pride of place was evident in all our interactions. Life was good.

When Jan and I were taken on excursions into the rainforest, lush vegetation crowded the forest floor and reached up into the high canopy. Such growth either thrived on its own or appeared as vines that crawled up trunks and tangled around branches of the great trees. The canopy was the thick, spreading foliage that made those of us on overhead flights interpret the rainforest as a solid mass. Occasionally we caught sight of startling red in the dense green—the bright face of a spider monkey or a stand of wild ginger.

With my limited exposure to some of the iconic great birds of Guyana, such as the macaws that I was busily embroidering on my vests, I was thrilled to see two macaw families in the wild as we cruised a river. One cluster of three Blue-and-yellow Macaws, perched high and distant, gave us ample view of their vivid yellow breasts and bright blue wings and tail feathers. This was probably a pair along with their offspring.

Macaw family

Another trio was perched on a horizontal branch with one bird's head tucked under the wing of another that gave an anthropomorphic narrative of an adolescent protected by watchful parents. Later, a single Red-and-green Macaw perched in such a way as to flash a posture-perfect view of its red, green, and blue plumage. I was an eager and appreciative photographer sporting a new camera. Now I could capture such show birds in distant locations.

On a forest trek, Ken nudged a log and gave us a jolt as a massive tarantula crawled out. The Goliath Bird-eating Spider was the largest of its kind in the world. It was truly scary with a hairy, gray-brown torso the size of a chicken egg. When stretched out, the creature was larger than a big man's hand with fingers splayed. Jan and I were so mesmerized by this creature that we forgot to ask if it was poisonous and really ate birds. At that moment, I was more focused on tinkering with camera settings, while keeping space between us. Later, online research assured us it was harmless for humans but did eat small birds, mice, frogs, lizards, and the occasional cockroach.

We spent many hours on the rivers birding and just enjoying the lushness of the rainforest, the bordering riverine vegetation, and all the wildlife that called this place home. Ken and Winston were thoughtful, knowledgeable guides. At one point, we stopped to fish with short sticks and a line with a bit of initial bait.

"Pull hard when you feel a bite," said Ken. I was the first to succeed and saw a small, red fish dangle from the hook. "Piranha," he said cutting it up for more bait.

Jan and I struggled to reverse our North American habit of playing a fish when we felt a tug. We were in piranha territory with a different temperament ruling. Tug, yank! Soon we were pulling up big black predators with the same round, flat body. Meanwhile, Winston quietly dropped a line at the rear of the boat and brought up a gorgeous spotted peacock bass, which was later grilled as our dinner special. I did wonder if he'd really caught it as we were busy with our piranhas, or if it was an earlier catch brought to impress us. Either way, it was a fish with glowing rainbow colours that delighted us and proved a tasty meal.

Our transportation was the small aluminum boat with a motor, but members of the Indigenous community paddled by in dugout canoes with sides only inches above the water. We'd exchange smiles and nods of greeting. The buildings along the riverbanks were mixtures of thatch, bamboo, wood, local brick, concrete, and plaster. The natural materials were more beautiful seen from a distance, especially in texture and colour, but the modern materials were probably easier to maintain and less subject to insect infestation and decay.

Our Rewa sojourn was a refreshing experience of life in the interior that nourished me at the beginning of my final month in Guyana. There was also more to the mechanics of planning this trip to be revealed later.

I thought this trip would be my last big birding adventure. I was wrong. Belated contact with Guyana's foremost birding group prompted me to count my remaining leave days and dollars and splice birding excursions with final work on the strategic plan. Then this winding down of my work and further sampling of Guyana's natural world led to my biggest birding adventure of all, which would inspire continued involvement in Guyana.

Chapter Seven

Life in the Wetlands

Guyana's Georgetown birding group didn't answer my request for help for five months. I was interested in arranging time with them as local guides. An email had finally arrived asking if I wanted to go birding. Of course! And where were they over the past months? The delayed response matched another handling of time in this culture. The so-called just now response could mean anything from right away to whenever.

In a phone call, I complained aloud about the belated contact, including a few swear words with cultural sensitivity be damned. My anger vented and an apology offered by the lead guide of the group, I booked an excursion on one of my remaining leave days. Andy was the Birdman of Guyana with thirty years' experience, and his name was mentioned in international books on the country's birds. He'd started his working life as a school dropout doing gold mining. His epiphany was summarized almost poetically. "I looked up and knew the real gold was flying above me."

Andy suggested an early morning trip eastward along the coast to the Mahaica River, a place that I knew boasted some distinct species. I asked Linton to take all of us, which turned out to be Andy, two assistants, and me.

Birds were everywhere and not the ones that I'd already identified. I handed Linton my binoculars, and he was thrilled by close-up views of birds. "I've seen these birds all my life and never knew their names," he said looking birdy-eyed when Andy pointed out yet another species.

The Spotted Sandpiper, with its mottled brown feathers and white breast dappled with black, ran along the riverbank on yellow legs. The Red-capped Cardinal with black feathers, a white breast, and a red head sat obligingly on a branch overhanging the river. It even gave me time to fiddle with the settings that enhanced my telephoto capability.

The Blue-black Grassquit atop a fencepost rose into the air time and time again flicking its wings showing a white under flash. Andy said this fencepost ritual meant that it was in breeding mode. Linton's jaw dropped in amazement with each new bird. Meanwhile, Andy kept up a flow of conversation about names, habits, and habitats.

The most memorable birds of the day were clustered on the far bank of the Mahaica. We studied several Hoatzin on the branches of riverine trees. This was Guyana's national bird, also known as the Canje Pheasant or Stinky Pheasant. What made it unique was a crop, an enlarged part of its esophagus, that was part of its digestive system. The crop fermented food with the aid of manure-scented bacteria. The young also had functional claws on their wingtips harking back to a time when dinosaurs and birds shared some characteristics. The Hoatzin had a crest and feathers of brown, shades of tan, white, and red. It also had a blue orbital eye patch and red eye. Linton was ecstatic. "Our national bird and I've never seen it!"

We found another bird that only lives in the mangroves. The Rufous Crab Hawk had reddish feathers, yellow legs and beak, and a red eye. Andy said this bird's sole habitat was the coastal area of the Guiana Shield. With an experienced birder, my exposure to and knowledge of the birds of Guyana was growing rapidly.

Gauging leave time and funds available, I played tourist one day and flew an hour into the interior on a visit to Kaieteur Falls. This was one of the longest single-drop waterfalls in the world at 225 metres or 741 feet. I was also interested in another opportunity to see the Cock-of-the-Rock known to live in the nearby forest.

I boarded a small plane along with other tourists, and we followed a winding river deep into the hinterland. Soon we saw a narrow stream of water flowing from a high ledge bounded by forest. After landing, we were guided up to a vantage point level with the Potaro River, which plunged to continue its flow to the ocean. With no barriers between our ledge and the waterfall in the distance, my courage only allowed me to belly my way forward to the edge and peer out. I photographed as much of the waterfall as possible but couldn't get a shot of where it splashed into the river far below.

Our guide said only a narrow stream of water was falling this time of year. At the height of the rainy season, water cascaded over the entire width of the ledge. I considered what I saw extraordinary and could only imagine the uptick to spectacular when the river was in full flow.

Andy had cued me to ask our guide in advance to take us into the habitat of the Cock-of-the-Rock. Our planeload of day tourists trekked into a forested area, and we spotted two bright orange birds. These were ordinary tourists, not birders. One man crawled forward with his camera. I cautioned, "Please don't move closer or the birds will fly." He ignored me.

"Oh, look! There's two of them!" said a woman flapping her hand and causing one bird to fly.

I tapped her on the shoulder and whispered, "Please stop waving and don't shout."

"Oh, they're just so bright and beautiful!" she said in a loud voice with both hands in motion.

Stepping even closer to her, I said, "Shut up!" She still didn't register anything, which was probably just as well. My outburst was one thing you shouldn't tell anyone at any time, especially somebody who was on holiday and clueless about birding protocol.

I did manage to snap a couple of photos and captured the grandeur of this remarkable orange bird with crested head and intricately arranged black and white feathering on its wing tips. I also reprimanded myself for my display of bad birding manners. Back aboard our plane in the late afternoon, the pilot flew an arc over the falls so we could have a parting view of Kaieteur as the sun was beginning to gift us with another golden hour.

In Georgetown, I was polishing the strategic plan for VYC for distribution and squeezing in time for more outings with Andy and company. Our regional director from Jamaica, Roberta, was in Guyana for meetings and had heard of my birding interest. "Are there any birds to see in the city?"

"Yes indeed. Can you be ready for pickup at a quarter to six tomorrow morning? You'll be back for breakfast by seven o'clock. The Botanical Gardens are only five minutes from your hotel."

"Yes! I can be ready," said Roberta.

I quickly rounded up our birding posse for the outing. Even with heavy early morning rain, Andy, his two sidekicks, his driver, Linton, Roberta, and I all met at the gardens on time. We slipped into a thatched benab, more of a gazebo, with its roof and pillars. Andy's assistants, who will remain unnamed for reasons that will become apparent later, set up the spotting scope and tripod.

I had visited the gardens many times prior but only midday with crowds of Guyanese. Now, with an expert assisting and an early morning visit, we saw species I couldn't have identified and none of us could have studied without the spotting scope.

I saw my first White-throated Kingbird. Andy pointed out a Festive Amazon, a parrot only found in Guyana in the Botanical Gardens. "This is fabulous," said Roberta on her first birding adventure.

The guides then set up the tripod and spotting scope in the open-air mausoleum with the elaborate sarcophagus of Forbes Burnham, Guyana's first prime minister.

An elderly expatriate craftswoman I had once met told me a curious story about Burnham's later years. "I was noted for my handcrafts and sent to a ranch in southern Guyana decades ago to learn leatherwork at government expense. Then I was commissioned to learn bookbinding and make leather covers for all the prime minister's books." I knew from experience in tropical climates that leather was subject to mold, especially if not aired regularly. I thought about Burnham's authoritarian rule and bizarre legacy that ended in such erratic whims.

Our guides encouraged us to admire the quartz embellishments on the sarcophagus. I took a closer look. They were only melted glass. I said nothing, except a whispered comment to Linton.

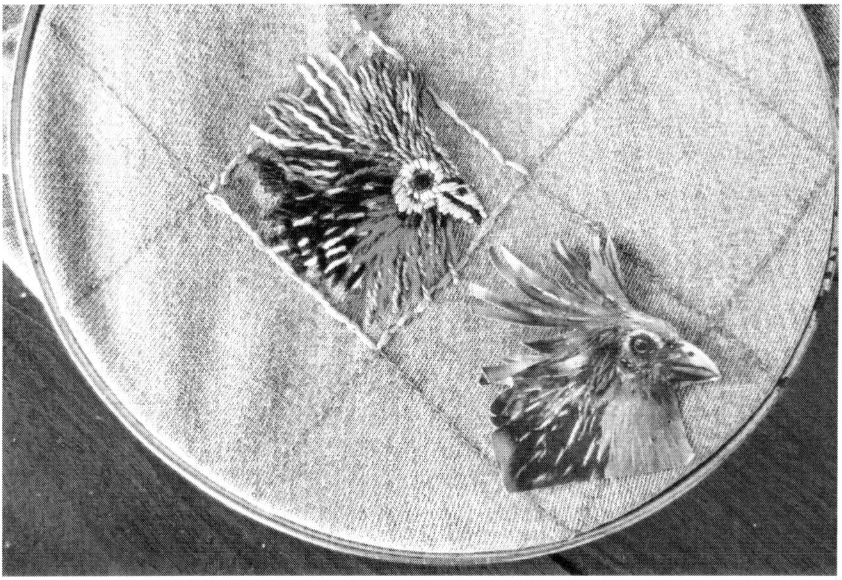

Embroidered Hoatzin

My guides and Roberta also noticed my birding vest where Guyanese symbols and new birds were hatching via stitchery. By this time, there was a toucan, a lotus lily, and the Guyanese flag in red, green, yellow, black, and white. Kaieteur Falls flowed in one square with blue and white stitching. Nearby was a male Cock-of-the-Rock in bright orange. A Jabiru Stork from the North Rupununi stood tall in red, white, and black. A Hoatzin took the place of honour in the centre. My vest was a fibre arts tapestry of my travels.

One iconic photograph in my collection of these happy days of birding is of Andy, a tall, lean man of Indo-Guyanese heritage, in the foreground leaning into the scope on its tripod. Muscular Afro-Guyanese Linton stands in the background holding my binoculars.

I also snapped another photo of what became one of my beloved images: a Striated Heron with water droplets glistening from its beak and feathers in the early morning light. We spotted twenty-three species in just an hour. Roberta was ecstatic.

Andy and Linton

My final birding excursion was based on the recommendation of a Peace Corps acquaintance I'd met at an InterNations event. He'd enjoyed his time at Adel's Rainforest Resort on the northwest coast in Region 2. I recalled the name of the resort and the British woman with the wild, curly golden hair. Andy couldn't accompany me because of a prior booking, but he'd send the two fellows who were with him on the earlier outings. They'd bring a spotting scope and tripod.

There'd be no flights for this trip, only road and river travel. Passage to this area would be in six phases. First, I took a taxi to collect my guides from the birding group's office where two toucans, rescued from illegal bird traders when young, squawked from their wire cages shaded with vines.

The guys hefted their packs and birding gear and we piled into a taxi for the short ride to Stabroek Market where we boarded a water taxi at an old warehouse with a rickety *stelling* or wharf on the bank of the Demerara. Ten minutes later, we were at Vreed-en-Hoop at a less wobbly structure. Exiting its vintage warehouse, we caught another taxi for the half-hour ride to Parika on the east bank of the Essequibo River.

There we walked through another ancient warehouse onto an equally antique wharf and boarded a speedboat, an enclosed wooden boat that held twenty or so people for the forty-minute ride over the estuary. Depending on weather conditions and the tide, I was told it could be a relatively smooth trip snaking around islands in the river's mouth or it could be a bronco ride.

After a calm trip, we disembarked at Supenaam, the little settlement on the west bank. Again, we climbed into a taxi for an hour's ride up the coast to Charity on the Pomeroon River. We sped along and I studied the seawall on our right and vast rice fields with pale green growth on our left. Midtrip, we veered south to Charity.

Once there, we waited on the creakiest *stelling* to date. Cell phones are the norm in rural Guyana, and I used mine to call a boatman recommended by Adel's. When Kurt's open wooden boat arrived, we made our way down slippery wooden steps lapped by brackish river water. When the boat was packed with people and all the packages and luggage were wedged in place, we started downriver. I was the only passenger with a life vest, a Cuso mandate if we were on water. I was a certified scuba diver, which I realized was a useless skill if we had a boating accident.

This forty-minute ride included stops on either bank to drop off passengers. Our six-part road and river journey took roughly four-and-a-half hours and gave me another experience of life in the coastal floodplains and a much more affordable way to experience the country's interior.

Adel's Rainforest Resort was a charming, rustic retreat on Akawini Creek that flowed from Indigenous territory deep in the interior and ended nearby at the Pomeroon River. This agricultural plot had been carved out of boggy land and the rainforest over two-and-a-half centuries ago. Frederick Dubois had escaped the French Revolution in the late eighteenth century and established a new life in the soggy coastal floodplains. Nearly sixty acres of land were now only partially cultivated and produced coconut, citrus, and vegetables. A descendant, a retired hotelier, had used boardwalks to link three old wooden farm buildings near the creek to form the quaint little resort named after her grandmother, Adel, who had lived to the age of 102.

When I visited, the resort was currently managed by Jessica, the English woman whom I'd met at InterNations. She handled the management and marketing of both the resort and its produce as a volunteer while conducting her private, informal program of ad hoc educational and healthcare services in the region.

Arriving in the late afternoon, our birding trio was greeted by Jessica and five guard dogs yipping and dashing around. We walked along a boardwalk over high ground and then over a little wooden bridge that spanned a narrow canal between the embankment and the resort. The agricultural property behind was called the backdam. This was natural wetlands like Georgetown. Creeks flooded at high tide or in rainy season, making berms and canals critical if the land was to be settled and farmed.

We learned that the bridge over the little canal was where first one puppy, and then another, had recently disappeared. Their fondness for cavorting on the bridge provided the noise and vibrations to lure a hungry anaconda. The killer, over four metres or thirteen feet long, was later dragged from the shallow water and hacked to death with a cutlass.

For our visit, all was serene as we approached the reception area with its waist-high wooden wainscoting and railing that served as walls with canvass curtains that could be drawn during heavy rains. We felt ourselves relax as we noted comfortable old sofas and stuffed chairs arranged in conversational groupings. To one side stood an immense plank table with benches that provided dining space. A massive, burnished metal bowl filled with grapefruit, oranges, lemons, limes, bananas, and a pineapple was the centrepiece.

"Come this way," said Jessica guiding us over a boardwalk to an adjacent wooden building with a landscaped lawn on one side and a courtyard on the other. "Your accommodations are here." Rooms contained two double beds with mosquito netting and bathroom facilities. Everything was constructed of Guyana's famed timber. I found myself enchanted by this creative repurposing of old farm buildings of unknown age.

Soon we were engaged in late afternoon birdwatching in the manicured grounds around the resort and further into the farmland laced with canals, which we crossed on wide planks. "Striated Heron," I said as I recognized a bird with mottled gray feathers and neck tucked in eyeing the canal for food.

David, an Arawak and Adel's man-of-all-trades, heard me and said, "Chao. That's what we call it here." We exchanged smiles and, in retrospect, I now realize we had immediate affinity. Since it was late in the day, we started hearing the chirp of the cicada. David again looked at me and said, "Six-o'clock bee."

The guys were delighted with the sumptuous meal Jessica prepared of local fish, spiced rice, and greens from what she called the shade house. She had commissioned a gardening area with a wood frame, plastic stretched for roofing, and planting beds constructed so the gardener could stand. Salad greens, peppers, tomatoes, and herbs from the garden were gracing our dinner plates. Dessert was an array of fruits from the plot.

The next morning, as we finished breakfast and were preparing for birdwatching on the creek, a Silver-beaked Tanager flitted around. It was a male sporting a silvery bill and reddish feathers. The Black-crested Antshrike was also present with its black, gray, and white-tipped feathers and distinctive long, dark crest.

When we climbed down into the boat, I noticed more steps than I had remembered from the day before. These waterways were subject to tidal action. The water was fresh when flowing from rivers connected to the Amazon. It became brackish when seawater from the Atlantic flowed down the nearby Pomeroon. Now the tide was out leaving a slippery, salty residue. The wooden boat was the same style as the one that ferried us to Adel's the previous day with three rows of wooden seats with backs. It was a steady boat and as comfortable as bench seating can be.

While we motored up the creek, I noted modest wooden homes scattered on either bank with small docks for their boats or dugout canoes. Blue Morpho butterflies with metallic-hued wings flitted across the water adding a flash of iridescence to the sun-glinted canopy of the rainforest.

A Little Chachalaca, with its rufous head, tawny-brown feathers, gray throat, and buff-coloured chest, made an appearance and then dashed off on red legs. In Georgetown, I'd learned to identify the Black-collared Hawk with its rufous feathers, white head, and black tail. It was one of the only hawks whose belly hue and wing configuration I could identify as it flew overhead and on into the marshlands.

I was delighted motoring along Akawini Creek with silky water and a gentle breeze. However, our early morning outing was interrupted by the motor sputtering to a stop. David removed the housing atop the engine and tried poking and prodding. No response.

Downtime was story time. With guests to entertain, Jessica regaled us with the nearby village of Wakapoa's ancient whale bone story. A family had cared for immense bones on a spot of high ground in the middle of the swampland during the distant magic times. Long ago a little girl, who had nurtured a fish in a nearby pond, encountered a big fish—a whale—that ate her. A man rushed to her rescue with a cutlass but was also swallowed. Then he sounded a horn from inside the whale and the little girl began to sing what was now called "The Whale Bone Song." Villagers rescued the pair by battling the great fish to death. They buried the body but kept the head. To this day, villagers sing the ancient song. While we listened to the tale, I noted similarities to the biblical story of Jonah and the whale. Had this story been influenced by Christianity making its appearance in the hinterland?

Soon another boat filled with villagers came from upriver. It pulled alongside and the motormen conferred. We saw nodding of heads. David plucked a twig from the leafy overstory. The other boatman poked around with the twig clearing the fuel line and the engine started. "Bush mechanics," said Jessica as we all eased back in our seats.

Continuing our journey upriver, we decided to find out more about rumours of the illusive and iconic Harpy Eagle's presence in the area. This was the world's second largest eagle with a wingspan over six feet. We spotted a distant homestead on high ground and veered up a narrow channel through tall grass to its *stelling*. It turned out to be the home of hunter and logger, Chris, a sturdy and serious Indigenous fellow who wondered about the boatload of people motoring up his way.

"The Harpy Eagle? Yes, there was a nest nearby. Some loggers chopped the tree, but I have four more nests on GPS."

"You have GPS here?" I asked startled that there was access to such sophisticated technology in tribal territory.

"Yes. Now come see some of the birds we have here," said Chris.

One of our guides identified a Gray-winged Trumpeter strolling around the yard. It had been adopted as a mother by three orphaned chicks of another species according to Chris. "I find injured or abandoned birds when I'm out and bring them home, so they'll survive," he said. "My wife Minerva and the kids and I like having them around." Minerva and their flock of children sat on the front steps enjoying our experience with their pets.

We watched this tall bird with black feathers, gray and brown wings, and gray feet ambling around the sandy area near the family's wooden house. The building was up on pillars at the front with the back resting on higher ground. "This bird usually walks around the forest floor," added Chris, "but when it's frightened, it'll fly onto a high branch." Meanwhile, we were mesmerized by this bird of the wild calmly walking around finding food for its little family.

"Let's see about checking those eagle nests," said Jessica in an undertone as she stroked a tame bird sitting on her arm.

I added, "We want to not only locate the birds but also support efforts to keep them undisturbed. Maybe this could help others experience this treasured species." What had I just said? I wasn't consciously thinking of species conservation. I then went on about this journey itself and not having to use expensive air travel. "I enjoyed seeing small towns and life on the river as we came here to your place," I said with David, our guides, and this family with ten children listening and watching us with the birds.

While enjoying the family's homestead, I noted that Jessica, like Chris, was also something of a benevolent adopter or perhaps kidnapper. She had spotted Princess, a lovely young daughter with long, flowing black hair. "Thirteen? She should be in school," declared Jessica.

There was a quiet exchange between the parents. Jessica continued with her commanding voice, "Get her things together. I've got the uniform and school supplies at Adel's. We're going up the creek for another hour or so and we'll return and take her with us. We're visiting the school over in Wakapoa this afternoon. We can register Princess."

Amazingly enough, this couple agreed to ready their daughter for the residential school in the neighbouring village an hour's boat ride away. It was in another tribal territory to the north and shared the Arawak origins of this family.

Later, we collected Princess, as promised, and headed back to Adel's for brunch and to equip this newest school recruit from Jessica's stockpile of school supplies. I was experienced with the paperwork of the Global North in the Cuso application process and all the planning and writing of reports involved with my posting. I was astonished at the quick decision and trust demonstrated by these parents here in the hinterland. I also knew the history of residential schools for First Nations children in Canada and Native American children in the US. For the moment, I kept my thoughts to myself. At least Princess would have a chance for more education, which I hoped meant something positive.

Back at Adel's, we had more fresh produce from the plot and shade house, plus the fresh fish. I had provided the fish. The previous afternoon, before boarding the boat in Charity, Jessica had asked me to pick up fish. "Just ask for Fisherman Jack and tell him it's for Jessica. He knows the kind of fish that I want and how much to send."

So, I'd arrived at Adel's with my personal kit, two guides, and two big fish. This was the first of my journeys in this river-based world and foreshadowed what would become my life over part of the next year.

After lunch, it was back to Akawini Creek and on to the wide Pomeroon for a fifteen-minute ride downriver to Wakapoa Creek. Then we motored for another half hour through the thick vegetation of the rainforest and on into the marshlands of this region.

Wakapoa territory is a cluster of high spots in the wetlands that house homesteads for three thousand people. These inhabitants are descendants of those who fled intertribal genocide and colonial invasion centuries ago. We headed for School Island, the largest of the settlements with a sturdy stelling of timber and steel. A sandy area had been cleared and contained the primary and secondary schools, dormitories, and playground equipment. There were also a few community buildings—including a clinic—along with a small gazebo and a couple of food shops. Wooden homes, some on posts, were scattered in the scrub land surrounding the community area.

First, we met the headmaster of the school and entered Princess in the school's registry. The matron, Aunt Hazel, escorted Princess to the girls' dormitory, a room full of bunk beds. We also took her to the main village shop where Jessica bought basic toiletries for the girl's new life as a student.

Jessica had established relationships in the village, which allowed guests from Adel's to experience a bit of Indigenous life. The mother and daughter of a family close to the marshlands were processing coconut and cassava. The father had designed and built a machine for grinding these foodstuffs into pulp. Little did I know that months later, I would be hanging my hammock in a corner of this family's home during visits to Wakapoa.

While we studied the processing of food underway, an elderly man had arrived at Jessica's invitation. He carried carvings of animals, birds, canoes, and paddles of the territory. I could identify some but not all the carved creatures. Jessica and I bought several items and this fellow's gap-toothed smile widened with delight.

Part of our village tour included meeting the toshao, or elected village leader, to discuss more about local life. "We live wherever we can keep high and dry," he said with a chuckle. "We mostly get around in our motorboats or dugouts. Sometimes we have boardwalks over short, swampy areas between high ground." When he spotted the embroidery on the back panel of my birding vest, he asked, "You made this?"

"Yes, I'm recording some of what I see here in Guyana."

"You have our country on your back," he said with a smile.

When we piled back into the boat, I had ideas bubbling from this typical show-and-tell. We were experiencing a bit of Indigenous life with interesting road and river travel and without the high cost of flights. I had heard one villager call themselves the "Cinderella county," the forgotten region. Could ecotourism be further developed for these remote villages?

We motored on until David stopped in a wide, shallow section of one of Wakapoa Creek's tributaries with no homes visible. "Time for a swim," said Jessica. I'd been alerted to dress for the occasion, so we women peeled down to our bathing suits. The guides stripped to their shorts and gingerly eased themselves into the water and paddled around with us. David steadied the boat near the embankment next to the tall grasses that were waving slightly in the breeze.

The water was warm and the bottom, sandy. We were like kids at a swimming hole. Floating on our backs, we watched birds fly overhead. "Great Egret," said one of the guides. A large bird with white feathers, a yellow bill, and long black legs trailing was flying to a distant area of the wetlands. We watched it settle down to stand alone waiting for dinner to swim by.

The next morning was our final outing on the creek. Our small boat motored through the rainforest, and we bent our heads away from overhanging tropical vegetation. A pair of Blue-grey Tanagers, distinctive with their pale colouring, flitted near the bank. A Smooth-billed Ani with black feathers and a prominent bump on its matching black bill perched on a riverine bush and eyed our passage. "Old witch," said David smiling directly at me.

One of the guides obliged me, the paying client, by saying, "Straight-billed Woodcreeper" as a russet-feathered bird darted in and out of thick foliage.

We chatted about bird views and news while David turned the boat back to Adel's for breakfast before our departure. We glided slowly down the river when suddenly David slowed the engine, set it in reverse, and backed into a small gap in the tangle of branches and vines on the bank. "What?" asked Jessica.

Tucked into the shallow channel, David cut the engine. He pointed and said, "There." We spotted two small birds deep in the forest with bright red heads and chests and black bodies. One flew, but the other remained. I saw a band of white at the forward edge of the wings.

"Take a picture!" shouted the guides while I climbed over the wooden seat to get firm footing at the centre of the boat.

"Stand firm!" I said to the nearest fellow as I readied the camera. "You're my tripod." I steadied my forearm on his shoulder. Easy. Shoot smooth. Click. The bird flew.

"What's that bird?" asked Jessica, breathing heavily.

"Firebird," said David.

"Did you get it? Did you get it?" the guides shouted. I fumbled with the review button and revealed one photograph with the firebird in focus dead centre.

"Yes!" I said.

"Show me!" said Jessica. "This is the first time I've seen a firebird!"

David smiled while starting the engine and returning us to the creek. I sat between the guys, and we stared in awe at the perfect image. Jessica kept saying, "Amazing! Amazing!"

The guides contacted Andy back in Georgetown by cell phone. From their description, Andy called it a male manakin, the elusive Crimson-hooded Manakin, always near water in thick understory. Later, in Georgetown, I emailed the image to Andy, and it was added to the group's website resulting in over five hundred hits within a day. Ideas were churning in my head, and I saw that Jessica was thinking the same way.

I was about to leave Guyana, but stories of eagle nests and seeing the manakins sparked an epiphany. The Harpy Eagle and the Crimson-hooded Manakin were species avid birders would travel far to see. I'd already experienced the toughness and expense of birding in Guyana.

Maybe careful sharing of more of the country's birding bounty with readily accessible and affordable transportation could be developed.

This could enhance the lives of these Indigenous people, help celebrate and protect wildlife, and expand ecotourism offerings for both the Guyanese and foreign visitors.

It was Sunday morning and after more early birding around the compound and breakfast, we'd be off. Flocks of Orange-winged Amazons, with flecks of the defining colour on their wings, squawked their morning wake-up calls. The Blue-chinned Sapphire, in iridescent green and blue, flitted about on its nectar quest as did all hummingbirds. David, sitting quietly by the creek, had showed me a Three-toed Sloth nestled in a tree across the creek from our stelling. It had eyed us with its characteristic sleepy gaze.

We had settled into a breakfast of an omelette of eggs from the chickens out back and tomatoes and greens from the shade house. We sipped coffee grown in Wakapoa and conversation drifted into talk of dreams and schemes. "The resort here could be home base," said Jessica. "I know the local toshaos and was a teacher with the Indigenous HEYS youth program last year. They're interested in building ecotourism in these territories."

"What's HEYS?" I asked.

"Hinterland Employment and Youth Services," said Jessica.

I looked at the guys and said, "You fellows and Andy would be the birdmen with expert knowledge. Adel's could be home base. Cuso could help with organization and arrange for training."

One of the fellows with neatly plaited hair said, "We would be the tripod, just like the stand that holds the scope."

"Exactly," said Jessica. "This is a relatively untouched area of Guyana. Resource extraction is mostly timber. Other areas of the country mine gold, diamonds, and bauxite—the messier industries. This would be clean development."

"Yes, ecotourism is about observing and conserving the natural world, not extracting from it. Everybody could learn both the local call names and formal book names of birds, which would link local and global knowledge," I added.

Excitement was building around the table. Ecotourism could reinforce efforts to maintain a healthy environment and share ancestral skills and cultural heritage. With thoughts buzzing and the clock ticking, we packed up our gear and headed for the stelling to start our homeward journey.

Would Cuso accept such a proposal for a placement in Region 2? Soon after my return, I broached the topic with Vanessa. She had listened closely and given the go-ahead to draft a description of how such an assignment might be configured. We both knew that this could be a strategic plan to get me back to Guyana. Long before this outing, Vanessa had asked more than once if I'd return to work in Georgetown. I had always declined, but work in the Pomeroon-Supenaam region's tribal territories was a different story for me.

Vanessa said, "The goal will be sustainable incomes for marginalized people, especially women and youth, without damaging their environment or cultural integrity." I suggested that the position be titled Ecological and Economic Development Advisor, which she liked.

I envisioned that the effectiveness of this placement would rest on how quickly a volunteer assimilated into the culture of the local environment. Work would be split between Georgetown and Region 2. After review and discussion, Vanessa sent the document on to Roberta in Jamaica. From there, and with a bit more tweaking, it went to Ottawa. Then we waited.

Chapter Eight

Native Cultures Aren't Static

After my time in Region 2, I got to thinking more about taproot in relation to the tumultuous history of Guyana. Nine Indigenous tribes were still represented but formed only a single-digit percentage of the overall population. They were the Arawak, Macushi, Carib, Warrau, Akawaio, Wai Wai, Patamuna, Wapishana, and Arekuna.

The taproots of the Afro-Guyanese and Indo-Guyanese were relatively short and twisted over the past two to four hundred years. The Indigenous tribes' histories spanned thousands of years in this region of Amazonian abundance. I had met the Macushi in the North Rupununi and the Arawak in the Pomeroon-Supenaam region. I realized that my glimpse of Region 2 riverine life gave me, a mere visitor, a deeper sense of what rootedness and authentic community meant as people blended lives of tradition with modernity. For example, some people travelled in dugout canoes and some in motorboats and often switched from one to the other with ease.

Now it was time to shift from such thoughts and say goodbye to friends in my partner organization. The process of developing a strategic plan was as complete as possible and ready for implementation by VYC.

The final Cuso event was the Annual Partner Review with all volunteers and staff along with Roberta from Jamaica and representatives of all partner organizations present. I was in a swirl of activity as Caroline had been in her pitch-n-pack departure. I was also drifting back absorbing the experience of less than a month exploring new areas of the coastal region.

The annual meeting was conducted the day before my departure. Hurricane Maria had been battering the Caribbean, especially Dominica and Puerto Rico. I was assured that I would fly as Guyana wasn't usually in the path of hurricanes. It was on the shoulder of the continent and that affected airflow. Also, flights were generally routed to the west of the Caribbean archipelago. Past performance was present reality. I exited on schedule and winged my way north.

Any prolonged travel is always meditation time for me and transition between worlds. Those few days at Adel's started a scheme for adventure-level activity in the interior. Questions drifted into my stream of thoughts. How worthwhile or feasible was the idea? Would Cuso support it as a placement?

I had accomplished more than I thought would be possible in six months. Partnership development with Volunteer Youth Corps was successful. Goldie was pleased with our work on a plan that included mention of a robotics program, a dangling project suggested by ExxonMobil but not yet funded. We'd prepared a plan that could be followed, evaluated, and updated in-house.

The Cuso community was perhaps strengthened by my encouraging walkabouts in Georgetown and stepping up for extra tasks in the country office. I'd weathered the difficulties experienced with VYC and carried on despite the stress from the destruction of the prison. I'd even done far more studying of birds than I thought would be possible.

Guyana had helped me build on strengths gained from long years in international development. The journey that I had anticipated in preparing a strategic plan for an organization in an urban area was enriched by just following my personal interests in birdwatching, fibre arts, architectural observation, and photography.

I departed Guyana stronger than when I arrived and coined what I dubbed activision. I might be able to return with an even clearer plan for community empowerment. I'd be poised to tackle opposition and challenges, build my strengths, and tame my weaknesses. I'd also let the process of the journey flow onward and keep not only my eyes but all my senses alert for development opportunities.

Back home I continued absorbing the experience while sipping award-winning wine from our Okanagan Valley. I savoured the ambrosia of grapes from our sunny region embraced by lakes and high country.

Cuso accepted the placement description. I applied. Cuso responded with an invitation. Hurrah! I was approved and didn't have to fly to Ottawa for another five-day training session. One inoculation of such training per annum was deemed sufficient. I would return in three months as an Ecological and Economic Development Advisor. I felt both honoured and humbled at the support and speed of the placement decision. The glow of accomplishment in the initial posting and opportunity for future involvement reigned supreme over my three months at home. I used the time to gear up for re-entry.

Initially, I needed to deal with the cause of my mysterious weight loss. My doctor had said, "Loss of more than ten percent of body weight is a cause for concern. Twenty pounds is thirteen percent of your normal weight." A subsequent full examination and tests registered nothing abnormal. So, we concluded my sudden shrinkage was probably a combination of factors. First, there was the exceptional high heat and humidity in Georgetown, even more intense than my years in India. My vegetarian preferences plus neglect of dairy might also have triggered the condition. The stress of my assignment was probably a contributing factor with civil unrest after the prison riot along with tensions in both the Cuso and VYC offices creating further pressure. None of these factors individually was likely to cause such loss of weight but combined could have been the reason. My remedy was to increase caloric intake and add dairy to regain ten pounds. I then levelled off and left, so to speak, the remaining ten pounds in Guyana,

Another odd physical phenomenon, the change in my sleep cycle that started in Guyana, continued. In Georgetown, I would wake up with ideas and work for a couple of hours in the middle of the night, a time I called creative insomnia. Maybe it was early-bird syndrome.

Back in Canada, I learned that prior to the advent of the Industrial Revolution in the mid-1700s, such a pattern of sleep was common. Some people would sleep three or four hours, then be awake for an hour or two. Sometimes this was caused by needing to put another log on the fire or check on noises. Then people would go back to sleep for a second phase of rest.

This pattern of interrupted sleep occurred in all cultures. If people remained awake, the time could be filled with art or crafts, cooking, sex, reading or writing, or maybe strolling out into the night. So, my biphasic sleep cycle was nothing new or unusual. It served me quite well in Guyana where I used it for reflection and work while in total solitude. It was during one of these nocturnal periods that I'd understood the essence of my proposed return to Guyana. My recreational birdwatching and handcrafts and even interest in architecture could serve as bridges in developing essential relationships in Indigenous communities.

With my physical issues of weight and sleep understood, I turned my attention to an event in Guyana that would happen without me but would set the stage for my return. It would be a quest for Harpy Eagle nests and assessment of river and camping conditions. We needed a preliminary expedition of a few days up Akawini Creek deep into the rainforest. Jessica would organize this with local guides plus a birding guide or two. I would send some funding.

Before I left, Jessica and I had decided that if Cuso agreed to post me again, she would organize such a trip. She would provide the boat, driver, and supplies for three days of camping. Chris would come with his GPS. One or more of the guides from Georgetown would be paid to return for bird identification. I would supply money for gas, funding for the guide or guides, and cover food cost for the expedition. If I was to continue work with Cuso, I would wire money back to Georgetown, care of one of the guides, with instructions as to how much he was to keep for transportation and other funding. The balance of the money would be collected by Jessica when she was next in Georgetown and would finance the balance of the venture.

The result was that she received only a small portion of the funds, the rest was pocketed by the receiver, and no guide or guides returned to Region 2. It was a bad choice on my part and another lesson learned: do not entrust money to an acquaintance in a struggling organization in the Global South. The temptation to steal can be too great.

The handling of money was often a challenge in Guyana as demonstrated by two incidents from the Rewa trip a month before my departure. Jan and I were only able to get to Rewa by paying for a full five seats for the return trip. When the day arrived, we were told we'd be flying south to Lethem to pick up more passengers and then fly north to Georgetown. That was fine with us as it didn't take much more time.

The bonus was that one of the men who boarded in Lethem received a surprise greeting from both of us, "Patrick!" He was a long-term Cuso South-to-South volunteer from Uganda who had married a Guyanese woman and was continuing work in agricultural development in the interior. Jan knew him because of a Canadian project that Patrick was working on and that she monitored. I knew him from Cuso meetings and from his input on Lydia's agricultural placement description.

We three chatted all the way to Georgetown and when we parted, Jan and I had a brief discussion. We knew the airline was struggling to fill flights with what Jan later summarized as "expensive fuel, lack of regular passengers, poor infrastructure, [and] telecommunications problems." However, this return flight had recently acquired more passengers for a profitable flight. We'd paid for a total of five seats for the flight, the minimum needed. We'd talked about donating those three seats if anyone needed medical treatment in Georgetown but couldn't figure out a way to make the offer. Now we should have our money refunded for those extra seats.

Jan asked me to sit quietly in the airline's office and let her handle the matter. That was fine with me. She was the one who was officially part of the diplomatic corps. There was discussion and some scuttling between the counter and the back room, but Jan made a solid case for immediate cash repayment. When we were outside, she handed over half the wad of bills to me and we exchanged smiles.

The other incident related to paying for accommodations and tours at Rewa. Despite several exchanges of emails, I was left with an understanding that the total was calculated for each of us. When it came time to pay, it was apparent the sum that I'd been quoted was the total for both of us.

Jan and I looked at each other and she switched to our country's other language, French, and asked if that was fine with me. "*Certainement!*" I replied. We each counted out only half the money we'd expected to pay and left big tips in appreciation for the overall experience. Later, I used the extra funds from the Rewa trip for the additional birding expeditions, including Adel's Rainforest Resort.

Now, despite the reduction of funds needed for the preliminary search for eagle nests, Jessica had scraped together enough money and pushed onward with the trip. It included David from Adel's, Chris and his GPS, and two young Indigenous women that the Akawini toshao wanted on the trip. Jessica and company managed to get the eagle nests surveyed and spotted a bird.

Jessica reported, "We were just having breakfast in the miserable rain when I happened to look up and there, in the clearing between huge trees, I saw a Harpy Eagle with its massive wingspread—a good six feet. Glorious!" This eagle was the second largest in the world, with the Philippine Eagle taking first place at often over two metres.

I was thrilled with Jessica and her crew's accomplishment. This was the critical preliminary trip with the authorization and support of the toshao and, presumably, the village council. A full expedition into the interior would be planned when I returned.

"What was it like?" was the constant question while I was back home in BC. I answered from many angles. Interviewed by local newspapers, I said, "I like to empower people, [but] I don't like to have power over people. Educate people, help them to be literate, help them to be healthy so that they can craft a better life for themselves.... I feel more alive when I am in less overdeveloped countries."

Why did I say "overdeveloped"? I was referencing the Global North's outsized ecological footprint and the selling of its definition of development to the rest of the world. It was not equitable and not sustainable.

I also did presentations about Guyana to two different groups. The South Okanagan Naturalists' Club had requested a presentation even before my initial departure. "Tell us what it was like, not only the birds, but life in Guyana," said Anthea who scheduled speakers. I was happy to oblige because this friend also shared my belief in the larger context of linking the natural and the human world in both the Global North and the Global South.

Someone in the audience said, "Those claws really are three inches long!" as they viewed Marcy maneuvering the three-toed sloth to hang onto the boat for a ride to the far bank of the Essequibo River.

I tucked in one slide with three images: a newspaper clipping of the prison fire underway, the aftermath, plus one square of embroidered flames on my birding vest. Sober silence reigned as wildfires were still raging in BC.

I continued the presentation with images of time at the Indigenous eco-lodge in Rewa and my outings in the final month of my posting. I included Andy leaning forward into the spotting scope and Linton using my binoculars.

I celebrated the Hoatzin with three images. First, it was the bird in the wild in the company of others. Then, its image was embroidered onto my birding vest along with a colour photo pinned as a stitching guide. Finally, the image of a huge, ragged Hoatzin made of papier mâché moldering outside a government building, the remains of its appearance on a float in a festival parade. Our naturalists' club usually showed birds in the wild, but I wanted them to see how birds were woven into the very fabric of Guyanese life.

A knock-kneed, fluffy little Wattled Jacana chick standing on a lily pad in evening's golden hour was the final image. The audience murmured with delight. I also used the occasion to announce my second posting and requested donations of used equipment, especially binoculars. "I'll take equipment back to Guyana to encourage development of wildlife groups as a basis for ecotourism efforts."

"Delighted to help," said a club member. "Let us know how things turn out." Donations started to flow at the next club meeting. This request empowered my birding friends to make contributions to Indigenous villagers. People who would never visit Guyana could contribute to my return journey and feel the satisfaction of involvement.

Contrasting buildings in Georgetown

I prepared another presentation at the request of friend who was a local architect. Chris had asked, "Can you show us what you encounter in Guyana that's architecturally interesting?"

"Sure, and it'll be not only some early Dutch and later British colonial architecture, but whatever I can find of Indigenous buildings, classic or contemporary."

The iconic photo that I shared to start the presentation was of a massive, three-storey, white concrete home with each level at least three-and-a-half meters high. This was a sampler of the classic porticos, gables, pillars, verandas, balconies, fretwork, arches, and a patchwork quilt of architectural styles in a huge house built at ground level. Over the top but educational.

In the foreground was a shabby clapboard house somehow holding together on weathered posts with crumbling steps and railings. The juxtaposition of these images needed no commentary from me.

I went on to show my audience of architects some beautiful renditions of the louvred Demerara window and lush tropical vegetation, which one could almost smell based on the beauty. A Great Kiskadee was perched on rolled razor wire that topped high iron fencing surrounding a classic Georgetown residence. A horse-drawn cart shared the road with a tanker truck. A plain turquoise minivan was lined up behind a van painted with tiger stripes and sporting jazzy hubcaps.

Market tables laden with fruits and vegetables promised good eating and vied with nearby tropical vegetation for vibrancy. A classic, cream-coloured Georgetown building housed Indigenous artifacts and showcased a tidy row of louvered Demerara windows upstairs tipped outward. I took the architects inside to see Guyana's rich, dark hardwood as flooring and wall panels. Display cases and wall hangings showed the artistry of Indigenous basketwork, fibre arts, pottery, and weaponry. Miniature architectural displays demonstrated the structural use of organic materials of the rainforest, savannah, and marshlands: timber, poles of saplings or bamboo, vines, reeds, and grasses.

Another image was of Marcy and me on Turtle Mountain overlooking the rainforest and the Essequibo in the North Rupununi. Marcy, with her bronze beauty, matched the majesty of the forest. The picture of Milner and me at Surama with the savannah and mountains in the background showed the varied and rich environment of the country. "You've given us a window into a completely different world," said my architect friend.

I shared snippets of the natural and built world that most of my audience would never see. Maybe I'd helped them understand my recent journey. Knowledge is power. Who knows what my presentation might have generated in this firm's future designs or the urge of its young architects to travel beyond their culture as many of the firm's foreign interns were already doing.

While packing my bag and chatting with staff, I realized yet again that I'd offered a window into life in what was considered a poor country but that was a rich experience. Do such presentations have any effect on rebalancing a world suffering from extremes of the haves and have-nots? I'll probably never know. I just share my experiences with an open hand and hope.

The most important book that I read in my three months at home was *The Inconvenient Indian* by the Indigenous Canadian scholar Thomas King. He focused on the "savagism versus civilization dichotomy…that North America trusts without question [and it is] so powerful a toxin that it contaminates all our major institutions. Under its influence, democracy becomes not simply a form of representative government, but an organizing principle that bundles individual freedom, Christianity, and capitalism into a marketable product carrying with it the unexamined promise of wealth and prosperity. It suggests that anything else is, by default, savage and bankrupt." (p. 79).

I continued mulling over Guyana and its Indigenous peoples' lives. The country's history was a distinctive blend of colonialism based on slavery, indentured labour, and a strong undercurrent of nine Indigenous cultures. It continues struggling to gain a measure of order, equity, and prosperity that some citizens feel had existed when it was part of the British Empire. Are memories really about a better time, or are they just a gossamer drape of imperial nostalgia? How does the increasing emphasis on indigeneity globally affect the future of Guyana and the world? Ongoing questions.

Thomas King spoke of his Canadian Indigenous people in a manner that I had perceived even in brief encounters in Guyana. "Native cultures aren't static. They're dynamic, adaptive, and flexible, and for many of us, the modern variations of older tribal tradition continue to provide order, satisfaction, identity, and value in our lives." (p. 219).

I continued reflecting on both the remembered past and the imagined future of my work in Guyana. I was careful to avoid harbouring a saviour mentality where people are viewed as objects who needed rescuing.

My role was now twofold. First, I would assist Indigenous villages in aspiring to however they saw themselves participating in ecotourism and whatever else they chose. Second, I would invite them to share aspects of their way of life in constructing a way forward. This sounded very manufactured—constructing—but it really did describe the process of mutual contributions.

I knew that Jessica and I would first have to clear all plans with Vanessa and Cuso along with the toshaos and village councils of both territories. I would be the liaison between Cuso and the village leaders. We needed expectations satisfied by everyone, and that would require settling on the details of the relationships.

Part of my return assignment would be to scout the country for other professional birders to assist with identification. Villagers could help but they would use local call names in English or Arawak. I would work with them to match these with formal book names. We'd empower each other. I didn't expect opposition in the Indigenous communities since they had already expressed interest in ecotourism. My challenge would be to encourage attainable, sustainable projects.

Some of my strength came from Jessica's good rapport with the toshaos and her eagerness to share information and insights with me. A weakness we both perceived for me in fulfilling the assignment was transportation. Akawini took an hour or more by motorboat from Adel's. The toshao was a reserved man and sometimes hard to reach by cell phone. This meant communication would also be a continuing challenge. Akawini boats would have to transport me according to their schedule as they passed Adel's with me paying the going rate. Travel to and from Wakapoa was shorter, more frequent, and cheaper.

Cuso had never worked in Region 2, the Pomeroon-Supenaam, whose names harked back to Dutch colonial days before the nineteenth century. Vanessa was eager to support and actively participate in this initial venture. She said that the country program office would serve as the official partner organization. When I returned to Guyana, we would make a special trip to visit the toshaos and the village councils and discuss what they would like to see accomplished in six months.

Jessica offered room and board at Adel's at a discounted rate for my Region 2 headquarters between visits to the villages and trips to Georgetown. Cuso would provide a per diem allowance and cover all my transportation costs. My challenge would be to arrange a schedule that maximized both my availability for meetings in Georgetown and work in the villages. Online work, printing, and getting supplies could only occur in the city. Cell phone communication would be my lifeline while at Adel's and in Wakapoa. Cell communication in Akawini would be intermittent.

Food, check. Clothing, check. Shelter, check. Transportation, check. Communication, check. Good to go.

Part Two

2018

Don't go in thinking you can solve someone's problem, that's arrogance.... Go in and receive the experience.

Lily Yeh, Philadelphia artist and activist

Chapter Nine

Eagle Quest

Barely two weeks back in Guyana, I was in Region 2. We wasted no time in organizing and setting the start date for a second quest for signs of the Harpy Eagle. Clement, our boatman for this expedition, navigated our craft from Adel's boathouse up to the stelling for loading gear. The plank seat in front had been removed to make cargo space. The fifty-gallon gasoline barrel was already wedged in the bow. Camping gear, food bags, the cooler, packs, and life vests were ready for stowing. The five guard dogs, with pure white mother Lily in the lead, dashed about, which added to the commotion.

"Start handing down," said Eon. Jessica and I grabbed containers and bundles and swung them over to the men. Eon, with the physique and dexterity of a stevedore, had positioned himself near the barrel and wedged items wherever they would fit. Clement stayed at the stern and stowed items under the rear seat. Jessica and I then climbed in and stashed the remaining bags as signaled by Clement and positioned ourselves on the back seat.

My waterproof pouch with all our tech equipment rested between Jessica and me. I stared at the gasoline barrel, my contribution, and the big-ticket item at GYD50,000 that was $333 Canadian or $250 US. It was an ironic investment: an ecotourism expedition fueled by gas. It also reminded us that we were under the dark shadow of ExxonMobil's offshore oil discovery oozing its way into Guyanese life and greasing the political system.

"Look!" I said as a tiny green frog, the size of my thumbnail, hopped from a puddle of rainwater on the floorboards, leaped to the side of the boat, and onto the steps. Clement said, "That's good luck for the trip.

Departure from Adel's stelling

"Good luck! Great," said Jessica, probably remembering the nonstop rain of the initial foray three months prior. "We welcome a dose of luck."

We left with our dogs barking and dashing around in dismay. Butch, the alpha male, was on the bottom step with his paws in the lapping creek. He wanted to leap in and paddle after us. "Butch, no," said Jessica. "We'll be back!"

With everyone and everything squeezed in for the long journey upriver, we motored forward. Reaching a patch of rainforest cleared for a small homestead, there was another sign from the natural world. I said, "Eon, there's a rainbow and, from where I sit, it ends just over your head."

Jessica laughed. "Your head must be the pot of gold." Eon turned and grinned before he resettled himself with muscled arms the colour of Guyanese mahogany draped over the seat back. I watched him absorb the embrace of the rainforest.

We were off for a five-day expedition deep into Akawini territory for more signs of the iconic and scarce Harpy Eagle. The name came from monsters of Greek mythology with the body of a bird and the face of a woman. Harpies carried evildoers off for punishment. Now this magnificent bird of prey was suffering from hunting and habitat loss.

It was synchronistic that I had picked up the latest issue of *National Geographic* at the Vancouver airport when returning to Guyana. It declared the Year of the Bird with a sharp-eyed Secretary Bird of Sub-Saharan Africa on the cover. The lead article, "Why Birds Matter," was in capital letters. The magazine noted that one in eight bird species is facing extinction. We were on a quest to locate one such species.

Jessica and I had used my time back in Canada to email each other a thumbnail sketch of our respective backgrounds and extend plans for work. She was a Brit who had gone bush a decade prior leaving a fast-paced London life where she was an innovative, high-profile marketer.

Months ago, when we met at Adel's, she had told me, "All that I was doing was getting people to buy more stuff. There had to be more to life. Here I'm involved in education and health care. This work matters and this is where I'll be buried."

She was initially based in Georgetown and had now been at Adel's for nearly two years offering pro bono service marketing and managing the little resort. Guyana, especially the riverine world of the Pomeroon, was her Eden. This area contained elements of Eden for me too, or I wouldn't have returned.

Jessica's skills also included time as a certified safari guide and cook when working in Australia at one point in her past. Besides the camping gear of woven cotton hammocks, mosquito nets, and tarps that filled our boat, there was a kerosene stove, pots, and necessary eating utensils. There was packaged food that could be prepared easily for what would soon be the seven of us.

Over coffee the week prior when we were both in Georgetown, Jessica had said, "I'm in the city for my birthday, plus there's someone I want you to meet." She exuded a radiant glow when she went on to say, "We're now making our partnership public."

I smiled and said, "Congratulations. Double celebration."

Eon was a surprise. He was a striking, muscular man with short, natty dreadlocks, glasses with thick lenses, and a strong jaw. He had joined us for coffee and when we shook hands, I felt the strength of his grip. Eon spoke with a British accent because London had been home for decades. I would learn his backstory gradually during the trip. Now he had been in Guyana nearly a year and was eager for this foray into the interior. "I'll be your Sherpa on this trip," said Eon with laughter in his voice. "Time to see more of my country."

"Great," I said. "We'll quest for birds and also your heritage. Jessica tells me that you've been gone since you were ten. There'll be much catching up to do."

Besides meeting Jessica with Eon shortly before our trip and buying some additional supplies, there was a swirl of Cuso activities. I was in Georgetown for the required week of in-country training for new volunteers. Vanessa had asked me to make another presentation on getting around the city and offer to guide anyone interested in an initial walkabout. She and I also met privately for a catch-up and ongoing discussion of my new assignment.

One thing that I needed was a haircut. I called Julia, the sister of Colin who had been my driver in Iwokrama the year before and told me about his close call with an anaconda. "I came back to Guyana for a good haircut," I said to Julia, who laughed.

"I have time later this afternoon. Come. I want to hear your news."

Ann from another Canadian aid organization, World University Service of Canada, or WUSC, had heard of my birding interest and wanted to meet as we were both a rare species in the country. I made time for a walk with her in the National Park and she was fascinated with my upcoming posting. She said, "I'm based in Georgetown, so do keep in touch with details of your rural life. My husband Phil will also be very interested in what you're doing."

"Sure enough," I said with good cheer as I was glad others were also intrigued by the interior.

My new apartment was across from the Cuso office. I was sharing with Andrea, my Cuso colleague from my original posting. She had returned to Guyana to complete her one-year assignment after an emergency exit for a few weeks. Her husband Claude, my other close colleague, remained in Canada to deal with a crisis in his family. Andrea said, "I told Vanessa I would only share an apartment with you. There's so much going on in our lives right now that I can only finish this assignment in the company of a friend. And, by the way, you look better not so skinny."

Vanessa had honoured her request. I moved in with my usual kit plus a second checked bag filled with supplies for birdwatching and fibre arts workshops.

Good news arrived about Lydia. Cuso had accepted her for the posting of Organic Tropical Agriculture Development Advisor. She was assigned to Wakapoa in Region 2 and would arrive in three to four months, a year after we had met at Captain's House of Flavours near Bourda Market.

I showed up at the regular Wednesday night gathering at a local restaurant for Quiz Night and acquaintances welcomed me back with a free beer and greeted the new volunteers that I'd brought along. One of our Guyanese staff members had helped start this event over a decade prior. It was another opportunity for locals and expats to gather and form teams answering localized questions of the Trivial Pursuit variety. This was always a lively night of matching wits and enjoying a sip-n-nibble. I had attended a few times the previous year and now resumed attendance from time to time.

While in Georgetown, my total focus soon became the expedition. I loaded my daypack with binoculars, a birding camera, my small digital camera, a cell phone, and the Cuso satellite phone. I packed cotton shirts and pants, running shoes, and rubber boots, and made sure that I had my antimalarial medication and water filtration bottle and tablets. I was good to go.

Eon was the surprise addition to how I had envisioned this new assignment and I appreciated his declaration as a self-proclaimed porter. This expedition was a momentous event on many levels for him. His parents split when he was young with his mother taking the six children to the US. It was dangerous times politically in Guyana with power struggles after independence in 1966.

His father, educated in the UK in electrical engineering, remained and provided critical technical expertise in establishing telecommunications for the fledgling country. Georgetown soon became the go-to place for other South American countries adopting new telecommunication systems. Now Eon, with training from MIT in mechanical engineering, among other skills, had returned and was rediscovering his lost Guyanese soul.

In further preparation for our trip, Eon had arranged for me to meet the Minister of Forestry, who knew his father, and was now also his friend. The minister, a large woman in a long, loose-fitting cotton garment, offered me coffee, which we sipped at her home.

Narrowing her eyes and lowering her voice, she said, "The forest is no place for amateurs."

I looked her straight in the eye and said, "I know. We'll be guided by Arawaks from Akawini who are hunters and loggers. We would never attempt such an exercise without Indigenous knowledge, and skills. We also have permission of the toshao and the village council."

Later, Jessica told me in a quiet voice as we were assembling gear at Adel's, "Eon's never been in the rainforest, much less in the hinterland. He's never even been camping anywhere and had an urban life when he moved to the UK. This might be make-it or break-it in our relationship."

I studied her bent over tying a hammock into a tighter bundle and said, "I'm betting on make-it."

That first day of the expedition, we'd headed into the interior with gear piled to the gunnels and the busyness of departure yielding to the calm of creek passage. We motored through dense rainforest with vines dangling and I watched for snakes on overhead branches. Jessica looked away, dragging her fingers in the water and studying the ripples. We experienced rainforest yielding to a fringe of bushes along the banks. Then the marshlands or wetlands of the extended coastal floodplains, thick with high grass, appeared on either side of the creek. Eon turned my way and, in a soft voice as he nodded toward the lush grass, asked, "Is that agricultural land?"

Akawini wetlands

I leaned forward and whispered near his ear, "No, it's permanent wetlands." I then realized how limited his knowledge was of the geography of his homeland having left as a youngster. He nodded again and turned back to absorb this new understanding of another reality of his country. He was regaining his taproot and letting his life in the UK and elsewhere in the world fade in importance.

With no sign of human habitation or adaptation, each of us eased further into the world around us. Jessica had settled in her seat with the far-off look that I noted when she was on the water. "This is where I'm most at home," she had told me when I'd first visited Adel's.

Clement, operating the motor and understanding the land and the river, kept the boat moving at a quiet, steady pace. Jessica had given David a five-day holiday from the resort to spend time with his family in Wakapoa. Clement's wife Rema was tending Adel's—with no current bookings—and feeding the dogs while we were away.

Eon sat with his dreadlocks resting like finger-thick springs on his head and continued draping his arms over the back of the seat. He turned his head occasionally to glimpse something far out in the marshlands. When a bird with long toes stepping across lily pads near the bank caught his eye, I said, "Wattled Jacana but spurwing to the locals." I was delighted to see this lovely riverine bird in the wild. It had been the first bird that I'd spotted and photographed the previous year when in the Botanical Gardens.

An hour later, we edged into Chris's home channel for assistance. Minerva and the youngest of their children were there to greet us. We would start this expedition by hiking in the highlands of Ykinipa, the largest of the Akawini settlements in the wetlands and only a few minutes ahead on the creek. At the stelling, we would collect the toshao's eldest sons, Jacob and Elijah—age nineteen and eighteen respectively—as guides and porters.

Elijah and Jacob

Now we picked up one of Chris's elder sons who would drop us at the settlement and take Adel's big boat back to his family's home. We'd rendezvous with Chris the next day when he'd bring two of his smaller boats for passage up the narrowing creek. First, we had to check the reported nesting site in the high country with the help of Jacob and Elijah.

The new Ykinipa stelling was impressive. It was less than two years old and a quarter mile from the creek to the dry land of the settlement rising out of the marshlands. With a sturdy steel frame and thick plank flooring, the stelling was engineered to last. Nearby was the old structure of rotted wood, still partially visible but totally unusable. President Granger had visited months earlier to dedicate the new structure, and it was the pride of the community.

We were kitting up when the young men arrived with their packs and cutlasses. Both were tall and handsome with bronze skin and thick, curly black hair. They moved with the grace and dignity of men comfortable in their bodies and their environment. We all hefted our gear and walked single file along the stelling and onto a dirt path through the settlement of small wooden houses with thatch roofs. For the next three hours, the six of us hiked uphill.

Eon had never experienced such a trek and certainly not with a backpack. He had bought the pack in Georgetown, but it was poor quality. I'd stitched to reinforce areas even before we'd left Adel's. Watching him struggle, I gave him bits of advice at rest stops. "Lock your knee for a moment at the end of each step. That transfers weight to your skeleton and gives your muscles, ligaments, and tendons momentary relief. Also, shorten your stride, if necessary."

Later, in a low voice, Eon said, "Works great! Have Jessica doing it now, too."

"Trick of the trek," I said as I again adjusted the straps on his pack so more of the load was carried closer to his wide shoulders and not hanging off his backside.

When we reached the end of the logging road hours later, Jacob pointed to a large nest high in a tree off the trail. While the crew was setting up camp, I cut through undergrowth and vines watching for snakes. Circling the tree looking for a roosting spot, I saw a fallen trunk with a clear view of the nest. I forced a path through underbrush and cleared seating space.

I heard noises from the campsite and caught glimpses of the brothers chopping poles and wedging them into the ground at set angles. Eon was busy with the hammocks and mosquito nets. Then the men were wrestling to unfold a large tarp to cover everything in case of rain. Jessica was firing up the kerosene stove while perched on an upturned plastic bucket. Clement was sitting on a log away from the campsite watching the sky.

First camp in the highlands

Tinkering with camera settings, I realized that Jacob was now standing a metre above and behind me on another fallen tree. These were obviously the rejects from logging operations focused on wallaba and greenheart and other prized species. With a cell phone in hand, Jacob answered my unspoken question. "Need a connection," he said with what I had come to understand as his minimal use of words. Akawini didn't have a cell tower, but Wakapoa, a few kilometres to the north, did. We were high above the rainforest and marshlands and Jacob was hoping to pick up a signal.

"What's the smart phone model you're using?" I asked.

"Samsung Galaxy," he said while moving the phone to various positions.

"What's your cost?" I asked preparing to think in local money.

"3,500 dollars. We pay somebody in the village to get a prepaid package." I did a quick calculation. That was about twenty dollars in Canadian or US money.

"What do you get in the package?" I asked.

"Calls and texting. Maybe videos and music. But one movie takes the whole 3,500. We just use basic service." This was my longest conversation with Jacob so far. At that price, no wonder he and others in Akawini could only afford talk and text.

Near dusk, when I wandered back to camp to see how preparations were going, Clement signaled me to head back into the bush. I struggled to get to my roost and focus the camera. A large bird was perched on a bare limb near the nest.

The female Harpy Eagle was larger than the male and was dark grey. This bird had a white head, breast, and upper leg feathers with black on the shoulders, back, and crown. Was this a male or an adolescent Harpy Eagle? I'd studied the drawings in my birding book and Harpy Eagle photos online but didn't know what I was seeing in the wild. What was the sex, age, and breeding stage of this bird? I really needed input from an experienced birding guide.

The bird scanned its domain and then stared down at me. I ignored the no-see-ums that were biting through my socks and three layers of clothing. Earlier, I'd slathered exposed body parts with pungent crabwood oil, but these invaders were again going for my juicy parts: abdomen and thighs.

After a few minutes, the bird flew while the cherished golden hour was fading. I retreated through the brush catching my foot in a mass of vines and nearly falling. Everyone crowded around with shouts of "Did you get it?" and stared over my shoulder for a glimpse of the camera's screen. Soon there were murmurs of delight and exclamations of "You got it!"

Yes, but what was it? We would have to wait two months for a definitive answer since my connection with the birders in Georgetown was ruptured with the earlier pilfered funds and no-show to guide Jessica's preliminary excursion.

Clement spotted the bird first, so Jessica named the area Camp Clement. I found it humorous that she had the explorer's desire to name key spots in our expedition as though this was a first encounter with this land. It was known for countless years by Indigenous people and had experienced hundreds of years of foreign incursions. Nevertheless, I enjoyed the sheer fun of the dubbing.

Jacob and Elijah were part of the expedition also for their knowledge of bushcraft and ability to handle the smaller boats. Another reason was that the toshao wanted to strengthen the territory's fledgling Youth Wildlife Group and get training for ecotourism. They were obvious candidates for this expedition. Just before dinner, the brothers were absent for a short time and returned to camp looking refreshed. They had known of a stream a few minutes away and had slipped off to wash and collect fresh water.

A vexed Jessica said, "We're all tired, sweaty, and low on drinking water. You're also here to take care of people like us who don't know the area. You should have told us about the stream and let us bathe and collect fresh water too if you're going to be guides." The young men had nodded and then stepped aside and become very busy double-checking the lines securing the hammocks and tarps. Jessica was now called The Boss, a named bestowed by Eon.

Dinner was standard camp fare with food from boxes, cans, and packages. We perched on logs, chatted, and then slipped away to refresh ourselves and refill our water bottles before hammock time. I popped a purification tablet into my special water bottle as I refilled it from the fast-moving stream. I skipped bathing and just stood knee-deep splashing water on my arms and enjoying the feel of cool running water on my tired legs and feet.

Darkness fell, conversations ebbed, and we climbed into our respective hammocks slung side by side. I tucked a small flashlight and toilet paper into my pockets and set my shoes nearby. Then I carefully placed my bottom in the centre of the hammock and pivoted my legs and torso in balance. Once settled, I zipped up the attached mosquito net. There I was, an ear of corn nestled in a husk.

One cannot toss and turn when sleeping this way. There was only one position possible. With an exciting day and my first time overnighting in a hammock, I slept lightly and only for short stretches. I resigned myself to just relaxing into yet another bout of creative insomnia. I conjured more details of a strategic plan for this project for the next few months and simply gave myself over to enjoyment of the cool and fragrant night air and the gentle breathing of my companions.

At dawn, the stirring started, and we had all climbed out of our hammocks stretching and preparing for the day ahead. We stowed our personal gear and dismantled the camp. Jessica cooked porridge for belly ballast and perked us up with a pot of steaming coffee. With the camp fitted into backpacks, we were soon underway with Jacob in the lead.

Suddenly, he veered off the path. He was looking up and had seen a large bird in the high canopy. Was it the same bird as last night? Its mate? A juvenile? I readied my camera and aimed overhead at a difficult angle as I didn't want to shift position and alarm the bird. Its back was facing us, and it only occasionally turned its head to peer down. Besides the awkward angle, I was dealing with morning mist and thick foliage.

Soon I felt my upper arm muscles weaken. Eon was standing closest to me. "Eon, stand behind me and support my arms so I can keep shooting," Without a sound, he stepped near me so we could use our combined strength to continue.

A few moments later, the bird flew, and everyone again crowded around saying, "Let's see!" This was a darker bird, but this could have been early morning light versus yesterday's bird in the full glow of sunset. However, I had a collection of record shots from both days.

Positive identification would have to come later, and it would be startling.

Continuing our downhill trek, I again adjusted Eon's pack for greater comfort. I now suggested, "Flex the knee. Don't lock it. Save the joint by letting the muscles, ligaments, and tendons help."

"Shorten stride, too?" asked Eon. I confirmed what he'd figured out with his knowledge of mechanical engineering applied to his own body.

Our trek, with occasional rest stops, proved nearly uneventful till near Ykinipa. Jacob was leading with Jessica behind. Suddenly, she turned with both arms straight forward and palms facing us. "Stop!" she said in her boss voice. She and Jacob then focused on what was on the path. The rest of us crept forward. I heard "carrot snake" and could see a bright green snake—the width of a thumb and at least a metre long—coiled on the path's warm, white sand.

"Carrot snake?" I asked.

"No, silly, parrot snake," said Jessica. Of course. It was green. Someone from the Global North was more familiar with carrots than parrots. What to do was the next question as Jacob had said that it was deadly.

Jessica continued in boss mode. "Clement, get a stick. We won't kill it, but we'll give it a good thrashing." Clement dutifully advanced from his rear position as our sweep, the man at the end of line. I had told him earlier about his job description.

"This means if a jaguar sneaks up from behind, it'll get you first and you'll save the rest of us." He didn't find my explanation very funny, and rightly so.

Now Clement stepped forward with a big stick—whack, whack—and hurled the stunned or dead snake off the trail. I sidled up to Jacob and asked how long, if bitten, one would last without medical attention. He looked over at me and said, "Maybe three hours." I nodded, gulped, and fell back in line.

We resumed our marching order with accelerated heartbeats and hiked on through the village waving to curious residents. The brothers stepped off the trail briefly to check in with their mother and the youngest of their little brothers and sisters in this family of nine not in primary school. The rest of us continued our walk on the footpath to the creek.

Jessica had phoned Chris and alerted him when to meet us. Gear piled high, we leaned on the railing and watched him approaching from downriver in his medium-sized wooden boat with its small engine and the big gas barrel. He towed a small wooden boat, blunt at both ends, with no engine. The creek would diminish as we continued our quest upriver, and we'd be paddling, pulling, or poling in the deep interior.

We managed to wedge all our gear, including Chris's chainsaw, and ourselves into the two boats. The rushing high waters of the recent rainy season had eroded banks. We would need the chainsaw to deal with trees that had fallen across the creek.

Soon we were underway leaving the settled highlands with the creek growing narrower and shallower. Tall grasses crowded our passage. Chris was at the bow with his cutlass hacking tangled masses of vegetation. Clement was at the stern monitoring the creek level so he could operate the motor for as long as possible. All was quiet except for the noise of our passing. Jacob looked upward often but didn't announce any sightings of birds.

By late afternoon, we had arrived at an already established campsite with some hammock poles in place. It was level with the riverbank, which was safe as this was the relatively dry season. To honour Eon's first venture into the deep interior, Jessica dubbed this Camp Eon.

Some of us tramped the forest on the opposite bank using Chris's GPS to locate another nest he'd spotted on earlier trips. We weaved between massive trees, often girdled with thick vines, and watched for snakes. Alas, no luck sighting nests or eagles or any birds. It was afternoon, not ideal birding time.

We crossed back over the creek poling the small boat and enjoyed the aroma of the dinner that Jessica was preparing. It was unmemorable as standard camp fare but filling. We'd had a long day of hiking and then passage on the creek. We chatted for a bit after our meal and were soon ready for our hammocks with mosquito repellent rings smoldering in various locations. Climbing into our respective hammocks, we heard "Aargh!" along with a loud thump when Jessica hit the ground tangled in her hammock, which hung next to mine.

I peeked out of my sleeping sling and asked, "What are you doing down there?" She was laughing and obviously not hurt.

We gathered and helped pull her upright while Eon studied the frazzled rope. There was a mosquito repellent ring wafting smoke attached to the hammock stake just below the singed rope. "Clement, your work?" asked Eon. The guilty look told all. No great damage done, but Jessica did have choice comments about Clement's judgment. The rest of us stifled our laughter as the culprit sidled back to his hammock without a word.

We crawled back into our respective hammocks, and I slept soundly this second night. It was a small sandbank, so hammocks were quite close. Chris and I found ourselves hip to hip all night. If one shifted, the other swayed in companionable harmony.

The next morning, we repeated our camp routines and watched birds flit by disturbed by our presence. I reminded myself that we weren't equipped nor could spare the time to trek deep into the raw rainforest for full-scale birdwatching.

Whack, whack. Chris cleared our path of low-hanging branches with his bare feet planted on the bow of our bigger wooden boat. He swung his cutlass with the muscles of his bronze body rippling as we pushed further into the tangle of rainforest.

One massive tree had fallen too low for us to lean down and pass under. We heard the whirr of the chainsaw until it came to a sudden stop wedged tight when the trunk shifted. Even with over an hour of manoeuvring, which included nearly everybody jumping up and down on the trunk in synchronized motion, the blade remained stuck. Finally, something shifted. Chris pulled the blade free and repositioned it to finish the job. Resuming a steady speed, we motored onward.

I sat midship next to the inflatable bag that held all our technical equipment, especially my camera, and gazed into the thick riverine vegetation tangled along the banks. "Duck!" said Jessica.

"Where?" I asked looking around.

“Your head!” yelled Eon. I focused forward just in time to lunge sideways and feel the fallen trunk brush my back. Our boat slipped forward, and everyone laughed.

“Birders!” said Jessica watching Eon slog through the shallow water pulling the small boat with Elijah while Jacob and Clement poled us in the big boat. “Thinking bird instead of action.”

Soon Jacob, from his standing position ordered, “Eon, get in the boat!”

“Why?” asked Eon still pulling the skiff.

“Eels,” shouted Elijah climbing aboard.

Eon leaped into the skiff with amazing agility. We’d reached a favourite place for electric eels that can generate five hundred volts. Several glided by with an aura of translucence in the sun-dappled flow of water. The creatures were over a metre long.

“They usually don’t kill,” said Chris looking back at Eon who had his hands clenched on the gunnel and was staring into the river. “But they can stun without touching.” The men of the interior could spot the eels in the shallow water, but Eon was urban Guyanese. He couldn’t identify them on his first trip into the heart of the hinterland.

Whirr. I watched Chris use the chainsaw again to cut a thick branch dangling in our path. Jessica held the gunnel of our boat until the branch crashed and the men pushed it downriver beyond our boats.

Tough going deep in the rainforest

Eon was now back in the water since we'd passed eel alley. Jessica asked the men to pole us up close to the bank. She grabbed a tangle of branches and slipped over the side to join the men in handling the boats. The river remained shallow and cool and the current, gentle. I stayed aboard with Chris and Jacob and continued photographing our passage.

By early afternoon, we had reached our third camp and the river—more of a creek—was growing increasingly difficult to access. I suggested that Chris, Elijah, and I head upriver using the small boat to see if we would be able to reach the next nest site the following day. The rest of the crew were left to set up camp. After an hour of much cutlass clearing, I felt the need of a go or no-go decision.

"Chris, why don't you walk forward for fifteen minutes or so and report conditions." He nodded and, with his cutlass, made his way through the thick riverine growth. Soon he returned with the verdict.

"More of the same ahead," he said from up on the bank as he slashed another tangle of vines to get himself back down to the creek.

"We're losing daylight. I suggest we return to camp," I said.

Chris and Elijah nodded and rotated the boat. I paddled a bit with Chris pulling at the bow and Elijah guiding from the stern. The current was with us, and we made steady progress. Dusk embraced us as we crawled up the muddy bank to the camp.

Dinner wasn't quite ready, so we gathered on the logs around the small campfire and talked about what to do. I looked around and said, "We've seen at least one nest, photographed an eagle or eagles, and we're getting tired. Other nests are confirmed by Chris, and an eagle was sighted on the earlier trip. Chris says the way forward will be as tough as we've experienced today. That means more chance of accidents. Do we want to turn back in the morning? We've seen enough on these two trips to judge this area as good for adventure ecotourism." Heads nodded and I heard murmurs of support.

Elijah and Jacob returned to the base of a massive tree where Eon was learning how to build a fire. He'd been shaving dry wood, adding other dry materials, and creating a small pyramid of kindling. Elijah had shown him earlier how to make a V-shaped notch in a large piece of wood and choose a spindle. He was to rub it between his hands as fast as he could while moving his hands up and down the shaft. Soon there was a spark and the notch started to smoke. Eon used his tiny tinder nest of dried leaves and wood shavings to catch the glowing spark and ignited his kindling pyramid. We watched him enjoying this bushcraft and noted the glow of satisfaction on his face. "I've done it! I've built my first fire!"

Jessica returned to stirring the pot of pasta. I overturned a storage bucket and sat nearby. She leaned over and said in a whisper, "I'm so glad you made the call. I'm totally exhausted." She'd been in the river much of the day helping pull or push the boats. I'd stayed in the larger boat taking photos.

Our communications equipment was useless weight. There was no cell phone reception. We needed a clearing and ability to pivot fully seeking a signal for the satellite phone. There was never that opportunity in the rainforest, which meant the device that was mandated by Cuso was of zero use. We were on our own whether dealing with fallen trees, medical emergencies, or anything else. I remembered the words of the Minister of Forestry, "The forest is no place for amateurs." I cherished the presence of our Indigenous companions.

Earlier, as we prepared for this trip, Eon had ferreted out a nugget of family history when he heard the toshao of Akawini's family name. He'd contacted an elderly aunt on his father's side about where his great-grandfather of the same surname was raised. She said, "Up Pomeroon way." Eon was related to Jacob and Elijah. At one point, he announced the link to the young men who responded with their usual reserved silence, something I was growing used to in Indigenous territory.

"Take a picture of me with my cousins," Eon had said. The family resemblance was in the curly black hair. The photograph captured Eon's smile with his arms around the shoulders of the fellows with their composed demeanour. I wondered what other surprises were in store for us on this expedition.

Chapter Ten

Risky Business

The next day promised a leisurely return floating with the current downriver. With no rush to depart, we munched breakfast and puttered around after bundling the hammocks and tarps. Eon tinkered with more bushcraft instructed by Chris, Jacob, and Elijah. Jessica collected the cooking gear for Clement to stow in the boats. I just plunked myself on a log on the bank and watched the creek flowing by while twiddling a twig. Then I took out my birding book and flipped to pages containing some of the birds that I'd identified earlier in Akawini territory. I was curious about local call names. Jacob and Elijah wandered over, so I handed them the book.

"Turkey Vulture. Check vulture," I said. Elijah's finger tracked down the index to "V". "The plate numbers are on the upper left of each page." He then flipped to reveal several species of vultures.

Jacob, now at his side, tapped the picture of a black bird with a bright red, fleshy head and yellow bill and feet and said, "Carrion Crow." Elijah nodded with Chris and Clement looking over his shoulder and grunting in agreement.

"Black-collared Hawk. Try hawk," I said.

Flipping pages, Elijah said, “There” pointing to a drawing of a hawk in flight with rufous chest feathers and black tips on its wings and tail feathers.

Black-collared Hawk

“Turn to the next few pages and look at the adult and immature birds shown standing. Do you think we were seeing an adult or an immature bird near the Ykinipa stelling?”

“There was a white head,” said Elijah, “so adult.”

“Right. Now do you have a local call name?”

“Fish hawk,” said Jacob.

“Ah-ra-pi-KO in Arawak,” said Chris, separating each syllable and emphasizing the last.

“There,” said Eon, “one bird with three names.”

So it went with several more birds. The Dusky Piha, grey with brown highlights, was fruit crow. A hummingbird zoomed by in a flash of iridescent green, blue, and violet and the fellows called out together, "Zwing!" So many of the names were witty, musical, and earthy.

We departed midmorning on this fourth day and drifted beyond the shallow waters with the electric eels. The brothers poled us out of thick rainforest into a narrow passage in the swampland. There was still some cutlass work for Chris, but the chainsaw remained at rest.

When lunchtime arrived, we tugged the small boat with Eon and Elijah closer and shared the bread, peanut butter, and jam. We gave them the sole butter knife. Then we lengthened the rope so that they could relax even farther away in the calmness of the current. I broke a twig from a nearby branch stripping off the leaves and used it to spread the blobs of peanut butter and jam on our bread. Nature was providing.

Fishing for dinner

Reaching the wider, deeper creek, we went from poling to paddling to motoring slowly. It was midafternoon and people were fishing for dinner. Indigenous territories were subsistence societies. Refrigeration, if any, relied mostly on store-bought ice. Forget freezing. Two men in a dugout canoe were fishing near the grassy edge of the creek and responded to Chris's wave. We savoured a panoramic view of the marshland with no sight of human habitation. The rainforest in the distance provided a dark perimeter.

The sun now cast a golden glow over our homecoming. As we reached Ykinipa, the brothers hoisted their packs and cutlasses. The long bench with a canopy on the stelling was filled with villagers enjoying the sunset and our arrival. "Wait! I want a photo of Elijah and me," said Jessica. "He was one of my HEYS students when we talked about tourism in last year's training." I followed with my camera as they stood at the railing with Jessica beaming a bright smile for both.

We motored on to Chris's home where he had offered accommodation for the night. His house was built of wide planks with large cutouts for windows but no glass or screening. Double beds had been placed around the house accommodating the family's nine younger children. The eldest son, his wife, and their baby lived in a small house near the family home. A kitchen was in one corner of the main house with an adjoining area built with only waist-high planking and a roof to allow for cooking in more open-air conditions.

We shared details of the trip with everyone crowding around to see the photos. When I brought out the birding book, the gathering was even tighter. Eon had heard teenage Simon mutter, "Who cares about birds," but he also joined the huddle peering at the drawings. My photos of the eagle were another big hit.

Even a trip to the outhouse proved an adventure. Minerva, a composed woman of great beauty who exuded calm and competence, escorted me through the kitchen areas and pointed to a path into the bushes that led to the outhouse. When I strolled back, I circled the house planning to enter up the front steps.

Suddenly, I stopped and stared in amazement and then went on to the staircase. Jessica and Eon were above on the landing leaning over the railing in conversation with some of the family. I motioned for them to come down. "What?" asked Eon with a hint of irritation. I simply signalled again more firmly, so everyone trooped down the steps.

A sheet of plywood was leaning against two posts of the several supporting the front of the house that was built on a slope. A flat, dry hide with holes where eyes had been was nailed to the plywood. Its fur was pale yellow dappled with tan rosettes bounded by black. "A jaguar!" shouted Eon as Jessica, Chris, and the family assembled around us.

"It was an old jaguar and couldn't hunt," said Chris.

"What happened?" asked Jessica as she stroked the pelt.

"It ran Simon up a tree. Neighbours heard him yelling and sent someone to get me. Other men came running from several nearby homes. We beat the poor old creature to death with sticks," said Chris looking down at the ground. "We hated to kill it, but now it was going to be a maneater," he said in a level tone looking at us.

"Where are the claws and teeth?" asked Eon as he inspected the end of a paw.

"Everyone took something to remember this old cat," said Chris.

"Does this happen often?" asked Jessica in a soft voice.

"Only sometimes. We don't like to kill jaguar. My last kill was maybe ten or twelve years ago."

"What will you do with the skin?" I asked.

"Anyone with 20,000 dollars can have it," said Chris. I did a quick calculation and figured that was a hundred dollars or more, depending on Canadian or US currency.

With the sun setting, we all dispersed to various places around the house or surrounding area to finish the day's tasks. Eon, who was also a chef extraordinaire, busied himself taking Minerva's fresh fish and cassava bread and making dinner for everyone. After camp fare, we welcomed the scent of frying fish and tasty bread.

When storytelling about the trip wound down, we all prepared for bed. I would share sleeping space with a young daughter. Jessica and Eon would have Chris and Minerva's bed and our hosts were heading for the nearby primary school where Chris was also a watchman with access to sleeping space. Soon peace settled on the home with an evening breeze bringing us cool, scented air.

We awakened with the sun streaming into the home this fifth and final day of our expedition and enjoyed a simple, leisurely breakfast prepared by chef Eon. He'd bought a can of mackerel from a small shop nearby and served it with cassava bread.

It was months since Jessica and I had first met Chris and the family. Now there were several more birds around the house and yard—foundlings, injured, and in various ways not able to live in the wild. There was the Grey-winged Trumpeter, which Chris called waracubba. Other young birds scampered or flitted around the house with the confidence of permanent residents. I didn't concern myself with their names and just enjoyed the antics, especially the chicks wobbling around on the plank floor.

Midmorning, Chris started the motor of his medium-size boat, and we chugged back to the creek and to another nearby channel to the northeast. We were to rendezvous with a tractor from the logging area upland that would take us to another nest site. Stopping at a small dock, Jessica, Eon, and Clement puttered around a decrepit building that had bits and pieces of logging equipment that intrigued Eon. Looking at me, Chris said, "Let's walk up. There's sometimes those manakins that we call firebirds." Up the trail, we crept through some dense shrubs to the side, but the elusive species remained out of sight.

Chris then stopped at a place where an immense tree had been felled. "There was a Harpy Eagle nest. Somebody even said they ate an eagle's egg for breakfast." He looked at me. "The toshao says nobody is ever again to cut a tree with an eagle's nest here in Akawini territory. Nobody is ever to harm the bird or its eggs." I nodded with a lump in my throat at the brutality and ignorance of the destruction. We walked on for a bit. Still no sound of a tractor.

"What's this?" I asked picking up a tiny tortoise with a pale greyish-green and yellow shell and positioned it in the centre of my palm.

"Where did you find that?" asked Chris in surprise.

"Right here on the track," I said stroking the ridges of its shell.

Chris laughed. "I'm supposed to be the tracker, but you're pretty good."

No tractor made it obvious that we weren't going to see another nest at high elevation. "It's okay, Chris. Let's go back."

When we rejoined the others and shared news of the felled nesting tree, Eon said, "What a waste. That nest could have produced more eagles for this area." I showed the tiny tortoise and deposited it near the stelling before we climbed back into the boat. There was no need for talk.

Chris pointed to an area beyond the marshland. "Lots of birds to see there on that bank another time."

Chris and family

Back at the house, we stowed our gear in the big boat from Adel's. Eon spotted a rolled hide, skin side out, in the boat. "What's that?" he asked.

I smiled and shifted it slightly so that it wouldn't get splashed. "For you. The jaguar." Jessica and Clement looked at each other in surprise. Chris and Minerva and the older children just smiled.

"Thanks," said Eon in a quiet voice as he rolled back some of the hide stroking the black and tawny, mottled fur. "My first jaguar."

The whole family again congregated on the dock while Clement backed us out of the channel. "We'll be doing more work based on our time here," said Jessica, "and we'll keep you in the loop, Chris."

"I look forward to it," he said.

We judged the expedition a success, coupled with results of the shorter quest three months earlier. As we left Chris and his family, we knew that this was eagle country.

An hour later we were back at Adel's with a symphony of barking from our lonely dogs. After unloading the boat, we all scattered for private time. Eon retreated to his quiet place, the kitchen. Jessica had downtime for herself with her dogs. I retreated to my room and scrolled through the photos of the trip.

Over dinner we discussed how we could have a range of itineraries for ecotourism trips: introductory tours, moderately adventurous excursions, and advanced experiences such as the Harpy Eagle nest quest. The challenge would be marketing and finding knowledgeable birding guides plus the help of local guides to find locations for experiencing a variety of birds and life far upriver.

Word of our expedition was doubtless buzzing through Akawini with the return of Jacob and Elijah. Mission accomplished for the moment, we celebrated with a tot of rum. The next day I was off to Georgetown to report to Vanessa where I discovered that I had an additional task.

Life is risky business anywhere but living and working in a foreign country creates additional challenges. Cuso had made sure that we knew Guyana ranked as a dangerous country according to international surveys on safety. We'd also had a full day of special training on the topic with an official from Ottawa sent to Georgetown.

Within three weeks of arriving in Guyana the previous year, I believed the rating. I had headed to a nearby restaurant for dinner, so that Caroline could prepare a meal with friends without feeling obliged to include me. Even though I was only four blocks from home, when finished, I called for a taxi and stepped outside to wait.

Suddenly, there were shouts behind me and a cluster of angry men were swinging what looked like Royal Enfield long rifles. I looked for my taxi. Nothing. I called the taxi company again but couldn't understand the dispatcher with all the shouting around me. Was this a gang war? Was this a drug deal gone bad? I decided to hike the few blocks home. When I passed a bar, a fellow came lurching out and slurred, "Why, hi there!"

"Get outta my way!" I growled as I stomped past. Later, I shared the incident with Caroline, the family in my compound, and staff at the Cuso office. Some guessed maybe it was rowdy miners in town. Carrying long rifles? I didn't think so. Nobody could come up with a plausible story.

Eventually I stopped by the restaurant while passing a couple of weeks later. I talked with the manager who said, "A customer was leaving and bumped a guard who thought he was being treated discourteously. Then the van with the shift replacement guards arrived, and there was a shouting match."

"So, no real danger. Just a guard's bruised feelings."

"Yes, and I'm sorry that you were frightened. Please visit us again. I can assure you that it'll be a better evening," she said.

Two other encounters in Georgetown had annoyed me but not to the point of fear. Both were incidents with taxi drivers and involved safety. In the first case, a driver started an angry conversation on his cell phone just as Eon and I were about to leave for a meeting an hour's ride away. I used the shoulder pinch made famous by Mr. Spock in the TV series *Star Trek*. "Give me your phone," I ordered using my firm, white woman's voice, plus my status as an elder. He did and I said, "You'll get it back when we reach our destination." He was sullen the entire trip, but I balanced the mood with my feelings of hope about arriving intact.

Eon loved the tactic and told me later, "I could never do that! I could never get away with what you did!"

The second event happened when a city taxi driver started sweet-talking some girl on his phone just as we pulled away from the curb. Again, Eon was with me. I leaned forward and said in a loud voice that could be heard by the driver's lady friend, "You romance this young woman on your own time. Hang up now." He followed orders and we were dropped off without further discussion.

Eon was again delighted by my handling of the situation. "That was great! He'll never do that again with a woman in his taxi to tell him off like his grandma would."

The only other time of possible danger that I heard about was what my friend Jan experienced on a weekend when she was strolling along a portion of the city's seawall. A middle-aged Guyanese man in shabby clothes approached her. She said, "Unprovoked, he came close to punching me in the face, while hurling misogynistic insults." That ended Jan's walks on the seawall.

Cuso headquarters in Ottawa had authorized my assignment in Region 2 but was uneasy about my posting as the first volunteer in the remote Pomeroon-Supenaam area. When I returned from the Harpy Eagle nest quest and gave my report, Vanessa was delighted with our results but had an additional task for me. "Cuso wants a formal risk assessment report prepared for Region 2. We don't have enough staff to fulfill the requirement. You know the area best, so would you complete the report?"

"Will do," I said, knowing the cart was before the horse on this assignment having returned without incident from far up on Akawini Creek. I scanned the spreadsheet grid with all its boxes, rating scales, and areas for extended commentary and wondered how to get the information.

When I arrived at Adel's and explained my assignment. Jessica said, "You're in luck. I'm the British Warden appointed by the High Commission." Noting my blank look, she continued, "That means in case of emergency, such as civil unrest or natural disaster, I'm the point person to connect with all British citizens in Guyana. I'm then empowered by the High Commission to help implement an evacuation plan, if necessary, especially here in Region 2."

"What about me? I'm Canadian," I said in an unexpected squeaky little voice.

"Oh, don't worry," said Jessica with a wave of her hand. "We'd help Commonwealth members and liaise with your High Commission too." Jessica proved to be my ace in the hole as I combined my research about Guyana with her ten years of knowledge of the country.

Civil unrest was the report's first concern. I knew from reading local newspapers and hearing Caroline's examples from her work with Women Across Differences that domestic violence was a greater concern than civil unrest. The example that she gave of a grandfather repeatedly messing with his five-year-old granddaughter and nobody in the family or social services doing anything about it was a particularly lurid case. Also, Jessica assured me, "No protests have been reported to me as the British Warden these two years."

When I worked with VYC the previous year, I had met a delegation from the United States Agency for International Development—USAID—assessing the work underway by this NGO. A small group of youngsters from the neighbourhood had been gathered at the officials' request to speak with children. Two interactions burned themselves into my memory.

"Do you feel safe in your community? In your home?" asked a delegate focusing on a young boy of eleven or so who stood in a corner with a downcast look. The boy shuffled his feet, looked up, and said, "No. I can be dead, shot dead, in my neighbourhood. I can get dead at home too." Silence reigned for a moment before the discussion continued with other questions.

Gang behaviour was also a critical social issue in Georgetown. Some of the USAID personnel had interviewed teenagers in an upstairs area of the VYC building. At the end of the meeting, delegates came down the steps with grim faces. When the children and teenagers departed, one official quietly said, "Some gangs have an initiation ritual that requires a young girl to have sex with both the male leader and the alpha female of the gang." Nobody said a word. Guyana's prison riot was a month or so in the future at this point, but turbulence and lack of safety in everyday life was obviously an ongoing trauma.

Besides domestic and community violence, the impact of the drug and weapons trade was also a greater concern than civil unrest. Just as I started work on the report, I saw a newspaper headline that said,

"Three held over Pomeroon double murder…weapons cache…link to drug bust." Guyana was a major conduit for Colombian drugs. This included the illegal weapons trade. Region 2 wasn't a high crime area, though not exempt from the illegal activities that spanned many regions.

Region 2 was sparsely populated and totalled approximately 50,000 people. I had passed through Anna Regina on the coast, the capital of the region, with a population of 16,000. Charity on the Pomeroon River where we boarded a boat for Adel's had a population of 1,300.

There were three police stations in Region 2. The only other policing presence was the gunboat that we saw near the entrance to Wakapoa Creek. It patrolled the short stretch of the Pomeroon to the Atlantic looking for drug and weapons smugglers.

Pomeroon River

One evening, I quizzed Jessica for more information about potential misconduct in this part of Guyana. She summarized her view of this world of riverine life while Eon was in the lounge area strumming his guitar. He was composing a song about his favourite primary school teacher, Miss Sugarbin. Musical accompaniment for our sober task was being supplied by a professional musician and songwriter. No end to this man's talents.

Jessica said, "The crime rate is relatively low and of the pickpocket variety, if it does occur. When crimes such as domestic violence, petty theft, and home or business break-ins occur, the guilty are usually caught and word spreads quickly through the settlement. There's strong community and upstanding Christian conduct here."

Health risks were relatively standard for a tropical climate—traveller's diarrhea, malaria, dengue fever, and chikungunya fever. Careful use of water, peeling fruits and vegetables, and eating cooked food helped avoid the first condition. The latter three were all related to mosquitoes with symptoms of fever, muscle ache, headache, and joint pain. Mosquito nets, repellant creams, oils, and smoke rings were advised. Cuso volunteers also took antimalarial medication.

Jessica filled me in about medical care. "Basic services and medicines for most common illnesses are available in the region's small cities and in tribal territories at the local health clinics. However, even getting to a clinic might require a boat ride, which happens mostly in the daytime."

"What about serious conditions or emergencies?"

"Major medical services must be handled in Georgetown and require road and river transportation. We can't count on flights in small planes. It's hard to reach local airports. Would there even be a plane, pilot, or money for a flight? The wife of a village council member in Wakapoa died recently. They say she died of high blood pressure. She didn't get a decent diagnosis or good care. That's often how life is in villages," said Jessica. I jotted that getting proper medical care in the hinterlands did involve some risk.

With so much river travel, Cuso was proactive about the risk of drowning. All volunteers were required to supply themselves with a Personal Flotation Device or PFD for river travel as part of their standard kit. I lugged along my orange PFD, wearing it like a horse collar whenever I stepped into a boat. I even used it when in shallow water during the Harpy Eagle nest quest to abide by Cuso's edict and elicit snorts from Jessica and Eon.

Working my way down the risk assessment report, I asked Jessica about drunk driving. "Not an issue where you'll be going," she said. "Akawini and Wakapoa are dry, Christian communities with dirt tracks and no vehicles except for maybe the village tractor."

"What about drunk driving on the roads between the cities such as Anna Regina, Charity, and Suddie or the river port area of Supenaam at the Essequibo?" I asked.

"With no streetlights, few gas stations, minimal available services in case of emergency, and no regular river travel at night, people tend to stay home. They might drink at home or at a nearby roadside or riverside bar, but they aren't doing much driving of cars or even boats," said Jessica. "Night means pretty much staying home or visiting nearby family or friends. People who have been drinking are no real danger to others unless it turns into domestic violence."

Communication was also part of this report. Jessica said, "Everyone uses cell phones, but phones have to be charged. You know our generator sometimes fails and our solar panels and the wind tower at Adel's can't always provide enough juice for recharging. And sometimes it's hard to get or maintain a cell signal for whatever reason." I summarized this section by saying that there was a degree of risk in Region 2 if we couldn't communicate for help.

"Exactly, and that reminds me, I have to make a quick call." She headed for the one corner in the lounge at Adel's where we could get our cell phones to work. The only other place was out on the stelling near the creek. When she finished, I quizzed her again.

"Should Cuso volunteers expect any risk in working with people here?"

"The projects benefit local people," said Jessica, "and they recognize the value. You're not contradicting cultural norms. You've contacted the toshaos and village councils. You're solid."

This report was humming right along, and it appeared that Region 2 was an inviting and relatively safe area for Cuso volunteers. Eon's song about Miss Sugarbin was also coming together and I found my foot bobbing in tune as I tapped on my laptop. "Inspirational music," I said looking over at Eon, who paused between bars and grinned.

Now I was on to assessing safety of accommodations. In Georgetown, there were precautions relating to strength of doors and adequate locks and grills. I smiled as I was able to assure Cuso that all was well in Region 2. I had arranged to hang my hammock with its attached mosquito net in the common room area of a family in Wakapoa. "Door locks are no problem. There's no door," I noted in the report.

Accommodations in Akawini were also secure as I would be staying with the family of the local acting headmaster. "The door is guarded by the family's Red-and-green Macaw that roosts nearby outside and is the watch parrot," I keyboarded with glee in the appropriate comment box. At Adel's, we had our five watchdogs.

Nearing the end of the report, I concluded that work in the hinterland of Region 2 was relatively safe. Success was anticipated because volunteers would be embraced by the local population and cared for as members of the community. Interactions would be conducted with mutual respect and support, thereby decreasing possible risk in operating in remote locations. Task completed, I closed my laptop for the night and enjoyed the tropical breeze wafting through the lounge.

"Come hear 'Miss Sugarbin' and tell me what you think," said Eon. "And let's celebrate with a spot of rum. Mine with one chunk of ice, please." The tinkle of ice, from a bag lugged downriver from Charity, blended with Eon's song as we three sipped our smooth El Dorado. His mellifluous homage to this cherished teacher with the snake eyes devoted to seeing quality education administered was captivating.

"Was she really called Miss Sugarbin?" I asked.

"I was a little kid and that's all that I remember," he said with another of his fabulous grins.

Wait. Did I miss something? No, the report didn't have a section on wildlife. No need to mention our recent encounters with electric eels and the parrot snake. I eased back into one of the old lounge chairs and deleted all concerns from my memory bank.

However, thoughts and images wafted up and gave me moments of contemplation as I basked in the pleasant atmosphere of this sparsely populated region of Guyana. Georgetown and the coastal floodplains were home to over eighty percent of the country's population. Region 4 was the shipping port and contained the major centres of business, industry, government, and education. Consulates of various countries were established in Georgetown. Outlying regions provided food and natural resources such as gold, diamonds, bauxite, and timber for export, but Georgetown was the pulsing heart of the country.

Soon an image resurfaced and imposed itself on me. It reminded me of ExxonMobil's growing presence with offshore operations preparing to extract yet more petroleum for global consumption impacting climate. The country was participating in potentially drowning itself.

Tanker and cart

Chapter Eleven

Local Talent

I continued settling down to work in the territories as outlined in the placement description. Making a living is always hard and it was worse in remote Indigenous communities like Wakapoa and Akawini. Many men, like Chris, were hunters and loggers. Others left for work in the gold or diamond mines of the interior. Women and youth were left at home with few opportunities for income. Some headed for Georgetown or other towns for work.

Vanessa was helping me contact key people at the Small Business Bureau, the Guyana Tourism Authority, and the Ministry of Indigenous Peoples' Affairs. I was gathering information to continue planning for ecological and economic development.

She also outlined another parallel task for me. "We need asset mapping of the area. We want to identify local talent that supports the villages' goals for livelihood and ecotourism development, especially for women and youth. Report what people are doing now to earn income and be alert for any future possibilities. We're looking for what can be shared within the community or beyond. Also, watch for any material or financial resources for development."

Vanessa was one of the best bosses that I'd ever worked with in my varied assignments. She knew what was needed, explained why, and outlined possible strategies in accomplishing tasks.

"I'm glad to do this mapping along with launching a couple of activities. Craft classes, specifically in fibre arts, can open communication and build partnerships in the villages. I think of it as craftivism. Birding fits, too, especially with Akawini wanting help in getting youth interested and trained in the natural world and ecotourism."

Vanessa's eyes brightened. As usual, she was open and attentive to new ideas, which I deeply appreciated. "You can blend all these tasks. Start asset mapping and set up craft classes and birding outings. You'll be fulfilling another mission that Cuso has requested of this placement: fostering Gender Equality and Social Inclusion, GESI. Your plan could increase your visibility in the communities and your ability to make some real progress. We also must get me to Region 2 so we can officially meet with the toshaos and village councils for their support and additional input."

Wrapping up my Georgetown life again for a spell, I told my roomie, Andrea, "You'll have the whole place to yourself for the next week or ten days. Enjoy!"

She watched me heft my bags—including my hammock—for another plunge into hinterland life and said, "Okay, and bring back more good stories from out there where I won't go." Her Cuso assignment was to devise a measurement and evaluation process that could be quantified for each of our assignments, mine included. Based in the nearby Cuso office, she slipped into her very high heels for work. Her environment was an office. Mine was the outback.

Returning to Region 2 was time for absorbing more of the lifestyle. The ebb and flow of the tides created the pulse of riverine life. River passage was an engine throbbing, water lapping the sides of the boat, and silent passengers just watching the world pass by like a slow-motion film.

My first mapping interview was in Wakapoa with Shana, whom I'd met a few months prior on my first visit to Adel's. She was a beautiful young woman with long, black hair, glistening eyes, and was pleased to talk about her food processing business. She showed me litre bottles filled with coconut oil. She also had bottles of cassareep, boiled juice from cassava processing that was used as stock for traditional pepperpot soup.

Shana was another graduate of the HEYS program the previous year. Food was Shana's focus because, as she said, "We have lots of coconuts and cassava." It was a business based at home, which made sense for a young woman with a preschooler and a baby.

We sat in a new building next to the family's small wooden home. The latter provided sleeping space for three generations: her parents, four of her five siblings, and her partner and their children.

Shana's mother Janet—a sturdy woman with the skin tone of polished mahogany—also worked in processing food for sale. She stepped into the new building. It had a kitchen and family room area. Janet brought me a sample of her cassava bread from a flat, round sheet a foot wide. I munched and said, "This is the crispiest and tastiest I've ever eaten." Both women beamed.

Janet then gave the history of the new building as she stood at the stove stirring a pot. "My eldest son is a mason, so he helped build this with a small grant we got from the government to get started on this kitchen for food processing." She shared the same calm disposition as her daughter, an innate quiet watchfulness that I'd come to expect in Indigenous people.

The building had a concrete floor on a bed of sand. The floor was covered with vinyl. One wall was cement blocks with two rows of decorative block near the top allowing light and air flow. The three remaining wooden walls had holes cut for windows. Some were bare openings. The two that faced the settlement's pathway to the creek had aluminum louvres with opaque glass panes for privacy.

There was a wooden sink and counter unit that had shelving below for dishes and pots. A stove, fueled by bottled gas, stood nearby. A huge homemade dining table with benches and some chairs was space for anything else the family needed as workspace.

A hammock hung across from the kitchen area, a hook on each adjoining wall. There Shana sat crosswise nursing her baby while rocking gently with her foot. Soon it would be my hammock hanging there when I overnighted in Wakapoa.

With the soup pot stirred, Janet said, "Come outside and see the grinding machine Matthias made for us." Now I took a closer look at the two-by-four frame holding a metal drum with a textured surface that I'd seen on my first visit with Jessica. Janet's husband, a compact man with a gentleness that gave hint of both wit and wisdom, stood nearby ready to respond to questions after I ran my fingertips over the drum.

Coconut and cassava shredding machine

Matthias said, “It’s handmade. A metal worker gave it teeth to make it rough for grinding.” With well-worn hands, he’d built a machine that helped the women with food processing. In a soft voice, he continued, “The pieces of coconut or cassava go into this chute and come out the other end. It’s much easier than grinding by hand.”

I marvelled at the ingenuity of this simple, efficient, and affordable machine. It was attached by a pulley to a gas generator with a small plastic jug for fuel tacked to the frame. “This is clever engineering, Matthias.”

Looking over at Shana, I asked, “Can you make more than one quality of oil?”

“Yes,” she said. “I bottle it as regular or make it extra virgin and sell it for more money.”

Janet stepped over to a long tube that hung from a tree in the corner of the courtyard. “This is the matapi,” said Janet, “our native way of handling cassava. We scrubbed and peeled this big tub of cassava root earlier today. Now we can use the machine to shred it. Then we load it into the matapi, made of local reeds, and wring out the bitter juice by twisting.” She pretended to twist the empty tube to show the process.

Shana held up a big tub of dry cassava pulp and Janet ran her fingers over the top. “We use this to make bread. See those big sheets of tin over there?”

I glanced over at the sheets on sawhorses. “Yes, we call it corrugated metal.”

Janet nodded and said, “We pound the breads flat, bake them over a charcoal fire, then lay them out in the sun to dry. We use everything from the cassava. The bitter liquid we squeezed out with the matapi could be deadly, but we boil it down for a long time into a thick syrup, cassareep for our pepperpot soup. You’re smelling it now and it’s for dinner tonight. You’ll get to taste it with the cassava bread.”

“Good, I often eat homemade soup and bread back in Canada, especially in the winter. I’d like to taste the Guyanese version.”

Shana tended her baby, Janet again stirred the soup pot, and Matthias drifted off to the boat shed behind the house to tinker with an engine. I pulled out my asset mapping notebook and added both women’s names and jotted details. Mother and daughter were thriving businesswomen in Wakapoa and the greater Pomeroon area filling orders for coconut oil, cassava bread, and cassareep. I also named Matthias as a creative mechanic whose skills were in demand in the territory according to Jessica.

With a solid chunk of asset mapping of this Wakapoa family completed, I was soon back to Adel's seeking more skills. Jessica suggested a short boat ride up Akawini Creek to see Alison and Raymond. Alison was a skilled baker of buns and sweets for the area. Jessica knew that she baked on Fridays, so she, Eon, and I visited on baking day.

Raymond was tinkering with the engine of their boat but stopped to welcome us to their home, an unpainted wooden structure on pillars. His love of their life was obvious. "This land has everything a person could want. I don't know why the rest of my family won't do agriculture," he said as he took us on a tour of the farm. Tidy trenches between crops provided both irrigation and drainage. It was fifty-two acres of varied crops such as coconut and fruit of all kinds.

Raymond was also creative in meeting the needs of his family and increasing their income. We strolled back from the farm tour and headed over to Alison's baking area near the house. I noted that her husband, with a last name that indicated Portuguese heritage, was skilled in what I called the farmer fix. With lumber and corrugated sheeting, he'd built a shelter with some of the plot's softwood trees as framing poles and a tarp lashed tight for the roof. Inside, he'd built a counter of solid wood and, nearby, a wooden cabinet lined with tin. This was Alison's baking area.

When we arrived, her apron was dusted with flour and the day's baking was well underway. She was of solid built Afro-Guyanese stock with arm muscles that proved she'd whipped up mountains of dough in her business. The men wandered off to water's edge talking agriculture, mechanics, and fishing. Jessica and I hovered around the baking area.

"Today I'm mixin' for cookies and buns. Last week, there was a big party out Pomeroon way and I baked cakes." Now buns were on tin trays ready for baking. She opened the door of the cabinet where an earthen pot at the bottom held a smoldering charcoal fire. She set the trays on shelves above and used a latch to tighten the door.

"I finished this batch of cookies earlier. Here, try some," she said handing us a bowl. Jessica and I each plucked a sample and started munching with delight.

"Um. Very good," I said, licking a crumb off my lower lip. Alison grinned and passed the bowl my way again. She was a thriving businesswoman who satisfied both family and local needs. I added her name and story to my list. Soon Alison pulled the batch of buns out of the oven. The seductive aroma drew the men to our area.

"Don't forget us," hollered Eon.

Asset mapping visits also produced local stories. Bits of information about early Dutch settlers deep in the interior sometimes surfaced. This was long before Britain wrested control of the colony early in the nineteenth century. "Come and now long gone," someone said about the Dutch.

The more recent naked Nazi tale was particularly intriguing. A man with blond hair and blue eyes had arrived shortly after the end of the Second World War. He paddled a dugout canoe down the Pomeroon River and far up one of the Wakapoa territorial creeks well away from any of the various homesteads. He dug into a hillside above the wetland and grew local fruits and vegetables, which he sold to creekside residents and sometimes upriver in Charity.

The most unusual feature of his life was that he lived naked in his remote home. He only donned pants and shirt when he was going to market. For a time, he had enticed an Indigenous woman to join him. She put up with living naked just so long and left. Some older people along the creek remembered him. He had left his hillside burrow at some point and settled in a city far away, where he died. Nobody ever knew his real name or his story. Locals just referred to him as "the naked Nazi." Sometimes he was called Lethem, the city to the south, which might have been his last home. I enjoyed adding vintage local stories in with the asset mapping exercise just for their ghostly presence.

Then I returned to tallying assets in earnest. When Jessica had volunteered to be manager of Adel's, she knew access to good, fresh food was an issue in the territories with minimal agricultural land in the marshland. She had done research on the shade house concept and paid for one to be built at Adel's. It was framed with sturdy timber and with heavy plastic sheeting as material for a pitched roof. Each side of the roof was at a different ridge level, so there was ventilation space at the top. The opaque sheeting reduced the intensity of both the sun's rays and heavy rains.

David in the shade house at Adel's

"These shallow planting boxes are waist-high making gardening easier," Jessica had said when giving me a tour during my first visit to Adel's. "They also mean fewer insects eating plants in this sandy soil."

At one point, I took a break from asset mapping and helped David's wife, Amanda, transplant three hundred vegetable seedlings for the shade house. We sorted sprouts for beans and peas, carrots, and tomatoes and transplanted them into larger containers. This meant we could give them more care before tucking them in place in the shade house beds.

We also used the time to exchange ideas about how a smaller version of this structure might be useful. “It would be easier to garden,” said Amanda. “I would have more good food for my family. I could also sell to neighbours.” I included Jessica, with her shade house, as a community asset well worth mapping.

Eon with his partially built Oven John

I also added Eon on multiple counts. First, he used his engineering skills to design and craft an outdoor oven mostly from local materials. I listened as he described what we called the Oven John to a group of villagers who motored over for a view. “These square, decorative cement blocks form the foundation with a zinc sheet on the top for the oven bottom. I’ve bent some angle iron for shaping a domed oven above,” he said, tapping his dried mud work as though it were a horse’s behind. “The overlay is chicken wire packed with mud from the creek bank. The door is scrap wood. This chimney is a column of tin cans worked into the wet mud."

"What do you burn?" asked one visitor.

"Coconut husks," said Eon. "They get piled in the foundation area below. See how there's open space at the front. That's so you can get the husks under the oven's cooking area above. The decorative square blocks for the foundation provide air flow to keep the fire going." This low-cost, homemade oven could both cook and bake. Neighbours were very interested.

Eon's second low-cost invention was a series of valves and PVC plastic pipe making an irrigation system controlled by gravity. This simple pump could provide water for a garden area up to four hundred feet away from a creek or river. Ideally, if we could get the Ministry of Indigenous Peoples' Affairs interested in the shade house, the Oven John, and the Easy Irrigation Pump, there could be paid work for people and considerable improvement in the foodways of the communities.

Continuing my search for local talent, I heard about a skilled woodworker in a remote area of Wakapoa's marshland. Casey was off the main creek in Mora, an area with a primary school, playing field, and assorted homesteads. After we veered off Wakapoa Creek, Jessica, Eon, and I walked up a path past the school grounds to a small wooden building painted pink with "Welcome" lettered on the front of the counter that was visible from outside.

There, lined up, were carvings that depicted Indigenous life. A toucan sat on a tree stump. Turtles of various sizes rested in a cluster. The place of honour was a carving of an Indigenous woman carrying a load on her back in a woven basket with the aid of a head strap. In the corner was a walking stick with a snake curling around its length and a carved bird roosting at the top. A jaguar stretched out on half of a club in polished dark wood. The half-metre-long club gradually morphed into an intricate carving of a bird at the other end.

Casey's work was imaginative and carefully crafted but he was faced with the eternal challenge of business: how to market beyond his immediate community. I admired his craftsmanship and asked the price of various items and the time it took to make them. "This is wonderful work. Is there something I could supply of equal value for the walking stick and the jaguar piece?"

After a moment of thoughtful silence, Casey said, "I could use more tools. I need chisels of different sizes and a blade for fine carving."

"I know a place in Georgetown where I can get good quality tools. You've given me the price of the pieces. Let me see what I can buy for you in the city," I said. He smiled in agreement.

I found the tools that Casey specified. When the club and walking stick were delivered to me, I gave the club to Eon and the walking stick to David. I wanted to honour Casey's creativity and need for more tools and have these items stay in Guyana as an example of Indigenous art. Besides, how was I ever going to get a long, heavy walking stick home to Canada the way that I travelled?

My next visit was with Lloyd, a retired teacher and a former toshao in Wakapoa. He was a delightful, engaging fellow involved with traditional crafts and ways of preserving the Arawak culture and language. Lloyd also had deep interest in visitors to the community, which inspired me to ask, "How did you become a teacher?"

"Strong paddling through the night to Charity," said Lloyd with a chuckle. "When I was a young man, another fellow, a young woman, and I heard there would be a government official in Charity the next day to administer a test for entrance into a government-sponsored teacher training program. We were all eager for the opportunity but knew nobody would take a motorboat out at night. We would have to paddle a dugout canoe at a furious rate to get there in time. So, we three headed down the creek to the river and paddled as fast as we could. Just the other fellow and I paddled. We let the young woman sleep. We made it just in time, took the exam, and all of us were admitted into the program."

Now he lived with his wife Pam, a primary school teacher, on a highland homestead at Masserie beyond School Island where she worked. Their two married sons lived in areas around the parental home. The short walk to each home maintained family connectedness as well as each household's privacy. Their daughter was in teacher training at the University of Guyana in Georgetown, and their youngest son was finishing high school.

Lloyd said, "I'm interested in the coffee planting tradition of this area—something that has ended. I'd like to help build efforts at growing coffee again."

"As an experienced teacher, how would you handle this?" I asked.

"Let's go walk around my trees," said Lloyd. We strolled a short distance from his home. "These are some of the mature ones," he said tugging a branch downward so that I could see the berries more easily. "I'm willing to nurture seedlings, sell them, and help oversee their care. I'm also willing to try new ways of drying the beans that Eon and I have been discussing. And Jessica says the Guyana Store in Georgetown is eager for good quality items to sell." Lloyd was added to my asset mapping list.

He and his wife had also built a roofed structure with a large table and benches near their home. There was shelving filled with educational materials at one end and a closed room as a storage area for more items at the other end. This was informal space for learning because educators may retire, but they never really stop teaching.

In addition, the couple had built a cottage with two bedrooms and a shared veranda nearby. These quarters had been used in the past by Peace Corps volunteers and other guests to the area. There were his and her outhouses at the edge of the compound along with a sink and a washing stall for bucket showers.

Lloyd and I discussed my documenting the two ité palm hammocks that his mother-in-law Eileen was making for me. I'd seen the hammock in his home on my first visit to Wakapoa with Jessica. When I returned to Guyana, I'd called Lloyd and placed an order for two. This traditional fibre art was dying as the palm was harvested from specific areas in the marshland and becoming scarce. The stalks were stripped, boiled, and then twisted and woven into material like rope.

Lloyd had arranged for Eileen to come to their home with one hammock completed and the second one nearly finished. On the day arranged for us to meet, we chatted about our similar interest in fibre arts. She would complete my second hammock that was lashed to posts in the covered teaching area. I was fascinated by the intricacy of the process. We also talked about asset mapping.

Eileen making a hammock

"Nobody wants to learn how to do this because there isn't enough money to be made," said Eileen with a sigh. "I do it for pleasure these days, but earlier I made hammocks and bags and lots of other things. I was widowed when young with four children to support, including Pam here. I raised them doing this work."

Lloyd brought us coffee and a copy of *The Traditional Art and Craft of Hammock Making in Wakapoa*. Flipping through the spiral-bound booklet, I saw a photo of Eileen a decade prior. I then turned to the cover and saw that this was a project of the School of Recreation Management, Acadia University in Wolfville, Nova Scotia. I had relatives who worked at the university! It was indeed a small world.

Lloyd also brought out his copy of *The Traditional Art and Craft of Canoe Making in Wakapoa*. "There were another two documentations, one on pottery and the other on basketry. Someone borrowed them with a promise of return and never did," he said with an even tone of acceptance.

"Lloyd, would you please trust me to make copies of both these booklets for myself and your family. I promise to return them to you."

"Yes. It would be a wonderful gift for my children and grandchildren to see Pam's mother plying what will probably become yet another lost art," said Lloyd as he watched me tuck the booklets carefully into my daypack.

With the weekend approaching, I had arranged to hang my hammock at Janet and Matthias's home on School Island. I routinely handed over my per diem allowance to Jessica at Adel's and the families that I stayed with in the villages. Vanessa had said, "We'll fund what you need to reach your assignment's goals." I valued her strong support. We both knew that it was critical for any degree of success in these remote areas.

With accommodations set in Wakapoa, I still had to deal with what type of hammock to use. Eileen's woven palm hammock was beautiful but too bulky and with no provision for protection from mosquitoes. I would have preferred a conventional woven cotton hammock made in Guyana, but it would be unsuitable for the same reasons. I could borrow the hammock that Jessica had loaned me for the expedition, but I wanted my own rig.

I had spotted a likely hammock while driving past a shop in Vreed-en-Hoop on the west bank of the Demerara. It was in lightweight nylon that fitted into a small pouch. I had brought a mosquito net treated with repellant from Canada and stitched that to the hammock. I also ferreted out a zipper over a metre long in Georgetown. The result was a sleeping cocoon.

My nightly routine was to wrap myself in a small, lightweight polar fleece blanket that I'd found in Georgetown. It could get chilly before dawn, even in the tropics. I then climbed in placing my bottom in the very centre of the hammock. The final step was pivoting my head and feet inside and zipping up tight. This was harder to do in a nylon hammock. The first night, I had a bottom-over-biceps backward flip onto the floor and a real struggle to untangle myself. There was then stitching before the rig was again usable.

My next candidate for asset mapping was Don, a young man in Wakapoa who had attended the HEYS program with Elijah and Shana the previous year. He had learned to mix the sandy soil of the region with cement and fashion decorative blocks. Don wasn't home when I visited, but his father and brother showed me around the brickworks. There I examined blocks that had been fashioned from various molds, fired, and now were drying. A church under construction nearby was using concrete blocks for the base and these decorative blocks in the upper level, just as at Janet and Matthias's home. Don's name went into my growing asset mapping list.

Not only was I inventorying skills already in use in the communities, but I was also laying the foundation for teaching or resurrecting fibre arts skills in the community. School Island was populated with both residential and day students and Aunt Hazel was the matron of the hostels. When I learned that she was skilled in embroidery, I asked Jessica to introduce us. Seeing some of her work, I said, "Aunt Hazel, these are lovely pieces. Your stiches are so even, and you've used one that I've never done."

She beamed with quiet delight and studied the back of my birding vest. "You do nice work, too."

Earlier, Jessica had offered her cloth and thread supplied by a Guyanese woman living in Suriname who'd visited Adel's on a couple of occasions. I'd brought hoops of various sizes and showed Hazel how to use them. I also told her about the craft classes that I hoped to start. "I'd like you to help as an instructor." She beamed another big smile, and I added her to my list of people with skills.

With permission of the toshao and village council, I started gathering interested young people for embroidery lessons and general conversation. I hauled out supplies and young people began to sketch subjects for needlework. I also left materials and equipment with Aunt Hazel to share with the students during free time when I wasn't in the village. In the evenings at home, I taught various family members to do not only embroidery but how to make necklaces of buttons.

One evening, I showed the Harpy Eagle nest quest photos on my laptop to the family and neighbours who had wandered over to chat. I also brought out my birding book for examination. There was quiet discussion and some questions. "Who would be interested in us way out here?" asked someone from the corner.

I turned but couldn't place the voice, so spoke to Janet. "When I stand out in your shower shed in the evenings and dip water from a bucket for bathing, I see the marshland at sunset with beautiful colours as far as I can see in either direction. I also see the fringe of the rainforest. I breathe in deeply the smell of the tall grasses and your pure air. There are people in the world outside Region 2, outside Guyana, who would pay big money to come to your country. They would want to spend time in the beauty of your village and experience some of your natural and cultural world. They would also want to meet you as the original people of this land." My friends in Wakapoa were silent and looked around at each other with amazement.

I heard another quiet voice from somewhere in the crowded room say, "We didn't know anybody cared."

Since I was appearing more frequently around the village and on the waterways, I was alerted to more people with interests and abilities worth recording. Ivan, an older fellow in the area, was put forward as the tech guru of the community. He was the school guard, called Uncle Ivan, who also ferried several children to school each day from his homestead area. He used a dugout with planks to heighten the sides. It had a very small engine and therefore used little gas.

Ivan was a short, unsmiling man, similar in build to many whom I'd encountered. When he heard that the toshao and village council wanted Cuso's help with technology, he perked up. Wakapoa had a cell tower but no way to connect with the internet. Ivan was delighted when he heard that I was helping with a formal request to have the Ministry of Public Telecommunications install an ICT unit—an Information and Communications Tower on School Island. Students could then study for examinations needed for advanced education. At present, they had to board at residential schools in Charity or Anna

Regina or elsewhere to do such preparation. Most families couldn't afford the cost.

The tower would also provide increased educational and economic opportunities for villagers, such as Ivan, who were eager for access to modern telecommunications. He was also interested in keeping the Arawak language and culture alive and was keen on having fibre arts and other skills taught. Here was a Renaissance man in the heart of the hinterland.

When Ivan heard that Akawini had used its annual lump sum of development money from the government to build a guesthouse for ecotourism, he arranged for me to visit an existing building that a relative in the UK had constructed inland some years prior.

One day he transported me by river, and we tromped by dirt track along with a friend caretaking the building to assess its possibilities. After travel down a narrow creek and a half-hour trek up a footpath through the forest and over parched ground, I saw a massive wooden building. It was gray with exposure to sun and rain and perched atop tall posts. There was a pitched roof with a wide overhang and a platform with benches at ground floor level with an elaborate staircase. The upper floor was one huge room with a locked area in the middle that held cooking and other miscellaneous supplies.

A leaning outhouse stood at the edge of the clearing. A tiny stream, now almost dry, flowed through short grasses. There was no other water source. "Ivan, there isn't enough water, no sanitary system, and no electricity. Everything would have to be carried to the site and, other than admiring the nearby forest, there's nothing to do." I mentioned that the building could be part of a backpacking adventure tour. It could be a combination of overland and river transport to various other locations of interest in Wakapoa and Akawini territory. Such a scheme would require much preparation and marketing to potential visitors.

Since creating a tourism package wasn't formally part of my assignment nor my skill set, I told Ivan that I could only offer general suggestions. I couldn't really assist with a proper business plan or promotional ideas. And so, I continued my discussions and explorations and grew my asset mapping list as I met other villagers in the territories.

My life continued to flow between Georgetown and Region 2. In the city, there were visits by Cuso officials from Jamaica and Ottawa and deep discussions about our assignments in Guyana. For me, nothing could beat time in Region 2 with its waterways and vast wetlands. Best of all was the company of its people with deep taproots in this part of the world and attachment to its merits tattooed on their souls. I found the appreciation infectious.

Chapter Twelve

From Omelette to Serpent

"Alex, here's some material on gender that you might want to use," I said setting some brochures and booklets on her desk in Cuso's central office. Her eyes brightened as she leafed through the pile. "Thanks!" she said. "I wondered what the Brits' VSO had been doing. This could be very useful."

I also found information on working with Indigenous people and emailed Mahendra, our Indo-Guyanese Canadian with his recent graduate degree in environmental science. He was preparing for work on issues in the interior. I wrote, "I've put some material in your mailbox. I'll add more items when I finish reading them."

Several days later, when Mahendra was back in Georgetown with online access, he wrote, "This is good information. I'm glad to learn their approach. Thanks."

At times development work is creating the new. Sometimes it's rediscovering what has already been tried. This happened one day while I was working in the Cuso office and had noted a dusty old file box at a desk that I was using. I found material on several topics that had been produced by the UK's Volunteer Service Overseas. This information dated from when both organizations worked in Guyana before VSO left. Development work is never a straight path. It's often a circuitous route with mingled starts and stops.

Volunteers shared the goal of leaving Guyana with something of value by departure time. The challenges of our various assignments ebbed and flowed. Sometimes we had periods of great happiness. For example, I remember a delightful day at Adel's, which I called a Sunday of utmost bliss.

Adel's Rainforest Resort

It was two weeks after the eagle quest. I was at the dining table sipping Wakapoa coffee. The courtyard was filled with blossoms. A pair of Blue-grey Tanagers chirped messages to each other. Jessica had visited the chickens in the backyard pen. "Here are eggs from our happy hens," she said as she set the basket in the kitchen. Eon was there humming and hatching Napoleon's favourite food, *oeufs de fandan*, an omelette created by French chef Auguste Escoffier. Someone had found the recipe in the chef's journals penned in the middle of the nineteenth century.

While providing scullery services at Adel's in my spare time, my cupboard cleaning produced a set of pale green, translucent glass plates. Eon used these to plate our breakfast of pampered eggs that took us back to the days of the Emperor and thoughts of his chef extraordinaire. Enjoying this dish, I said, "Let's salute the general's good taste with another cup of Lloyd's coffee." Cups refilled, we toasted with a hearty "Here! Here!"

Ideas swirled around over that breakfast. We eased ourselves into another day in paradise and dreamed of projects. Could a smaller shade house be built in Wakapoa? David and I had calculated the materials needed. What about Eon's Easy Irrigation Pump? He had just about finished rigging a prototypical unit that could draw water from the creek to the shade house. He just needed one more valve from Georgetown. Could the farm be brought back into full production? Jessica knew there was outside interest in expanding the agricultural potential of the land behind Adel's cluster of buildings.

Sunday is the traditional day of rest, so each of us backed off from thoughts of development projects and just puttered about. Jessica headed for the kitchen with an urge to see if ingredients were available for a dinner featuring Yorkshire pudding.

Eon was still in French mode but switched focus. He was making minor repairs on a handcrafted nineteenth-century wardrobe built by one of the property owner's ancestors with French heritage. This massive piece of furniture was an example of exquisite workmanship in native hardwood. Eon, who had also been a builder in London, called me over to appreciate the design and craftsmanship. "Here's a beveled mirror fitted into the door, which reveals a closet. You open the matched door and see shelves and small drawers. At the very bottom are wide drawers that still operate beautifully." He demonstrated the smooth, quiet action. "Now step back and check the molding that's both a base and a cornice at the top," he said adjusting the top molding and returning the wardrobe to perfection.

"It's a beautiful piece of furniture," I said with the appreciation of one who had once been a partner in a small furniture design studio in the US.

For my Sunday rest, I was leafing through a fibre arts book given to me by a relative just before I left Canada this second time. I immersed myself in the section on embroidery and practiced some stitches I hadn't done for decades.

The three of us tinkered about with muted sunlight filtering into the area and its array of sofas and easy chairs all made comfortable by long use. A breeze wafted through with floral undertones and brought an occasional hummingbird. One such little bird hovered in front of its mirrored image at the wardrobe, and we caught flashes of blue, green, and purple. I wondered what species I was seeing. Then, as a birder becalmed, I settled for just admiring it without concern for its name.

Jessica alternated sending and receiving text messages with rummaging in the kitchen for ingredients for the pudding. Eon switched to strumming his guitar and continued work on his song about Miss Sugarbin. I created a sampler of various embroidery stitches.

We three, a multicultural tripod, were truly having a fine Sunday. We contributed to each other's visions and projects as well as daily activities. I'd prepared the technical documentation for Eon's Oven John. Jessica's contacts in Region 2 and Georgetown helped Eon and me with our projects. She handled transport arrangements with calls to our favourite Pomeroon boatman when we needed to travel to Charity. She also stood on the stelling, hands on hips, deciding what to purchase when the fish man stopped with fresh catch from the Atlantic. "What's good today?" she'd ask.

Savouring our Sunday, Eon glanced over at me and said, "Just like Jessica and me, you're never going to leave Guyana." Oh, to be so lucky to continue enjoying this little piece of Eden but there was work to do in the villages and a life to maintain in Canada. I smiled and remembered when I'd said, "I came back a second time because I left part of myself here, my heart."

Life in the hinterland was not always easy or so blissful. No life ever is. At times there was real danger that required immediate action. One day, I was at work with papers spread out on the dining table. Jessica sometimes asked David's wife Amanda to help with housework. This day she was cleaning cobwebs in the rafters of the lounge area and spied Guyana's most lethal snake, the lightning fast labaria, more commonly known elsewhere as the fer de lance. "Labaria!" shouted Amanda. I knew from my study of Guyana's snakes that this was big trouble.

Jessica ran in from the shade house where she was tending seedlings. Eon was out of earshot on the *stelling* at work on a new song about Guyanese river life.

"Eon doesn't know how to handle this snake," Jessica said as she looked at me. "We need David." I knew that he was in the backdam from the sound of the chainsaw.

"I'll get him," I said kicking off my sandals and yanking on my rubber boots. I raced over the wooden bridge and tore along the path on the raised bank of the creek toward the whirr of the chainsaw. Out of breath, I reached the edge of the property and stared down at the irrigation canal. It was too wide and too deep to cross. I started jumping up and down waving my old cloth hat and timing my shouts to coincide with pauses in the sawing.

When David finally spotted me, I shouted, "Snake! Snake!" When he reached the canal, all I could say was, "Labaria…house…run!" My hands were down on my knees as I tried to catch my breath. David raced back on his side of the canal along with his eldest son who was helping that day. Devon turned to look at me. "Go! I'm okay."

It was tense work as David got a ladder and nudged the snake out of the rafters with long kitchen tongs supplied by Eon who'd heard the commotion. At last, the labaria dropped to the ground and the men thrashed the thin, metre-long snake to death.

Using the tongs, Eon held the snake by its head. Froth was dripping from its mouth. Just as he was about to touch the snake, Jessica shouted, "Don't! That's the venom!" The white liquid from this serpent could mean death without quick medical attention.

Eon studied the snake a moment longer and then walked over and dropped it into the creek. We watched it sink. In a quiet voice, Jessica said, "It was probably after eggs from the bird nests in the rafters. Have to clear out those nests."

A few days later, there was another incident involving human encounter and the same backdam land. This time it was a group from an agricultural program funded by another agency of the Canadian government. I'd been on the stelling when a boatload of people motored up the creek and prepared to dock. I tied off the boat and helped them up the steps. Most were young women in city clothes and sandals. I was given expressionless faces and limp fingers for handshakes. When Jessica and Eon arrived, I slipped away.

The tour was to include the resort, the shade house, and the backdam area on the sandbar that David had been clearing for evaluation of its agricultural potential. The group was escorted around the resort and the shade house without incident, but then there was a question about the sandbar. "It's too hot to walk back there. Can't you show us a site closer to the resort?" asked one of the princesses.

"But the sandbar *is* the site," said Eon through gritted teeth. "Where are your boots? Where is your testing equipment? This is a field visit not a walk in the park."

The princess gave him a blank stare. Jessica gripped Eon's upper arm, said something soothing, and got the group trudging in the direction of what they seemed to think was wilderness.

This was a visit to see whether this site was suitable for growing onions for export. Not only were the office workers inappropriately dressed, but they were also clueless about agriculture. It was excursion time out of Georgetown with a Canadian development organization picking up the tab. The group was staying at a posh resort elsewhere in Region 2 that required road and river travel to reach Adel's. Not only did they make this costly trip once, but they were returning the next day. They could have stayed at Adel's, but obviously it wasn't up to their standards for an office outing.

The whole point of the exercise was to provide development ideas for local farmers who met monthly at Adel's. Farmers in the cooperative were present the second day. Eon made himself scarce. It became obvious that the farmers thought the whole experience a joke at best and a waste of time and money. Jessica continued to conduct an orderly and respectful tour. No gain in having a shouting match.

After their departure the second day, and with local farmers watching the whole fiasco and departing with wry comments, Jessica, Eon, and I were all in foul humour. I said, “My country is paying for this kind of foolishness. I don’t intend to let this waste of my tax dollars pass without comment.” Jessica and I reported the debacle and word sifted back that there were repercussions for the holidaymakers.

Synchronicities were high-water marks of my assignment, such as meeting Peter who helped me secure proper birding equipment and then my discovering Lydia and her desire to come to Guyana and assist with agricultural practices. At one point, I was on my way back to Georgetown in a speedboat over the Essequibo estuary with ocean and river turbulence. This day I was wedged next to a young woman. We exchanged glances and smiles and then leaned over and talked into each other’s ear over the roar of the engine.

“That’s my mother and aunt up front. We’re from the UK,” she said. We exchanged names and brief sketches of our work and reasons for this ride as the boat bucked and heaved. Samantha worked in community development with youth in the UK and was intrigued by my involvement in Region 2. “Our young people with Guyanese background in the UK are eager to experience this place,” she said. “Is there any way they could come on a work-study program?”

“I’ll do some checking, but—as ever—the issue will be money.”

Jessica later said, “If they came to Adel’s, they could be housed in the dormitory upstairs, but who would pay for their lodging and food? When would we have time to train them to understand and help with the agriculture or any other work around the property? How would we pay for the gas to ferry them around the Indigenous territories?”

Samantha and I exchanged emails several times but couldn’t make progress on such a plan. People on both sides of the Atlantic would have to mobilize resources to create such a cross-cultural exchange for youth of the diaspora. So many dreams die for want of dollars.

What was it like constantly shifting between urban and rural life? What did I miss when out of Georgetown? I missed machines. There was a printer and Internet access at the Cuso office. In the apartment, I could also use the Internet plus the washing machine. With laundry done, I would load a duffle bag with clean hinterland clothes, handcraft supplies, reading material, and some canned and packaged food as treats for host families. With such provisions, I could sustain myself in the territories for ten days to two weeks.

With life expanding in Region 2, there were more moments of pure pleasure. On one occasion, I'd made my way to Wakapoa for a few days and arranged to meet Lloyd. Talking about the merits of shade-grown, bird-friendly planting techniques, I said, "And speaking of birds, I brought something for you. We've talked about the birds of Region 2 and ways of showcasing them. The Wattled Jacana was the first bird that I saw in Georgetown. Now I see them on your lily pads." I then reached into my daypack and pulled out a cup with the imprint of one of my photos of the bird.

Lloyd accepted it and said, "Beautiful. Thank you. Our spurwing. Named for the defensive barbs at the elbow."

"The cup was expensive and I'm not sure there's value in making more consumer goods for anticipated visitors. I'd rather have them invest in the experience of Wakapoa coffee rather than add to their stuff. However, a jute bag filled with your great coffee beans would be a great item to take home. This cup is for you to enjoy."

"Thank you. You're probably right. Better to improve the coffee labels and natural packaging. Coffee would be a consumable item for the visitors that we hope to have."

"Plus, as you know, the Guyana Store near Bourda Market would probably like to sell your coffee, if you can provide a steady supply." Lloyd nodded.

At this point in my assignment, travel arrangements were easier, and I was known by more people in the interior. Linking Georgetown, Adel's, and Wakapoa with a population of three thousand was going well. It was time to also strengthen connections with Akawini's population of eight hundred. The latter was a more distant community, both geographically and in relation to the toshao and the villagers.

Vanessa had come from Georgetown for official visits to both territories. In Wakapoa, we met with the current toshao and village council. They were already comfortable with my comings and goings as well as the handwork classes. The toshao said, "We need help applying for an information and communications tower, an ICT unit, and whatever help with agriculture that Cuso can provide." The territory also had a dream of developing ecotourism.

I'd heard these requests informally earlier, so Vanessa was prepared to commit to assistance. I would help prepare a letter to the appropriate ministry about the tower. Lydia would be arriving within a couple of months to assist with agriculture. Help with ecotourism might be a stretch, but we'd provide input when possible.

The power structure in Akawini was different. The toshao had remained aloof, though he had responded favourably to Jessica's request for help with Indigenous participants for the initial search for eagle nests. He'd also arranged for his eldest sons to accompany us on the second, more involved expedition. This toshao had been the leader for nearly twenty years. He doubtless had been the force in getting bleachers erected near the playing field and the construction of the new stelling. Now there was a guesthouse under construction on posts next to the bank of the Ykinipa settlement near the stelling.

These were only the physical features of development in the village. I was certain there was much work behind the scenes with the Ministry of Indigenous Peoples' Affairs over the past two decades about which I was clueless. The toshao's moniker in the territory was Captain.

When Vanessa and I arranged a formal meeting before I began my official involvement in Akawini, the toshao said that we were to meet at the bleachers. He marched up with Jacob and Elijah, one carrying his father's briefcase. All three climbed up high into the bleachers and peered down at us. Vanessa and I twisted around for the discussion. I'd anticipated this situation and wasn't surprised by our positioning. I'd also come prepared with an icebreaker and cued Vanessa in advance about what I proposed. She'd smiled in agreement.

I looked up at this father of nine—handsome and athletic—probably in his late thirties. He wore football socks pulled up to his knees and his feet were fitted into plastic sandals. Shorts and a T-shirt completed his outfit. Vanessa greeted the delegation. I opened my laptop to a PowerPoint presentation, carried it up the bleachers, and handed it to one of the young men. "Here. Let the toshao see the eagle expedition."

I then turned and stepped back down to sit near Vanessa. With a son on each side, the trio clicked through the presentation with a murmur of comments. When the toshao finished, he nodded as the laptop was brought back down to me. Vanessa then continued her remarks about Cuso and willingness to assist Akawini. "We're here to support projects that you and the village council would like to see developed."

The toshao's degree of reserve lessened. "We want to start ecotourism. You saw the guesthouse when you arrived. We want a stronger Youth Wildlife Group and have them trained to help."

"We can work with you toward this goal," said Vanessa and they discussed ways and means of proceeding with me as the go-between. She also raised the issue of accommodations. The toshao said that he would make the arrangements. I was again prepared to hand over my Cuso per diem allowance for hammock space and meals and pay for whatever boating arrangements were necessary. Usually, I could be wedged in the packed market boat going past Adel's.

We never did meet the village council, but I had briefed Vanessa in advance on the dynamics of power here in Akawini. Captain as a title indicated how things were run in this settlement.

Vanessa wasn't the only visitor at Adel's. My friend Ann from the World University Service of Canada—WUSC—and her husband Phil had holiday time and decided to visit Adel's. All three had attended the village council meeting in Wakapoa as part of experiencing life in the territory.

Jessica had put on her tour director's hat with the arrival of these guests and thought a trip to Chris and Minerva's home would be interesting and had contacted them in advance. Unfortunately, the tide was out and the channel off the creek to their place was very shallow. Some of us tried slogging through the marshland next to the channel. Vanessa was game enough to accept an offer of a ride in a dugout canoe.

The whole venture turned into a source of howling laughter as those of us in the swampland brigade got hopelessly stuck and knew we couldn't make it to the stelling. Vanessa's fate was the tipping of the dugout and her plunked, bottom first, into the knee-deep channel. Ever the photographer, I snapped a picture of Phil graciously stepping down into thick mud pulling Vanessa to her feet and helping haul her up onto the boggy bank with Eon and Jessica pitching in to tug.

To Vanessa's credit, she was laughing the entire time. Slogging back to the boat on the creek, we had hauled our wet and muddy selves aboard. We signalled farewell to Chris and his family all waving in good cheer with a grand story to tell of the aborted visit.

The return to Georgetown provided unexpected drama for Vanessa, Ann, and Phil. They'd opted for a slow return on the ship that passed around the islands of the Essequibo estuary from Supenaam back to Parika instead of the speedboats. Just before departure, they suddenly found themselves amid prisoners in chains being transported with armed guards. The trio prudently found seats in another area of the ship.

When I later returned to Georgetown, I told Vanessa that I could now, if ever necessary, blackmail her. She had tipped overboard wearing no life vest, which contravened Cuso regulations. Ever sporting, she requested a copy of the photo to share with her family who thought the whole episode as hilarious as we did.

For the next three months, I was made to feel at home with the designated Akawini family whenever I was present in the territory for a few days. They lived in a typical wooden house painted the popular lavender of the bleachers and a church. The latter two were within a stone's throw of the simple, unpainted house of the toshao.

The acting headmaster's house was elevated on posts with an enclosed area at the rear for storage on the ground floor. I guessed this space had once been a shop. The large front balcony, unusual in the village, looked out over the common footpath. A canopied wooden staircase led to a small living room with well-worn sofas on opposite walls. Two bedrooms—doorframes hung with curtains—were off this common area. There was an extension at the back of the house equipped as a spacious kitchen and dining area on one side. Studs framed the other half of the space that would become two more bedrooms. For now, two sturdy hooks were placed for me to hang my hammock.

The outhouse was in the bushes in the back. I was given a small plastic bucket for night use. A large black plastic water tank rested on a wooden platform next to the house. There I would fill my water bottle and pop in a water purification tablet. The wooden shower stall was nearby, and I'd fill a bucket with water using a dipper for bathing just as I did in Wakapoa.

Living with a family gave me added insight into life in a small community and ways to communicate and make progress with my assignment. Tristan and his wife Latoya established our dinner routine. The children would be fed earlier, before I arrived. Latoya would set the table for Tristan and me. It was usually a simple meal with maybe eggs in some form and potatoes, another root vegetable, or rice. If I had brought canned fish, such as tuna, that would be served. The couple were thoughtful and gentle hosts.

EPA trainer at acting headmaster's home

Tristan, an educator, was the most comfortable in speaking with me. He was an amiable man, probably in his thirties, and one of the two trained teachers in the territory. "I'm not from here. I'm from another community on the Pomeroon, upriver from Charity. Latoya is from Akawini and related to many here, including the toshao."

"I've met three of your four children and enjoy their company," I said over one of our dinners.

"Thank you," said Tristan. "Our eldest daughter is at a residential school in Charity because Akawini doesn't have secondary education. I oversee the primary school you passed just before reaching us. The clinic is in another part of the territory a short distance upriver."

The children and other young relatives were usually outside playing, in the living room, or on the balcony entertaining each other during our dinners. Nisa was their next oldest child. In the late afternoon, I'd say, "Come sit by me, Nisa, and I'll show you how to get started on beading." She was a shy girl of eleven but responded when I brought out arts and crafts supplies. We began to communicate through projects, and the family's balcony became a beehive of craftwork.

Their son Josh wasn't very interested in fibre arts. However, once we got to talking about birds and I distributed paper and coloured pencils, he drew a marvelous picture of their pet, Lester, a Red-and-green-Macaw.

Alece was the youngest. She evolved as the day progressed from being grumpy when she got out of bed for nursery school to being a sweet child with a winning grin and a dimple. She coloured a bit but was mostly interested in watching others.

Latoya's parents lived across the footpath and her brothers and other relatives wandered in and out regularly in this relaxed household. All were interested in my presence, so we chatted back and forth about why I was in Akawini.

Latoya's brother Fabian was a stunning twin of Fabio, the model who graced the covers of romance novels of the 1980s and 1990s. Such works of fiction never interested me, but I do remember those book covers with that sleek, muscular physique on full display. It was Fabian who often was the helmsman of the village's marketing boat. I was impressed by not only his looks but also his quiet dignity.

Relationships evolved and relaxed. Life with this family became a springboard for connecting elsewhere in Akawini. It was in discussions with Tristan that I began to envision details of what assistance I might, or might not, be able to give the village in the time remaining.

The guesthouse was now being sided. This was to be the start of the toshao's vision of ecotourism. The building was situated on stilts in the wetlands and had been in skeletal form when I first arrived for the eagle expedition. It was probably being built with Akawini's yearly allotment of funds to do with as they pleased from money administered by the national government.

Now that I was staying a few days at a time, I watched it being framed. It was a conventional building that looked like a square, 1960s North American home with a hipped roof angled on all four sides. There was a sliding glass door as the entrance. Later, the building was painted lime green. I winced.

When I explored the interior with no workmen present, I couldn't figure out the layout of the rooms. A guesthouse with no toilet or bathing facility? Very odd. Probably a bathroom block on dry land would be added later. However, if it was a pit toilet, it would be too close to the wetlands. I made no comment as I hadn't been asked for input. I would help in developing ecotourism from a human resources perspective.

Lorenzo's Indigenous crafts with local materials

Since I was using handcrafts as a way of connecting with villagers and still engaged in asset mapping, I was introduced to Latoya's brother Lorenzo. He was skilled in making costumes and jewellery, especially for the national Indigenous festival held every September. The traditional headdress for toshaos sported upright red and blue feathers and a band of smaller feathers in various colours along with local seeds as beads on the headband. "Lorenzo, macaws weren't killed for these feathers, were they?"

"Not these days. These are found feathers, or I've dyed some with powders I get in Georgetown. We honour our ancient culture but don't kill to make modern day versions of ancient crafts."

Then he showed me carved calabash bowls and grass skirts where he'd experimented with raffia palm fibre and yarn. "The yarn doesn't lie like the palm grass, but I thought I'd give it a try." There were skirts and halters for women in grass and yarn versions. Tibisiri fibre made from the ité palm, the same material used for hammocks, was woven into belts and headbands. Lorenzo was the start of my Akawini asset mapping.

A disabled woman who did handcrafts lived in another of the settlements nearby in the wetlands. Her sister showed me some of her work that included valiant attempts at jewellery and hats. The latter were carefully woven but so stiff that they wouldn't fit anyone's head. I praised her efforts and hoped that there were occasional sales. I guessed at the challenges for this woman in the hinterland trying to keep occupied and creative. However, she couldn't be on my asset mapping list without some guidance.

I welcomed tips about talent elsewhere in the territories. I'd heard from Lloyd about another young woman with artistic ability living in the general area of Tristan's school. The closest contact I was able to make was gathering a variety of drawing and painting materials in Georgetown and giving them to Tristan to pass along. Sometimes the best one can do is gift with an open hand and hope that it helps.

The toshao had spoken earlier of nine sewing machines and a teacher that were promised for Akawini by the Ministry of Indigenous Peoples' Affairs. We waited, but it never happened, much to our disappointment. However, discussion of machine sewing did encourage me to visit one of the homesteads in Wakapoa. Again, it was Lloyd who continued to keep his finger on the pulse and possibilities in the community and made the connection for me. "A relative has rigged an electric sewing machine for my mother-in-law Eileen. It can be used as a treadle machine at her homestead, which has no electricity, and can run with our generator when she's visiting us."

Later, I learned of such a factory-produced machine used by someone in Georgetown but couldn't track the location for details. I passed the information on to both Lloyd and Janet in Wakapoa, who were both interested in getting such a machine. It could make a huge difference in the villages where people wanted to gain or regain skills. They could then provide more clothing and household items for their families and for sale. Such ability could even lead to items for tourists if they could be drawn to the area.

I continued tramping the thoroughfare of Ykinipa, often with several children of various ages as company. I'd observed woodworking underway under a large tree at the side of the path. A dugout canoe was almost complete with the telltale burn marks as signs of curing the timber for leakproof transportation.

I stopped and chatted with the woodworker. Dameayon was a well-built man with wary eyes, probably in his early thirties. I asked about his training, details of his work, and sources of his materials.

"I taught myself woodworking over these fourteen years," he said.

"How do you get wood?"

"It's free harvesting when used locally. We call it self-used."

"How much are you charging for this canoe?"

"40,000 dollars." I calculated that was roughly $250 Canadian or $200 in US dollars. I added Dameayon to my asset mapping list.

Chris, whose homestead was between Adel's and Ykinipa, remained a key figure in our discussions about ecotourism. At one point when we were visiting, I commented on the huge cargo boat that was now nearly finished and resting in its building frame in the yard. "That's a fine boat. For work, right?"

"Yes. For hauling logs out from here. They must be milled. Could you take a photo of the boat and Minerva and me and get a printed copy? I've taken out a bank loan and need to show the boat's done." Chris was quite the enterprising fellow. I also added him to my asset mapping list for Akawini.

I continued finding fascinating people dwelling in the villages. They generally didn't have much formal education, experience outside Region 2, or much in the way of contemporary possessions or technology. They did have practical knowledge, ingenuity, and varying degrees of humour and wisdom. They also had a willingness to live with what I called good enough elements of the building blocks of life: food, clothing, shelter, transportation, and communication. Since coming to Guyana, I'd added the last two items as essential. The provisions for education and health care were also basic in obtaining quality of life.

Transport in the Akawini wetlands

One evening, a villager and I ended up sitting on the steps of the Akawini stelling at sunset and got to talking about the values of the subsistence lifestyle. He said, "I wonder if people really want to do the work to get ahead, or do they just want to complain."

After a few moments of silence, I said, "You know those people in dugout canoes fishing on the creek late in the afternoon? Where I come from, that's called the gone fishin' lifestyle. For lots of people, that's their dream of the good life in the busyness of my world."

He nodded, forearms on knees and rolling a twig between his fingers. We sat in silence and watched the glow of sunset in all its dusky pastel hues. I thought about this community-based way of living and strong interpersonal values. There was much in village living to recommend it.

Chapter Thirteen

Training for Empowerment

When I'd been back in Penticton between assignments, my friend Elmie and I were on a trash pickup detail for a local festival. Armed with a big plastic bags and latex gloves, I had stepped closer to her and fingered one of her dangling earrings while she just grinned. "Those are great earrings! Are the beads wired into the aluminum tabs from flip-top cans?"

"Yes, indeed," she said with satisfaction as she flicked the other earring. "Got 'em at an art fair somewhere, a craft item from Africa. Clever, eh?"

Clever indeed. Beadwork was one of the handcrafts I had done on and off since childhood. Elmie had inspired me to collect an assortment of aluminum tabs and pack them along with my tools for making jewellery. I also whipped up a pair of what I now called pop-top earrings for myself as a sample and for Jessica as a gift.

My plan for rapid connection with villagers was to wear these earrings when talking about craft classes. I knew both Wakapoa and Akawini were interested in economic development, and I needed a way to gauge interests and existing skills. I would also use these sessions to honour skills often pooh-poohed as women's work and frivolous. This was using the sense of touch to reach heart and head. It was also my take on an assignment including what Cuso called Gender Equality and Social Inclusion or GESI as an organizational acronym.

It worked. Once a little boy in Wakapoa had rushed up behind me, tucked a couple of pop-tops into my hand, and dashed away with a shy grin. "Thanks!" I shouted after him. Soon new earring designs were underway.

Initially, with more embroidery supplies than beading equipment, I started the classes with secondary school students in Wakapoa after the school day. I invited them over to sit in a shaded area near the school's water tank. Learning can take place anywhere.

Even teenage boys were willing to give embroidery a go as soon as I passed around instruction sheets that showed stitches. When I set out hoops, cloth, thread, needles, scissors, and pictures, hands flew into action. I made a point of wearing my embroidered birding vest with a growing sample of Guyanese flora and fauna on the back and invited everyone to identify the images. When we were given permission to use the village's craft and resource centre with tables and chairs, classes also filled with women and their young children. We spread materials around in glorious disarray with someone always asking, "Who has the scissors?"

I shared more samples, including some of Aunt Hazel's pieces, which made her blush with pride. I chuckled at the little boy who sketched and embroidered the outline of a car. There were no roads, much less cars, in the territory—only rivers and boats. The automotive dream runs deep, even in the most improbable places.

Everybody got to keep what they made, and I encouraged them to take supplies for more work at home. Craftivism for communication was well underway. I shared meals and hung my hammock with Janet and Matthias's family. Each evening, when the generator was turned off, Alpha and Gaynor, the youngest children, strapped on headlamps and continued their handwork.

Back in Georgetown, I always searched for more supplies. When my cotton blouses from India were nearly as thin as cheesecloth, I found replacements in a small shop operated by an Indo-Guyanese woman. A small rack of cotton blouses was tucked in a dark corner in the back of her shop, and I bought several.

Shanta had a gorgeous array of colourful beaded and sequined garments for special occasions. She was intrigued by my hinterland projects. She said, "Come next week. I'll have sorted through some of the jewellery that was damaged in shipping. Take it to the villages and let them have fun tearing things apart and creating new things of beauty." I took her up on her offer and villagers found great inspiration and pleasure in doing exactly what she had suggested. Someone made little Alece from my host family in Akawini a headpiece that turned her into an Amerindian princess who giggled with dimpled delight.

With more villagers and me working together on whatever crafts they enjoyed, many revealed their skills, and I added them to my asset mapping list. Our relaxed time together let me savour the Indigenous lifestyle, absorb its merits, and build friendships. I also reflected on the world's everlasting emphasis on money. In Guyana, these villagers were rated at the bottom of the country's income scale. I thought about their strong sense of community, which was appealing, at least to me.

In contrast, my upstairs apartment in Georgetown had been rigged with heavy grills and thick wooden doors. There were nine locks and bolts on our flat's back door to the caged laundry area below. My current apartment mate Rhonda and I never used more than two bolts. The caged area contained two washing machines and a generator. The house was fenced with razor wire coiled along the top and a locked gate.

In the villages of Region 2, we were free from excessive fear of theft or attack. This was a huge social plus to balance the economic minus. I quietly wove this thought through conversations in the villages.

In Akawini, handcrafts were only part of my plan for stimulating creativity and growth. I'd also came equipped with binoculars from the South Okanagan Naturalists' Club. There was great excitement among the young people when I shared equipment donated by friends in Canada.

"Can we go look at the birds by the creek?" asked Tabitha, the boldest of the young women whom I'd met in Akawini.

A group of us went to the end of the stelling at dusk when birds were getting ready to roost. I would call out book names and hear local names. "Great Egret," I said with my birding book open and people looking over my shoulder.

"Crane," came a voice from the group.

Youth often milled around the house where I was staying. In the mornings, when I appeared, someone would call out, "Can we walk to the playing field to see more birds?" These were the youth of secondary school age with no school for them in their territory. The government had promised a boardwalk over the marshland to the south that would let them walk to the secondary school at Kabakaburi. The walkway wasn't yet built, and the wetland was too shallow to use boats. If parents couldn't afford residential school in Wakapoa, Charity, or other areas of Region 2, education ended with grade six at Tristan's primary school.

I always brought *Birds of Northern South America*, and everyone was delighted to match book names with the local call names. The youth learned Silver-beaked Tanager, Striated Heron, and Black-collared Hawk, and I learned weso, chao, and fish hawk or arapaiko.

Even the toshao was interested in the book, having heard about it from his sons. Once he had quietly asked me, "What would it cost?" and then asked me to purchase a copy for the Akawini Wildlife Group and he would pay me back.

Adel's remained a hub of activity with tourists from Guyana, Canada, the US, and the UK who came for a sample of life in the interior. They were escorted by Jessica and Eon to more accessible Wakapoa for tours. They also cruised the Pomeroon and nearby creeks to enjoy the wildlife and ambiance of the region. If I was available, I would tag along and share information about my presence as a Cuso volunteer and some of what I'd learned about Guyanese life.

I also helped a bit with the tours of the development projects at Adel's. An official delegation from Akawini, headed by the toshao, had shown up one day for a view of the shade house, the Easy Irrigation Pump, and the Oven John. These prototypical features of Adel's were ways for people of the interior to visualize what might be possible for improvements in their territories.

And so my Guyanese journey continued. During one of my short stints in Georgetown a couple of months after the Harpy Eagle excursion, I had met Wally, one of Guyana's birding experts. He studied my eagle photos, leaned back in his chair, and announced, "I've seen many Harpy Eagles in my life, but I've never seen what you photographed. This is the even more rare Crested Eagle." Now it was my time to sit back in my chair and feel both astounded and delighted. The news soon flew through the Guyanese birding community as it had with my photo of the Crimson-hooded Manakin six months prior.

While in the city, I learned that Vanessa had communicated with a team from Guyana's Environmental Protection Agency about a visit to Akawini for two days of training for the Youth Wildlife Group. She had also contacted the Bina Hill Institute Youth Training Centre in the North Rupununi about an introductory session on ecotourism. These two encounters would be critical in helping Akawini reach its development goals.

We were also making progress in Wakapoa. The toshao and I discussed how a letter to the Minister of Public Telecommunications should be worded. He and the village council wanted the territory's request to be a priority. We decided that I would draft a letter for them to review and, if satisfied, sign. I would then deliver it personally in Georgetown.

The craft classes continued as happy venues for learning. It was heartening to see interest and ability grow. For example, Molly attended the classes with some of her children. She did intricate embroidery and amazed me. She took a colour copy of the pair of Blue-and-yellow Macaws that I had photographed and made a beautiful rendition of them using stitches I didn't even know how to do.

Molly's husband George was part of the masonry crew building a little concrete house behind the snack shop of a member of the village council. The new house faced the marshland with the panoramic view of the sunset. George was a friendly and easygoing man. We talked construction details such as the ratio of sand and cement, boring for most people but interesting for us. George supported his wife's craftwork and had told her, “Just do it for fun too. Everything doesn’t have to be for money.”

Later, when Lydia was beginning agricultural work in Wakapoa, I had introduced her to George and Molly. The three of them stepped over to an area near their plain little wooden house where they wanted to plant a small garden. I slipped away and left them to talk about soil remediation strategies, not a skill in my toolbox.

At one point, Molly introduced me to her sister-in-law Skeitha. She was part of the University of Guyana’s training program to retain the Arawak language, called Loko in the territories. She was also very concerned about access to fresh water for the village. Her dream was to raise poultry.

She had submitted an application for initial funding as part of the Ministry of Communities Sustainable Livelihood and Entrepreneurship Development program—long in name and lacking in response. She had delivered the application in Georgetown a year earlier but had heard nothing. Yet another urban disconnect from the rural.

First house on School Island

Skeitha also wanted to build a benab of wood and thatch similar to her elderly parents’ home. There she could display crafts and offer local food to visitors. As always, dreams and schemes aplenty. How to have visitors come to Wakapoa and visit her shop was the monumental challenge. In a word: marketing. Then Skeitha invited me to the home of her parents, original settlers on what was now called School Island.

I was particularly interested because this was a traditional Indigenous wooden house framed with four-by-four timbers. A measure of privacy was maintained as the height of the building was two feet or so above ground level. Partial walls, waist-high, blocked direct view of inside activities. The kitchen was in one corner with a pair of planks placed above and beyond the wall and braced on struts secured to the outside of the house. These planks provided open shelving for pots and pans.

An old metal wheelbarrow, stripped of its handles and wheel, was set into a four-by-four timber stand. It contained charcoal for cooking. The thatch roof was lashed to framing poles. There was no door. A breeze blew through the house unhindered. Visits such as these gave me a glimpse into a way of life and the structure of homes before the introduction of concrete, windows, and doors.

One day I accepted an invitation from Miss Pam who was Lloyd's wife and the senior primary school teacher on School Island. The large wooden school building was a bright, beautiful space filled with lively children. It was divided by bulletin boards for different grades. Her daughter was an intern finishing her teacher education in Georgetown at the university. I was delighted with the look and feel of this learning space.

Challenges in Akawini continued. Transportation remained a major issue along with having no civic building for gathering and working together. The toshao's reserve was mirrored in Jacob and Elijah. Despite our sharing the eagle quest experience, it took time for them to even acknowledge me when I visited the village. With friends, they would tromp single file down the dirt path in front of Tristan and Latoya's home looking neither left nor right. "Is that Jacob and Elijah I'm seeing?" I had called out one day from the balcony.

"Yes," came a reply with no adjustment of stride or turning of either head.

Things began to change when the toshao and I met in Georgetown to discuss the upcoming EPA training session. "What topics would you and the village council like covered in addition to the standard training?"

The toshao's response was quick and clear. "How to stop pollution of our waters, and how to save our fish and other wildlife for ecotourism."

With plans for the training underway and the dates set, I continued asset mapping in Akawini. One morning, I noticed Latoya using a cooker I recognized from my time in India. "What a great cooking device! It looks as though you started with just a small enamel dishpan," I said. "How did you make this?"

"I filled the pan with special clay from a wet area back of the village," she said, her face beaming with pleasure. "Then I built up the sides and left a hole on one side near the bottom for air to come up. I set the pot on the big hole on top for cooking. Today it's rice."

"I see you burn charcoal, which you make here in Ykinipa. Your father and your brother Fabian showed me how they dug the pit and layered cut small trees to burn down into charcoal." As I crouched studying the details of her device, I said, "This clay stove is called a chula in India."

"We don't have to use as much cooking gas," Latoya said stirring the rice. I stepped around taking various shots of her and the stove and added her to my asset mapping list.

Another person whose personality and ingenuity I treasured was young Tabitha. She was sixteen—bright-eyed and gregarious, an unusual village girl. The toshao had chosen her to be on the original Harpy Eagle expedition that Jessica said was three days of miserable rain with one eagle sighting. Since then, Tabitha desperately wanted ecotourism to come to Akawini.

Her story was heartbreaking. "I was in boarding school in Charity, but my family couldn't afford it. Now I must stay home. I started a girls' football team, but I'm not involved now. The toshao wanted a Youth Wildlife Group, so that's where I spend my time. He wanted to call it a club. I told him that I thought calling it a group would be more inviting."

I wanted to adopt this young woman and provide a scholarship for her schooling. Of course, I couldn't. Later, in surprising circumstances, I found out why she was such a dynamic, driven person.

One day, walking with Tabitha and other village girls on the stelling, I leaned over the railing and saw the trash of modern life: plastic bags and bottles, paper and cardboard. With debris floating by, I said, "It's almost World Environment Day. What can we do?"

"I'll organize the wildlife group to do a village cleanup," said Tabitha.

"Good. I'll supply the collection bags and plastic gloves" knowing that they'd become part of the debris.

The more that I saw and heard about Tabitha, the more I was impressed. She was forthright when she asked for help for her budding group. "Can you help us get bush clothes?" she asked after watching me in cotton shirts and pants and a birding vest with many pockets.

Later, Miss Lam, my former landlady and a continuing friend in Georgetown, had taken me to the vendors who regularly received the blue bins—huge barrels filled with used clothing from the Global North. Prices were cheap, so I'd loaded up on shirts and pants and lugged a full duffle bag back to Region 2 for the next gathering of the Akawini Wildlife Group, which was all girls at this point.

"Tabitha, everyone is trying on clothes, but you look disappointed."

"I meant your vest with pockets," she said with a sigh.

"Oh, my mistake." The next time I saw her, I gave her one of my pocketed vests in mottled brown that could serve as a birding vest. Then I received a wide grin. We both chuckled to see that she had bought herself a brown camouflage cloth hat that was a perfect match. Now she was properly kitted up for propelling the AWG onward.

Back in Wakapoa, the toshao had arranged a trip to the community garden, something he'd asked me to do well in advance and before Lydia was due to arrive as an agricultural advisor.

The Guyanese government, through the Ministry of Indigenous Peoples' Affairs, granted money from the Amerindian Development Fund each year. The 128 Indigenous territories could use the funds as they saw fit. Some territories invested in development projects such as Akawini's guesthouse and Wakapoa's community garden. Some territories just divided the money among families. The toshao in Wakapoa told me that they'd used last year's funds to clear twelve acres about a half-hour's walk from the nearest stelling after a short boat ride from School Island.

After motoring up a tributary from the main creek, the toshao and two members of the village council and I docked and followed a path through scrub grass. The village tractor and trailer also used this route to haul timber. When we entered the forest, I counted eleven ruts with many that would reach my knee or thigh, if I stepped down. Reaching the site, I saw slash-and-burn acreage gouged out of the rainforest with charred tree trunks and brush scattered about the site.

The toshao sat on a felled trunk and waved his hand toward various planted areas between the remains of trees. "The fund paid to clear the land and provided wages for nine villagers to work every other day. You can see cassava, pumpkins, and red beans here. Over there are watermelon, yams, and bananas. Farther over there's bora and okra."

"That's a good variety of crops," I said with as much cheer as I could muster.

"Later we hope to plant pears—what you might call avocados—and coconut, limes, and lemons." When I asked to see the water source, I was taken down a steep slope and shown a creek with only a tiny trickle of water.

The men had brought a large pineapple for food and drink. While we sat on a felled tree trunk in the shade, I learned that the funds had run out and now nobody was tending the plants. Villagers were being encouraged to move closer to the garden, but lack of water, shelter, transportation, and further funding meant this was a hopeless scheme. I also learned that the village tractor needed a new alternator, battery, and starter. The trailer needed two new tires with tubes and new bearings for the axel hub. Limitless need.

With no business plan for the garden, it was now at a standstill after only a few months of start-up activity. The rainy season would start soon, so the community garden might grow. However, the rutted road would only get worse. There was no way to get produce from the garden except by people carrying it.

I was sad for Wakapoa. One glimmer of hope that I shared with the men as we enjoyed the last morsels of the sweet and juicy pineapple was about Lydia. "A Cuso volunteer with organic tropical agriculture and soil restoration experience is on her way to become an advisor here in Wakapoa. She might have ideas to help you realize your dream for the garden." I had also casually mentioned the possibility of small plot development by individuals within the village at various homestead sites as a way to more readily boost agricultural development.

After visiting the community garden and me not offering high hopes for success, it was a relief to return to my Wakapoa base. I chatted with Janet and watched Shana swinging in the hammock and nursing her baby. I could hear Matthias in the shed out back helping a neighbour with a mechanical problem.

That day Janet and Shana were tending their cassava business. Disheartened about the community garden, I just hunkered down in the courtyard and helped scrub the cassava roots that were soaking in a big pan. It felt good having handwork instead of the day's tough headwork.

Shana's younger sister Faith was working as a teacher in the village this year. She was about to apply for medical school in Georgetown and stepped over to ask Janet a question. They were making plans to travel to the city so she could seat the entrance examination—exciting news.

This was also the night that I had provided unplanned entertainment for the family during dinner. It showed that cultural differences could even affect a simple meal. The conventional red and yellow plastic squeeze bottles for condiments that I recognized from childhood were in the middle of the table. I assumed that red meant ketchup and squeezed a blob onto my plantain chips. Wrong! For this family, and probably most Guyanese, red meant hot pepper sauce and yellow was ketchup. I only made that mistake once. Meanwhile, the family laughed as I gulped water and wished that I could just leave my tongue dangling in the cool liquid.

At Adel's, eagle identification notched up another level with a flash of additional birding news about Region 2. Wilderness Explorers, one of the country's biggest and best known tourism companies, had arrived. Tony, the managing director, was accompanied by the operations supervisor and a guide. Jessica took them to Ykinipa and repeated our first trek up into the high country to see the nesting site where I had photographed the eagle or eagles.

No bird appeared, but the nest was studied and, along with my photographs, the second authoritative verdict was given. The experts agreed that it was indeed a Crested Eagle, a juvenile. The presence of a young bird meant adults were also in the area. The challenge was how to craft an adventure ecotourism itinerary around this phenomenon, yet preserve this species' desire for solitude. Preparing to leave with gear piled on the stelling, Tony had turned to me and said, "Tourists want activities. Develop additional exciting activities as well as the birding."

I purposely hadn't gone on the trek with Jessica and the men because I knew I would be leaving in six weeks and couldn't pursue establishing adventure tourism. It was better left with Jessica to orchestrate with the villages and Tony or other tour operators since there would be no Cuso volunteer continuing my work in Region 2.

Jessica and Eon accompanied the visitors back to Charity while I resumed my tasks as kitchen wench. I ruminated about the scuttlebutt picked up on the creek earlier when travelling with villagers. An area a short distance up the creek from Adel's was being eyed for an upscale resort complete with a helipad. Adel's offered a light-on-the-land experience. If this new development went forward, it would be to alight on the land. Helicopters would deposit wealthy guests into a gussied up river and rainforest venue. My head swam with the contradictions of intent while I scrubbed. Better for me to clean pots and pans at this point than plot the finer points of possibilities for tourism and other endeavours in Region 2.

Since Cuso was the official partner organization for this fledgling effort in Akawini, Vanessa had found enough funding in her budget to provide a training excursion into the heart of the country in the North Rupununi. Four young people and I would be flown in to study the operations of two eco-lodges, one owned and operated by the Indigenous village at Surama—the same place that I had visited the previous year—and the other, a private enterprise. We would also visit Bina Hill Institute that trained Indigenous youth for a variety of careers, including tourism.

I met with the Akawini toshao again to detail this plan and discuss the choice of the four youth. He made the final decision: three young women, including Tabitha, and one young man, Jacob. We were cautioned by a Bina Hill board member, who was helping organize this introductory training session, to select individuals already outgoing and able to handle cross-cultural communication.

Sometimes I went off on divergent projects of my own and not only spent my money on craft supplies but also made investments in people. We were receiving a modest stipend while volunteering with Cuso along with accommodations, health care coverage, and flights to and from our assignments. I decided when I accepted this second assignment that the extra money I brought for travel and whatever was supplied by Cuso would stay in Guyana.

At Adel's, David and I appreciated each other's knowledge and skills. Jessica had helped his daughter Shondel attend a postsecondary technical school in Region 2's capital, Anna Regina. This was a two-year program on document processing and, at age sixteen, she was in her first year. Jessica had done much work securing study materials so that Shondel could take the entrance exams needed for the program. Now the young woman was complaining to her parents about eye trouble and extreme fatigue. We learned that she was staying up late to borrow a laptop from other students in the dormitory to do her homework. She desperately wanted and needed to work at normal times.

After speaking with David and Jessica, I'd offered to pick up Shondel for a weekend on my way through to Georgetown. We would price laptops and I would teach her how to use email. It was a whirlwind weekend of touring the city, shopping, eating out, and an email lesson at the Cuso office. A couple of weeks later, I delivered a laptop to an ecstatic Shondel.

Cuso had advised against spending our own money on projects, especially for big ticket items. However, I believed that sometimes one needed to invest a chunk of money in the future of a person or a project, and let it play out in whatever manner.

With the increased flurry of activities underway, it was important to insert moments of peaceful rest for myself that made Guyana of the hinterland such a remarkable experience for me. At one point, when I was about to leave Wakapoa, Matthias borrowed Ivan's small boat to ferry me back to Adel's. This was the tiniest boat that I'd ever experienced and had a small motor. The heightened plank sides gave me confidence because I was always concerned about toppling overboard and soaking my technical equipment and documents.

Wakapoa Creek shortcut through mangroves

I remembered this particular ride because Matthias had taken us down Wakapoa Creek to the Pomeroon using a shortcut. The sky was clear blue with the wetlands of green grasses waving in the breeze. Birds flew overhead and I quizzed myself on their names. Scrub brush lined the creek banks until we glided under the canopy of the rainforest with slivers of sunlight reaching the smooth surface of the waterway.

We passed large trees buttressed with trunk extensions that let them lead both a terrestrial and aquatic life. This was determined by the tidal flow and the water coming from the Amazon. Matthias veered sharply to the right near a grand old tree with its hipped trunk embedded in the gently flowing creek. There was a narrow waterway with mangroves crowding each bank. This was the quiet little shortcut to the great Pomeroon that could only be used by small boats.

My helmsman angled our little boat between the tangle of mangroves and drooping branches and vines in this fairy-tale foliage. Then, akin to the light at the end of a tunnel, we approached a portal of sunshine, a clear blue sky, and the gleaming waters of the big river. We felt the chop of wind whip up small waves—*kchonk, kchonk.* Matthias kept close to the bank of the Pomeroon avoiding the wave action of the bigger boats that sped by. Calmer water prevailed under the overhanging branches.

We glided along and soon neared the mouth of Akawini Creek. Matthias motored slowly to Adel's and aimed for the wooden staircase of the stelling. The dogs started their frantic welcoming antics while Jessica and Eon strolled down to greet us. Matthias and I parted with smiles as I handed him passage money and something extra. "Wonderful trip. Thank you." The three friends chatted for a bit longer before I heard the engine start and glimpsed Matthias backing the boat into the creek and heading home.

I always found it marvellous to be home with like-minded, spirited mavericks Jessica and Eon. They were also making frequent trips back to Georgetown now that the local TV station learned of Eon's cooking and singing prowess and asked for a proposal for a TV series. I saw the outline of episodes before it was submitted and applauded the enticing range of culinary topics celebrating Guyanese cuisine. I knew that Eon would add captivating commentary and music to the mix. Several episodes were now filmed and at the editing stage. Eon hadn't liked the title of the proposed series, but Jessie told him, "Embrace it. You know that's what people are going to call it." And so The Singing

Chef was launched. Jessica, with her history in marketing, became the ad hoc producer and both were involved in the editing.

If I happened to be based at Adel's for a day or two with guests present, I would join the ritual cruise near dusk for a ride downriver on the Pomeroon to the Atlantic. We would catch glimpses of the Scarlet Ibis winging their way for roosting in foliage inland after a day of feasting on crustaceans on the mudflats of the Atlantic. This diet gave them their vivid red plumage that contrasted with the clear blue sky and the lushness of tropical growth. A river cruise at dusk meant we also absorbed the cool, salty ocean breeze and the precious light of the golden hour.

Life was good. Work was continuing with the two territories' craft groups based at Ykinipa and School Island. I was nurturing Akawini's birding excursions and plans for the ecotourism training sessions. Wakapoa's request for a tech tower was in Georgetown. Lydia was about to start agricultural work in Region 2. I was luxuriating in hanging my hammock in homes in the hinterland with friends and enjoying my travels in this country of natural beauty and bounty. Suddenly, I was brought up short by a misstep in Georgetown.

Chapter Fourteen

Ecotourism Indigenous Style

Whenever I was back in the city, laundry was at the top of my to-do list. It had just rained and I was in flip-flops headed down to the laundry room on exposed, slippery steps. Zap! I fell backward. Oh, the pain! I guessed that my ribcage was bruised but not broken. Hauling myself up the staircase backward in crab-like fashion, I knew there was no bending or twisting possible. Spying a broken mop handle when crawling into the apartment, I used it as a crutch.

After time in bed, I got to a sitting position without moving my torso and pivoted on my bottom swinging my legs to the floor as a counterweight. Using the handle to stand, I shuffled into the kitchen. There were enough basic provisions for a few days. Rhonda would soon be back from a week's vacation at home in Jamaica.

I called Vanessa saying that I'd weather a few days of disability at the apartment and would call for help, if necessary. "I don't need a doctor at this point."

"Are you sure?" asked Vanessa with worry in her voice.

"Yup," I said with unjustified certainty.

Homebound, I found periodicals saved but not read. Many articles touched on my work and general thoughts about life in this former

British colony. One headline read, "The world's richest 1% are on course to control as much as two-thirds of the world's wealth by 2030." Did this mean the fate of the Global South would spiral downward at increased speed? Where did Indigenous people fit in this prediction?

"Gulf stream threat to world weather." Guyana's coast was six feet below sea level at current high tide. What was the country's future with climate change underway?

Continuing my passive life, I read an article linking quantum physics and Eastern religions. Maybe so. I could see the possible connection of some scientific and ancient religious thoughts about the material and immaterial worlds. How would this affect the science versus religion debates that continued tearing humankind apart?

A few days later, I was closer to feeling normal. I found that wrapping a tensor bandage around my lower rib cage limited stretching or twisting and eased pain. I headed for the Cuso office. Only half in jest, I told staff and colleagues, "Kindly don't tell any rib-tickling jokes. Laughing hurts."

Soon I was back doing some errands and making up for days of solitude. I stopped by a local shop to top up cell phone minutes. I headed for Phagoo's dry goods shop, which stocked the best selection of embroidery floss at a good price. I visited Austin's Bookstore and spotted a book for one of the girls who was sponsored by Jessica at the residential school in Wakapoa. I knew that Alicia was keen on Guyanese herbal plants and would welcome this slim volume.

Meanwhile, there were shifts in staffing at the Cuso office and established volunteers were deputized to help with operations. We were losing Indranie, a crackerjack accountant. She could carry on a detailed conversation while simultaneously counting a fistful of dollars. In her customary plain talk, she said, "I can be the accountant, but I can't also handle volunteer oversight. That's two different skill sets, and I don't have that much patience with people." Good point. I certainly knew when I was out of my depth, such as matters of tropical agriculture.

There was also another in-country training session beginning for new volunteers. I provided the group with some basic information but left space for people to find their own way. Lydia was part of this batch, so I shared some specific information with her on travel and Wakapoa and left the rest for her to discover.

Everything for me was now calculated in countdown mode. Logistics of hinterland travel and accommodation were crucial. I would accompany Lydia to Region 2 along with the EPA trainers. The following week, I would collect the four youth from Akawini for the North Rupununi training.

With Indranie gone and replacement interviews underway, Vanessa had asked me to create and oversee the budgets for the two programs and make all the arrangements for travel and accommodations. I wrestled with the budgets and realized that the only emergency funds available would be the extra personal money that I would carry.

I had hoped to have funds for training for five youths but could only cover the flights for four plus me. We'd visit Surama, a second trip for me to this Indigenous eco-lodge. We'd also visit Rock View, a privately owned eco-lodge. Both resorts would provide free accommodation. Cuso would cover meals, flights, and land travel. After making final arrangements for the EPA training and with my ribs healed, I would soon be back on the road and back in the boats heading for Region 2.

My association with colleagues and staff enriched my experience with Cuso as we swapped information and perspectives. However, my focus always returned to what was planned for Region 2. This was the dramatic other bookend of my assignment in Indigenous land. Seeing the Crested Eagle was the start. The trainings would provide the finish.

Deuel and Saliqa from EPA were experienced trainers, but this would be their first visit to Region 2. The agenda they had sent showed a thoughtful progression of topics on how to conduct environmental education in rural areas, keys to forming a group, and tips on maintaining momentum. Akawini was a fledgling group, so the young people could compare what they had already done with what was recommended. There would be a nature walk with our binoculars and a biodiversity lesson to conclude the first day.

The second day would start with an icebreaker exercise that looked like fun. Challenges for maintaining the group and the need for reporting group activities to the EPA quarterly would be stressed. Later, there would be sessions on specific topics requested by the toshao: water and sanitation, and waste management.

I would accompany the EPA trainers to Adel's along with Cuso volunteer Mahendra who had asked Vanessa if he could be part of the training in Akawini as an observer. I welcomed his presence for both his professional outlook from environmental science and his interest in the lives of his Indigenous countryfolk.

The plan was that Vanessa would arrive a day later and, with Lydia, would head for Wakapoa for the required Cuso inspection of her accommodations. Deuel, Saliqa, Mahendra, and I would await the boat from Akawini for the EPA training.

I do love good organization and held high hopes for the EPA program. I'd managed my initial part, which was to get everyone to Adel's on time, intact, and ready for the training. Jessica hosted a lovely dinner prepared by Eon that featured local fish and produce from the shade house.

Early the next morning, our group was ready at the appointed hour. We waited. We waited a bit longer. Then I made a phone call. The unapologetic news from the toshao was, "There's no gas." I was stunned. What to do?

Jessica had gone into emergency mode and called around the Pomeroon. "We need a boat at Adel's right away. To Akawini. The cost? Uh-huh. Uh-huh. Just a minute." She held her hand over the phone and said, "I can get you a boat and crew now for 30,000 dollars. There's 29,700 dollars worth of gas available that will get you there and back." Nearly 60,000 total—$400 Canadian or $300 US dollars. Ouch.

"Get the boat and we'll take all the gas," I said. In my brief conversation with the toshao, I'd made a deal. I would pay for transportation if he promised full reimbursement. He agreed. Yeesch! I was pushed to trust him on the strength of a phone call. I now had committed most of my emergency funds for both trainings first thing in the morning. My careful calculations were wrecked, and time was slipping by. The boat arrived and we piled onboard, departed at ten o'clock, and made the hour's journey through the rainforest and into the wetlands to the Akawini stelling at Ykinipa.

I'd arranged with Eon earlier to make a cooked lunch at my expense to treat the training group this first day. He'd prepared cassava pizza, chicken chow mein, and vegetarian cookup. We had run out of bottled gas at Adel's, so Eon cooked everything in his outdoor Oven John and with a campfire behind Adel's. Big cook pots and utensils were now wedged in along with our personal gear, plus the EPA training equipment.

Approaching the village, I peeled off the 60,000 dollars for our boatmen. Members of the wildlife group had come to help lug everything, except the gas, the half mile uphill to the village's meeting hall. "Tabitha, I knew you'd be here," I said as I gave my favourite young woman a big hug. Young men from the village, including Jacob and Elijah, started to decant all the gas into the village's containers. "Guys, remember this is my gas for our ride back and the toshao has promised full payment."

They nodded as the plastic jerry cans were handed up onto the stelling and stowed in the locked shed built out on stilts on the opposite side. Then we all trudged single file through the village, watched by everyone, and headed up to the meeting hall. We made quite the procession with Tabitha and me in the lead followed by Muslim Saliqa with her hijab. Then came Afro-Guyanese Deuel, Indo-Guyanese Mahendra, and Akawini's Jacob bringing up the rear. We almost made the "Land of Six Peoples" just in our gang.

The community hall was a new building painted light green with bare wood flooring and waist-high siding with spaced planking to the ceiling providing light and ventilation. Though far from the settlement and on high country scrub land overlooking the creek and wetlands in the distance, the building was elevated on stilts. This was probably to decrease insect invasion from the sandy soil.

The toshao had said to expect twenty to twenty-five people. The trainers had encouraged inviting villagers and not just youth, so the invitation was made in advance. Eon had prepared lunch for thirty. We learned that the toshao had forgotten to mention the training at the last village council meeting. There were only seventeen youth the first day and no villagers. Hmmm, I thought to myself. Late arrival at huge expense and now a small group. Not the start we had all expected.

First day of EPA training in Akawini

Lunch became the first order of business as it was now midday, and Deuel and Saliqa needed time for setup and discussion about how to shorten two days of training. There were no chairs or benches, so we just sat on the floor with our backs against the walls, literally.

After lunch, the trainers mixed discussion with activities that demonstrated how to build a strong environmental group. The goal was to spark environmental awareness and action in all villagers for their own good and for starting ecotourism in their region.

The late afternoon stroll in nearby nature and biodiversity training got everyone outside and roaming the grasslands and rainforest surrounding the meeting hall. The young people were sharing the binoculars and teaching each other how to adjust them. Then we experienced the seasonal afternoon rain and a rainbow to wind up the formal part of the training day.

"Remember the bonfire at the playing field this evening," I said as the young people departed. "And we'll start at nine in the morning. Please come on time." The bonfire was the toshao's idea. He wanted a pleasant evening with local talent. There was to be singing, dancing, storytelling, and poetry recitation. We visitors headed downhill to our accommodations to drop off our gear, reconvene to eat the rest of our lunch for dinner, and prepare for the toshao's invitation.

If transportation had caused me stress in the morning, then accommodations provided matching stress in the evening. We were to sleep on three new double bed mattresses still in their plastic covers in the unfinished guesthouse. I had spoken to Tristan earlier to adjust the plan. Saliqa was a young Muslim woman, and this was her first time in the interior. I decided she must have more private accommodation than bunking in with me and a couple of guys in an unfinished building. Tristan agreed that she would use my hammock at his home for the night. I made introductions as we walked by the house and left her to meet the family and get settled.

Meanwhile, Mahendra, Deuel, and I trudged down to the guesthouse and walked the plank over the marshland to reach a platform. We steadied ourselves and entered a building with only some walls completed. I'd carried sheets and mosquito nets borrowed from Adel's figuring that we better have at least basic bedding.

I'd also cleared with Tristan that we could use their outhouse and shower shed. We accepted the family's invitation to join them inside to eat our dinner. I said, "Come everyone. We have so much food from lunch that there's dinner for all of us. Ah, more family from across the way. Come, there's food for all." Latoya ladled out the chow mein and the chicken cookup, and the family took up slices of Eon's cassava bread pizza with great interest.

With dusk settling on the community, villagers gathered on the bleachers. A traditional fire of long wood poles set in tepee fashion would be ignited. Wood shavings and other dry materials were tucked into the base. Traditional spinning of a stick between hands was used to create a spark. The toshao and some young people, including Tabitha, were the fire starters. Soon we had a blazing pile of poles. All those who stepped forward to sing, recite poetry, tell stories, or dance were illuminated by firelight, mesmerizing everyone. It was a lovely gesture on the toshao's part, and we visitors all thanked him. It provided entertainment for the community. However, I was still grumpy about all the stress and disappointments of the day, especially the low attendance for the training.

By midevening, we visitors showed signs of exhaustion and started our way back to our accommodations. Reaching Tristan and Latoya's home, Saliqa bid us goodnight and climbed upstairs. Continuing on the dirt path, we three walked the plank to our oddly furnished accommodations. I left the fellows to sort themselves out. "G'night, guys!" I called into the dark. All I heard was a couple of umms.

Later, when I needed to pee, I had to plot how to get myself from under the net, slide the glass door open, and move to the edge of the wooden platform without toppling into the wetlands. What a gesture at an environmental training! Later, I heard scuttling around my mattress and thumped the floorboards. The next morning, I roused myself and heard the fellows stirring and asked, "How was the night?"

"Too hot," somebody said.

Ah, no Georgetown air-conditioning and no fans. Just pure tropical night air. With no place else to go, we accepted Tristan's invitation to come upstairs where I made a friendly call to the toshao about breakfast, "It's cooking. Just now." Click. I hoped this wasn't going to be another boat story.

Gradually, the rest of the family awakened. Nisa, ever the shy preteen, edged out the front door to the outhouse without a word. Little Alece was her grumpy, early morning self. She rubbed her eyes and headed for her mother who was preparing coffee for us. Josh handed me a drawing of Lester, their pet macaw. Saliqa joined us just when breakfast arrived: cassava meal porridge as basic belly ballast.

We returned to the meeting hall and found that our numbers had dwindled by four, down to thirteen. The trainers started with an icebreaker exercise, an odd term knowing we were so close to the Equator. Trainees formed a circle and tossed an awara seed, the size of a plum and native to Guyana, from one to another. Each person who caught the seed then recapped a memorable moment from the previous day.

Deuel spoke of how important it was for the EPA and the Akawini Wildlife Group, or AWG, to keep in touch each quarter. Saliqa outlined the challenges in keeping such efforts alive and growing. A written evaluation session followed and then the election of the board of directors for the group. Tabitha volunteered to be secretary saying, "I can get more done there than being the president." After a break, the presenters discussed one of the topics that the toshao had requested: water and sanitation. I remembered what I did in the night off the guesthouse porch platform and felt a twinge of guilt.

Lunch arrived as the toshao promised: vegetarian cookup. More good belly ballast. The wrap-up was again a toshao topic: waste management. By midafternoon, the training was concluded in preparation for a promised upriver tour of Akawini Creek.

Heading back down the trail, we paused at Dameayon's woodworking area, and—with a flourish—I asked him to show the attendees the storage cabinet for the group's reference materials and the binoculars. The cabinet was a metre high by a metre wide with bas relief hearts and diamonds on the doors, a lock, and carved decorative work on the cornice at the top. I thanked him for both his design and construction skill and handed him the envelope with the balance of payment. Another investment in people.

Fingers were running over the cabinet with keen interest when I asked the new board of directors to stand by the unit so that I could commemorate the occasion. I also asked Dameayon to stand with the group for another photo, which he did with his ever-wry smile. Jacob then hoisted the unit onto his head and carried it to Tristan and Latoya's home as the AWG library site.

With pots and pans, bedding, our kit bags, and training materials gathered, and with an abundance of helping hands, we made our way down to the creek. The toshao was standing at the motor, but the boat was pointed downriver. "No upriver tour?" I asked. He nodded and started the engine. Harrumph, I said under my breath as I settled in with gear piled around our feet, under the seats, and in the bow cubby. We made it back to Adel's at warp speed nearly achieving hydrofoil status.

When we reached our destination and our welcoming committee of barking dogs, we all dutifully thanked the toshao. "I hope you're pleased with the training," I said. He nodded. When we all disembarked, I turned and aimed a look directly at him. "We'll talk later about the money you owe me, right?" I got a tiny nod and a look that conveyed his turn in expressing harrumph.

With the EPA training concluded, our dinner gathering at Adel's was filled with Akawini stories that stole the spotlight. Vanessa had arrived that day for inspection of Lloyd and Miss Pam's accommodations for Lydia's posting. I stood and said, "I offer a toast to Deuel and Saliqa." Glasses clinked and there were smiles all around. "Also, the photos of the eagle in Ykinipa have now been confirmed twice by experts as a Crested Eagle juvenile. Akawini could become prime territory for adventure ecotourism."

Eon added, "Wilderness Explorers came up to check the eagle nest. They're offering a reward of $200 in US money for anyone who can locate a Crested Eagle or another nest."

Conversation flowed and a mellow glow of satisfaction brightened the dinner gathering. Then the trainers and Mahendra excused themselves to prepare for return to Georgetown in the morning. Vanessa and Lydia found a quiet place in the lounge to discuss their next day's trip. Eon and I returned to the kitchen for cleanup.

After our three EPA guests departed the next morning, we heard another engine slowing down with the dogs racing to fulfill their greeting ritual. It was Jessica returning from Georgetown with news from the official celebration of the Queen's birthday at the British High Commission. We chuckled at Jessica's experience of the royal and the rural all in a couple of days. Sabine, a friend of Vanessa's and mine and a board member of the Deaf Association of Guyana, DAG, also had arrived for the weekend. Cuso was creating crowds at Adel's.

After breakfast, it was back into a boat and off to Wakapoa with a range of tasks to be completed. Jessica was given little time to catch her breath or hear much of the latest news. Vanessa and Lydia would travel farther up Wakapoa Creek on an inspection tour. Jessica and Eon would accompany them and discuss a few more details about marketing Lloyd's coffee in Georgetown. Sabine would stay on School Island and meet the deaf in the village and convey news of DAG. I would stay with her and drop off more handcraft supplies care of Aunt Hazel and, when Vanessa and Lydia returned, introduce them to more members of the community. Gas was expensive. Each visit into the settlements needed to move projects forward.

With all the comings and goings of people and the mixture of itineraries and agendas, later in the day at Adel's I found myself not good company for anyone, including myself. I chose a medical thriller from Adel's collection of dog-eared paperbacks and settled, with no guilt, into the hammock at the far end of the veranda. Hours later, I was rested enough to enjoy another dinner by master chef Eon. A musical interlude followed the meal with sharing his recent songs focused on Guyana. No wonder the cooking show that was now being filmed for TV was doing so well. Soon Vanessa, Lydia, and Sabine excused themselves as they'd be catching an early morning boat for a return to Georgetown.

The next morning, I awoke early with kitten Otis leaping through my window and skidding down the net curtains that I'd hoped would cat-proof my room. He was on some sort of quest with all the expertise of a silly little cat. "Come here, Otis," I said scrunching down, plucking him out from under my bed, and depositing him outside. "Go look elsewhere." I then crawled back under the mosquito net and flopped back onto my fluffy pillow.

The toshao was to arrive with the four youths at 7:00 a.m. I needed to get us to Georgetown today for tomorrow's early morning flight on our way to Surama Eco-Lodge. I held my breath. This time the toshao arrived on time, despite driving rain. Jacob, Tabitha, and Candacy were aboard along with villagers going to market. "Where's Daisy?" I asked. She was the fourth trainee expected.

"We'll meet her in Charity," the toshao said as someone flipped up the corner of a tarp and motioned for me to crawl under. We needed protection from both the rain and the waves for the forty-minute ride down the churning Pomeroon. When we reached the town, the girls and I scrambled up onto the stelling and dashed into an old warehouse. We sat on benches inside while father and son visited a nearby restaurant in a wooden shed. We could smell breakfast cooking, but it was only the males eating. I'd grabbed my breakfast sandwich of cassava bread and a hunk of last night's fish and hoped that the girls had managed some food earlier.

"Where's Daisy?" I asked again.

"I'll phone," said Tabitha. Rain caused a delay in the connection before I heard the murmur of conversation. She turned to me and said, "She's halfway back at Barker's landing. She waved but we didn't see her."

"What? We're expecting her to be in Charity." I marched over to the toshao to convey the news and caught him mid-bite Setting down his fork, he reached for his cell phone. I said, "She has to get here herself or we'll leave without her." Turning on my heel, I rejoined the young women to fret.

The fellows soon appeared beside us in the warehouse. "She'll come," said the toshao now turning on his heel and leaving with Jacob at his side. So, we waited and waited some more. I asked the girls to take turns standing out on the stelling so Daisy would know where we were. I loaned my umbrella as my contribution to the vigil.

The toshao had selected Daisy. I'd never met her. At just minutes before the time that I'd said we must move out, Daisy appeared. "Just in time, Daisy. Five minutes more and we'd have been gone. I'll find a taxi and we're on our way. But where are the toshao and Jacob?"

"Oh, they've gone ahead to the bank in Anna Regina to get your money," said Tabitha. I was glad that at least one of us knew what was happening.

We piled into the taxi of a driver I'd recognized from earlier trips. Within the hour, we stopped at the designated bank. I stepped inside, saw the toshao in line, and walked over to touch his elbow. He looked over at me and I saw the first smile ever, actually just half a smile. He motioned for me to take one of the seats near the entrance. A few minutes later, we exited the bank and rendezvoused at the back bumper of his taxi where he started peeling off bills. "Looks like a drug deal," I said. I then got the other half of his smile as he handed me fifty percent of the debt. I watched him roll the other half of the wad and stick it into his pocket. I eyed the pocket and asked, "The rest later?"

"Later," he said as he climbed back into the taxi. I caught sight of Jacob in the back seat looking neither left nor right. I wondered how many other deals he'd witnessed in the company of his father. The toshao was heading for meetings with the Ministry of Indigenous Peoples' Affairs in Georgetown and Jacob would stay with him at his hotel overnight. I would have a taxi collect Jacob and bring him to the airport in the morning for our flight.

Business transacted, the girls and I were again off down the coastal highway. Ever curious about residential architecture, I noted that some homes were built high on wood or concrete pillars and others were at ground level. I'd first noticed this contrast when Linton and I attended the Housing Expo south of Georgetown the previous year. Now I was seeing it with waves splashing over the seawall. I knew most of these houses were built before climate change became a global issue. This was the tropics, but I shivered.

When we reached Supenaam, the speedboat touts scrambled for our business. I'd travelled this route enough to recognize some of the good and bad boats and chose one that might give us a better crossing of the Essequibo. The boat held fifteen or twenty passengers depending on their size and the amount of baggage. On one trip, I'd sat next to a woman supplying a poultry business with stacked boxes of cheeping chicks at her feet.

The girls reached for life vests, and I donned my PFD horse collar. Soon we backed away with exhaust fumes filling the cabin and choking us until the motorman switched to forward gear. For the next forty minutes, we lurched through the chop of ocean meeting river. We weaved between the various islands that dotted the estuary and made a zigzag passage to the settlement of Parika. Some of the girls braced themselves when the boat crashed through waves. I gave them my oft-repeated advice about rough rides on land or water. "Relax and go with the motion of the pitch. It'll be easier on your body than fighting."

When we reached our destination, we were again surrounded by touts wanting our business. I listened to prices and smiled at the fellows giving inflated figures aimed at tourists. "These young women are coming, too. Now how much for all?" I asked. When I heard a good price, we hoisted our bags and trod over century-old timbers. We passed through the old warehouse darkened with age and hard use. The air smelled of oil and exhaust fumes. Finally, we came out into the parking lot and bright sunshine. I sized up the driver introduced by the tout and gave my customary spiel. "You'll be driving this car but under my direction. Understood? If you're driving too fast or we're feeling frightened in any way, you'll change your driving, so that you don't scare us. Agreed?"

"Yes, ma'am, you the boss," said the driver as he tapped the brim of his baseball cap. When it came to safety, I used my white prerogative, my age, and my woman's bossy-pants voice to maximum effect. "Good. We're looking forward to a safe and pleasant ride with you," I said with a smile.

At Vreed-en-Hoop, the taxi entered another ancient warehouse with massive, creaky floorboards and pulled up alongside an area clear of shops. There we walked out onto yet another stelling for the water taxi that would take us over the Demerara for a ten-minute ride to Stabroek Market.

Again, the girls and I made our way onboard and donned life jackets. This ride was much smoother than the one on the Essequibo. When we docked, it was once more a quest for a taxi and just a short trip to near the seawall to the north where the Cuso office and my apartment faced each other.

I'd alerted my landlady, an elderly Indo-Guyanese woman with eagle eyes, that the girls would be staying with me for the night. She'd watched for us and came out for an introduction. It was smiles all around as we took the stairs up to the apartment. Rhonda was present, so more greetings, and then I showed the girls into my huge bedroom with its king-size bed. "You three get the bed and I'll take the couch," I said as they looked with wonder around a room larger than some of the houses in their village. Why I was provided an acre of bed in a country in the Global South left me clueless. One of the bedrooms in my apartment the previous year was also furnished with another king-size bed that meant getting around it by sidestepping. I'd kept to my original little room filled with only a queen-size bed.

I said, "Our Cuso regional director is here from Jamaica and has invited us all to dinner, so just relax, have a shower if you like, and we'll head out later."

While the girls were settling in and treating themselves to a shower with hot water, I caught up on news with Rhonda and retreated to the balcony with a glass of rum on ice. What a day! And an early morning flight tomorrow. I reminded myself to check everyone's bag weight again.

Soon I called for taxis to carry the young women, Rhonda, and me to OMG Restaurant. It was the very place where I'd experienced the ruckus with the chaps battling with the Royal Enfield long rifles over a year ago. Bygones and not-shot-down be bygones, I thought to myself.

Roberta greeted us with a big smile and hugs as we settled down to study the menu in this spacious urban restaurant. She and I helped explain some of the items to these village girls. The variety of meats, vegetables, and other items piqued curiosity to varying degrees. Tabitha and Candacy, girls who lived in different settlements on high ground in Akawini's marshland, ordered known items. Daisy, who was older and spent time in Charity and Parika working and staying with relatives, ordered more unusual dishes.

Dinner was filled with stories and questions, responses, and laughter. I was grateful for Roberta's gesture but concerned that Daisy had left much of her meal on the plate. Roberta had noticed. "Don't you like the food?" she asked. I don't remember what Daisy said, but I was annoyed enough with her to have a private word later. It was about want and waste and good public behaviour when one is a guest.

I'd earned the nickname "Mother Merle" when serving as the tutor in residence at the women's dormitory in my first posting with Cuso in Jamaica. I guess the tendency was still apparent.

Time with Roberta was important because, as Vanessa's supervisor, I knew she was one of the Cuso officials who'd authorized this training trip. I suspected the excitement that she'd felt when I'd arranged an early morning birding trip for her at the Botanical Gardens the previous year had helped persuade her and Cuso in Ottawa to make this investment in the training of Indigenous youth for ecotourism. When we parted, Roberta said, "I'm eager to hear what happens in your training. Have a great time."

I had a surprise for the young women when we reached home. They lived without refrigeration, so I had bought a large container of vanilla ice cream and we all dug in for dessert. Breakfast was oatmeal and more ice cream, much to everyone's delight. Why not!

I'd arranged for a taxi to collect us from the north-central area of the city where I lived. We were deposited at Ogle, the regional airport near the Atlantic coast. Another trusted taxi driver was to deliver Jacob from his father's hotel. Everyone convened on time, much to my relief. Bags went on the scale and then each of us was weighed. All went well. Only Jacob had ever been on a plane before, probably with his father on Indigenous business. I wondered if he was heir apparent to his father's position.

The three young women were wide-eyed experiencing taxiing, acceleration, and liftoff. They looked like I'd felt when on my first flight to the US Virgin Islands for a volunteer assignment fifty years prior. Then the young people studied the world below. We flew south over miles of carefully platted sugarcane fields. King Cane was in a very long death spiral here in Guyana as it had been for decades in other Caribbean countries.

As we flew onward, one of the young women asked, "The canals and rivers are white?"

"Yes, probably reflection off the water," I said.

Jacob leaned toward me and asked, "And the red lines? Roads?"

"Yes, the red laterite soil of the interior," I said. I'd recognized laterite as the same soil of southern India.

He nodded and turned back to the window. We gained altitude and experienced a panoramic view of the thick carpet of rainforest. Green then receded and the land began to undulate into high country interspersed with dry brown savannah and mountains in the distance. In less than an hour, we were on the same dirt runway I remembered from the previous year.

A pickup truck was there to fetch us. I was directed to the cab and the young people piled into the back with our bags and a plank across the sides of the truck for a seat. Miles of rugged road and clouds of red dust swirling behind us brought us to Surama Eco-Lodge in Macushi territory. Would it be a life-altering event for them as it had been for me?

Chapter Fifteen

How It All Ended

"Knees bad. No more high-country hiking for me," said Milner, the older Macushi guide with the wide grin when he recognized me. I extended my arms for a big hug, and we laughed as we embraced.

I said, "I'll stick with you on flat land, and we'll let these Region 2 youngsters from Akawini scale the heights."

Staff greeted us with the warmth that I remembered and escorted us to our various cabins built like benabs raised on stubby wooden posts. These small wooden units were designed with shutters hinged at the top to fit window openings. Both the shutters and wooden doors were painted with scenes of local life and the natural world, the birds and animals of the savannah. Conical thatch roofs capped the cabins. Interiors were painted white and furnished with simple furniture, spotless linens, and mosquito nets rigged on overhead cords. Bathrooms had toilets that required little water, and tiled shower stalls were built a few inches below floor level for drainage. Everything had been carefully designed and built for basic comfort and utility. I watched the young people snapping cell phone photos.

Staff had gathered in the large, two-storey benab that I remembered from my first trip. I observed the youth absorbing their surroundings and guessed that they were wondering how such a facility could be built and staffed in their village.

Surama benab

Jackie was the manager, the current toshao of the village, and served on the board of the Guyana Tourist Authority. Gary and Milner were senior guides. Anthony was the current operations and duty manager on a monthly rotation schedule, so that other villagers were also given opportunities for income. He oversaw welcoming guests, organizing camps away from Surama, and general oversight of day-to-day operations. There was also a tourism management committee that worked alongside the village council to create tour packages. Surama Eco-Lodge was part of the North Rupununi Tourism group and presented an impressive organizational structure.

The Akawini group listened with attention, knowing that Surama was the ecotourism model for the country. Established in 2004, it was a success story in Indigenous endeavour. Alexander was a driver and mechanic, a critical role because of road conditions. Chelsea did the accounting, and Compton handled all odd jobs. Lisa handled reservations and booking. This month Adel was head cook, and Berlinda was cabin attendant in charge of laundry.

We paused for lunch and headed downstairs where we were invited to seat ourselves at the long dining table set with a tablecloth, locally woven placemats, cutlery, and plates and glasses turned top down. An array of local food was arranged on a side table with a blackboard listing the offerings: chow mein, beef, roast chicken, fried farine, okra, macaroni and cheese, and mango juice. Dessert was *goiabada* or guava. The young people, the only guests at Surama these two days, were enchanted by the array and ate with great appetite. Gary, one of the guides, joined us for lunch and fielded questions.

"How did you become a guide?" asked Jacob.

Gary smiled. "I joined the village wildlife club when I was eight and loved it. I learned everything I could and, most importantly, I learned to cherish my environment. Now I wake up every morning doing a job that I love." Jacob and the young women were soaking up every word.

In the afternoon session, Jackie said, "There are formal reports every quarter so that the village council and the tourism management committee are fully informed about each other's activities and concerns." These were the sobering finer points of operations like those shared during their EPA training.

Anthony added, "Former village councils started to study natural and human resources back in the late 1980s and early 1990s, so Surama is a carefully planned operation."

Jackie went on to say, "There are direct and indirect benefits of our operations in terms of revolving employment whenever possible. A guest fee for each person is paid to the village for general use, which usually goes for improvement of health care and education. There's also a social service aspect to this operation. We provide a food hamper annually for each elderly person in the village." I saw the young people's eyes widen with interest.

They were reminded that a primary goal was job opportunities within the community. The lodge tried to employ young school leavers and find their strengths and interests. What traits, talents, and temperaments would best fulfill various roles. This was like the First Nations in Canada and the Native Americans in the US observing their youth and gauging those most likely to fill traditional roles in their communities.

This comment took me back nearly twenty years when I met Grandfather Semu Haute, the last of the four Chumash people's elders. The tribe's traditional land was the central and southern coastal regions of California. He told me, "I was born the eighth day of the eighth month of the eighth year of the twentieth century, 1908. The elders watched me grow up and decided that I would be taught the medicines of the tribe. Yes, I was the medicine man."

As my time with Grandfather faded from memory, I returned to the discussion underway. I thought about Akawini's toshao and how he had handpicked these four young people to participate in this training. I would like to think that the village council was also involved but knew enough about the power structure in the village to guess that the toshao had probably made the selection on his own.

Anthony said, "However, tourism isn't for everybody and there are still different levels of support and buy-in locally in this village of three hundred."

"Being a leader isn't easy," said Jackie. "Community leaders, whether in the village council or on the tourism management committee, have to be strong and able to take criticism. They also must learn to listen. The goal is to have the village feel a strong sense of ownership of the tourism business in their area."

Staff acknowledged that the favourite jobs were work in the office and guiding. The office was housed in the large benab we had passed as we drove into the compound. Two-thirds of the building's lower portion was local brick, above were upright poles of local wood spaced to provide light, ventilation, aesthetic appeal, and security. The roof was traditional thatch. All the communications and other administrative functions were housed there. Jackie said, "Catering and housekeeping aren't as popular, but villagers know that these tasks must be done and will provide income. If there are many guests, there's pressure on the kitchen and the housekeeping staff, which can be stressful."

Surama's greatest challenges were in communication and transportation, exactly what the Akawini youth and I had experienced in getting to the North Rupununi. I'd also identified these as core challenges in the country, whether in urban or rural areas.

Anthony added another piece of information that showed how Surama managed to have operations run as smoothly as possible. "Part of how we address communication challenges is a daily meeting, so everyone knows the day's activities. Everybody must be prepared for the planned and the unexpected." I took to heart the comment about the unexpected and hoped the Akawini young people did, too.

"What were the initial challenges in establishing this business?" I asked.

"Marketing was a big issue," said Jackie. "We needed to get the word out that we were here and what we had to offer. We also needed a variety of activities depending on interests and how long our guests were staying."

"Birding is a main activity," said Gary. "People are often very experienced birdwatchers. Our guiding must be top-notch. Staff must fulfill the expectations of our visitors to build a solid reputation for us."

Jackie added, "Sampling local food is also important to many guests. Staff must know about food preferences, allergies, and balanced meals. Sometimes there are unexpected guests, which is part of being prepared for anything and everything as much as possible."

Gary mentioned the importance of having good drivers and mechanics. "You got a sample of our roads on the way from Annai, so you know what I mean." Heads nodded.

"Finally," said Jackie, "costs and rates have to work out if we're going to stay in business."

I watched the young people absorbing this information and observed the wisdom of the staff in providing rest breaks. Milner had appeared and gathered us for a stroll through the savannah and into the rainforest for some birding and other wildlife viewing.

We made our way through what was a novelty for Akawini residents, a dry savannah. Everyone relaxed and slowed their pace. Macaws squawked from perches in the high canopy. They flew with their multicoloured feathers in full display. Mealy Parrots, with their rackety cries, swooped around the forest at midcanopy. A large rodent with a humped back and long legs scooted across the path ahead of us. "Agouti," said Milner.

On the way back, I overheard Jacob say to Milner, "That was a marvelous walk." I had misread his facial expression earlier as detachment or boredom. Maybe I needed to rethink how I had perceived and interpreted the way he and Elijah and others conducted themselves in Akawini. Maybe they were innately reserved, or had just been shy, or simply didn't know what to say to me.

I'd noted that all four of the young people wanted to be guides, but Jacob was also interested in business management. Maybe he saw the link between handling village business and managing ecotourism operations.

During another rest break, we studied crafts for sale. There was an array of embroidery, beadwork, basketry, and wood carving. I was drawn to the small, embroidered tapestries of Indigenous life. The stitching was superb and surpassed any embroidery I'd ever seen. The intricacy was matched on the reverse, too. No knots in evidence. One piece that I purchased was a sampler of local wildlife. The other piece was a depiction of the stages of cassava processing.

Later, when I'd returned to Canada and showed these tapestries to others, one woman had said, "Oh, these stitches are so perfect even on the backside. They must have used sewing machines."

I'd replied, "No, this is all handwork. They don't have sewing machines. They don't even have electricity in the remote village where these pieces were created.

When the young people had finished taking pictures of themselves against the backdrop of the savannah, they drifted over my way. The young women admired the handwork while Jacob and Gary were leaning against the bar talking about guiding. The shelves behind the bar were empty. On my previous visit to Surama, in the evenings I'd seen a few bottles of beer and Guyanese rum available for sale. None were displayed now. These items were for guests and not available for possible sampling by employees or visiting trainees.

Vanessa had arrived for another meeting elsewhere in the area and joined us for lunch. I conducted a short debriefing for her benefit with each trainee asked to share a key point of the day's meetings from their perspective.

Daisy said, "Jackie's manner is a model of leadership. She's very thoughtful and organized in everything she says and does."

Jacob followed with, "I liked the way everybody talked about their job here and some of the regular problems they have."

Tabitha added, "I like the fact that this place helps the community with education and health matters."

Candacy smiled and, in a soft voice, said, "The walk was wonderful."

I added, "What struck me most was that communication and transportation are key challenges, which is exactly what we experienced with our EPA training and also getting here." Vanessa beamed with delight. The investment in this training was producing solid results and she nodded in my direction.

Akawini trainees with ancient petroglyph

The next day, Gary took us on a tour of the village, including the airstrip. At the latter, a sign said, "Rehabilitated & lengthened to 4,300 feet using…soil solutions surface sealer." We learned that this was applied two years prior. No wonder this airstrip was less bumpy than the one at Annai. The village was also proud to note that it had hosted a visit by Prince Harry a few months prior to our arrival.

When we visited Surama's meeting hall, Gary told us of an unusual decision. "The village said no to a cell tower because where we were told it should be built would have disrupted wildlife. Technology isn't allowed to overrule the importance of the natural world here." I glanced over at Jacob to see his reaction. There was no visible response, but I knew that he and the young women had heard this remarkable bit of news. I remembered the first day I met Jacob when he was in the Ykinipa highlands trying to get a cell signal from Wakapoa's tower. Gary didn't say why an alternate site wasn't proposed. The trainees now had a different reaction to consider with their territory struggling to embrace ecotourism and technology.

The next day, there was more interaction with staff, including a tour to see how Surama did cassava processing, weaving, thatch-work, and other crafts. The finale occurred after dinner when our hosts introduced the local wildlife club. The performers were dressed in Macushi costumes crocheted in white cotton by the village women. The young women wore short, fringed skirts and halter-tops that were decorated with embroidery and beadwork in red, green, and black. They also sported matching headbands, bands on their arms and legs, and matching earrings and necklaces.

The young men wore embroidered, fringed panels of white cloth that stretched from their waist to below their knees. The bird stitched on the panels was the Savannah Hawk. This was an artist's conception of the same bird that I'd photographed outside my benab earlier in the day. The male dancers wore large crocheted, beaded, and fringed neck pieces that continued below their waist. Their costumes kept to the theme of white with embroidery and beadwork in red, green, and black. Everyone carried items woven of palm and fibre. Some held carved and decorated sticks with calabash tops, also carved and decorated. The troupe of half a dozen dancers sang in Macushi. Part of one dance included a pause while one young woman knelt and demonstrated spinning in the traditional manner.

The Akawini trainees were watching intently and after the formal presentation, spent a long time talking with fellow wildlife club members. I purposely sat to the side. I wasn't needed to facilitate this meeting of young people from the two territories.

The next morning, we said farewell to staff and climbed into the pickup truck that would take us to Rock View Lodge in Annai. After heavy rain, the road was now a soggy, red bog. We passed a freight lorry with its hood up and parts strewn around. The driver-mechanic said, "I've been like this for two days. I'm waiting for a part. You go on. Nothing to be done till it gets here."

At Rock View, we were greeted by Colin, who owned and operated this lodge. Blocks of rooms were built of local brick and stone with wooden rafters supporting a clay tile roof. Window openings could be closed with louvred wooden panels. All the furniture was wicker and local wood. A wooden frame above each bed held a mosquito net that could be flipped down to provide protection. The embroidery that caught my attention in Surama was framed and hung in the rooms and common areas. I studied and photographed each one. Rock View was a comfortable resort offering a different feel from Surama.

Daisy volunteered to be my roommate. When we were shown our accommodations, we were told not to be disturbed by the discoloured look of our toilet seat. The attendant said, "The seat is scrubbed for each new visitor along with a thorough cleaning of the room. We keep this seat as it ages in honour of a former guest who visited several years ago." She tapped the faded, framed photograph on our bedroom wall when leaving. Daisy and I stepped closer for a look, then burst out laughing. There was young Prince Charles in safari clothes feeding a tapir through a chain-link fence here at Rock View.

I said "Oh, poor Prince to be so remembered! I guess this was the honouring of the occasion. It certainly gave the word throne a different meaning." Daisy giggled again while wiping away tears.

Once we were settled, with Jacob having the luxury of a room to himself, we were invited to a nearby patio area. Colin spoke of the development of Rock View and the tourist industry over the past three decades. Looking each of us in the eye, he said, "To do ecotourism, you must have passion, leadership, training, and communication skills." He then shared stories of Rock View's history and the development of the tourist industry here in the heart of Guyana. Daisy, Tabitha, Jacob, and Candacy gave full attention to all that Colin was hammering home.

We toured the compound and convened again for lunch. Meals were served family style with large platters and bowls placed at the centre of the table. The room was decorated with Guyanese art and crafts and doubled as a gallery. The tall wooden statue of a pork knocker, a Guyanese term for a gold miner, intrigued us. After lunch, we were invited to climb upstairs to view more of the gallery above.

I was particularly interested in the chess set with Indigenous figures as pieces. The king was a toshao with a tall, feathered headdress, and the queen had a shorter headdress of feathers. The knight was a warrior with a spear. The bishop was portrayed as a shaman waving a cluster of leaves overhead. The rook was a benab and birds were pawns. I noted the last pieces with special interest.

Several more framed examples of the intricate regional embroidery lined the walls. Every detail—common tasks, hammocks, thatched shelters, birds, animals, trees, and plants—was carefully stitched. A riverine scene showed a fisherman holding the arapaima, the world's largest scaled freshwater fish. It could reach three metres and weigh up to two hundred kilograms. Now it was a catch-and-release fish for the tourist industry.

Guide Hendricks took the young people for a walk to see the arapaima in a nearby pond and said they'd scout for birds. Again, I wanted them to have private time with a fellow Indigenous person who was deeply involved in crafting the tourist experience here in the hinterland.

I opted for staying at the lodge with Colin and chatting over another cup of aromatic Guyanese coffee. We compared backgrounds and discovered that we were of similar vintage as the post Second World War generation. His stint as a British VSO volunteer in 1969 matched my involvement with the US Volunteers in Service to America in

1967. Colin fell in love with Guyana, married and started a family, and established Rock View in 1992. He also helped organize ecotourism in the North Rupununi. During these same decades, I had a life in and out of North America with more development work in the Caribbean, the US, India, Canada, and now Guyana. I mentioned my admiration of the embroidery he showcased.

"It's done by the women of Massara deep in the interior."

"That's where I'll head if I ever have the opportunity of exploring Guyana again."

When the young people returned and shared their fish tales, we were again loaded into a truck and taken to Bina Hill Institute that provided higher education for Indigenous youth. Our interest was the tourism training program. We were welcomed by a chorus singing a welcoming song in Macushi before formal presentations by the staff.

Community-based tourism was emphasized with the dual goals of development and conservation. It was obvious that there was great pride and a sense of empowerment in Macushi ownership of their land and crafting appropriate learning programs at Bina Hill. In the tourism program, the need for good management and financial accountability was also stressed. Another tenet of successful tourism was called FAM—food, accommodation, and marketing. Elements of the equation had already been stressed and demonstrated at both Surama and Rock View.

We learned that the North Rupununi Tourism Programme, NRTP, was the first of its kind in the country and was started with a grant from the Canadian International Development Agency or CIDA, the same agency that helped create Iwokrama. The purpose of NRTP was to maintain networking relationships on both regional and national levels and provide high visibility for travel and tourism, the largest industry in the world. This visit was part of the organization's mandate. The Akawini youth were particularly attentive when the presenter said new destinations and attractions needed to be added. Region 2 could help address this need.

Bina Hill Institute also operated a radio station with local reach and an interview had been scheduled with a member of the faculty who obviously loved his role. We trooped into the small recording studio with the control panel in full view. Microphones and headsets were dangling from armatures above head level when interviewees were seated.

I was asked a few introductory questions about this training session, Cuso, and my role in the project. Then Tabitha volunteered to be the first person interviewed. She wore the birding vest that I'd given her back in the village along with her brimmed hat that matched perfectly. When the interview got underway, I suddenly understood this sixteen-year-old's extraordinary articulation, focus, and drive.

"I'm the great-granddaughter of Stephen Campbell."

Tabitha

"What!" exclaimed the announcer. "Ladies and gentlemen, I'm nearly falling out of my chair in surprise. Listeners, this young woman's great-grandfather is our legendary fighter for Indigenous territorial rights. Stephen Campbell was our first Indigenous Member of Parliament in 1957. This young woman from Region 2 is here with us today with friends from Akawini territory near the Pomeroon river. Tabitha and these three other young people are here to see how they can ignite tourism in their territory. Indeed, we have a powerful Arawak girl right here in the studio."

After Tabitha listed the features of her territory that could promote ecotourism in her remote village, Daisy offered to speak. She didn't currently live in Akawini but stayed with relatives in Region 2 and Region 3 where she worked in local shops. Maybe Jessica's hunch was right. The toshao might be thinking of training in tourism as a way of bringing bright young people back into the village if they could have meaningful work. Daisy, at twenty-one, was spunky and her radio interview also focused on the highlights of life in Akawini that lent themselves to ecotourism.

Jacob, this handsome young man with a shock of bushy hair, volunteered next. As he clamped on the big headphones, I noted how long he kept his hair on top and how it sprung out on each side of the headset. No wonder he had hoisted the wildlife group's new library cabinet up onto his head and carried it to Tristan's house so easily after the recent EPA training. His thick hair was a cushion.

"Listeners, this is a son of Akawini's toshao with us today," said the announcer. "What strikes you as most different here in the North Rupununi, Jacob?"

"You've kept your heritage more than we have. You speak and sing in your language. You dance in Indigenous costumes. You've kept learning traditional arts and crafts. Your buildings remember the old style. We've lost so much where I live," said Jacob.

The announcer said, "Well, thank you for saying that. It's great to hear praise from another Indigenous region here in Guyana for what we're trying to maintain and celebrate as the first people of this land. What else strikes you about the North Rupununi?"

"I really like what I see about your way of life. I might just come back and find a Rupununi girl to marry," said Jacob.

With a sparkle in his eye and merriment in his voice, the announcer said, "You hear that, all you young ladies out there? I have a toshao's handsome young son who says he might be back looking for a wife!"

Meanwhile, it was my turn to nearly fall off my chair with Jacob's bold comments broadcasted all over the Rupununi. This reserved young man had celebrated so much of the wisdom and beauty of traditional life in all its manifestations that I'd noted was usually lost in the quest for Western modernity. I realized that Jacob was blossoming at warp speed these past few days.

He was manifesting a blend of boyish and adult behaviour in both his physical and verbal language. His "Yah!" was imprinted on all of us, even me, as a response. He was also the only person who mentioned interest in management in relation to tourism. I wondered if I was witnessing the beginnings of a leader. Would efforts in creating ecotourism affect how he and the young women conducted themselves in future? Would there be opportunities for them to grow into leaders?

Candacy couldn't put off talking any longer and had continued to be terrified by this whole training experience. She was gorgeous, with a model's build and grace and an exquisite smile but so reserved. That morning, I'd loaned her one of my blouses with long sleeves when I noticed her shivering at breakfast. I sensed that it wasn't just a matter of chills.

She put on the headset and stared at the microphone. She then began to speak in a rapid, mechanical manner and at low volume. "I like seeing everything. It's very interesting," was all she managed to say. I wondered if Bina Hill Institute training could work magic on someone so ill at ease outside their customary world.

With the interviews concluded, the announcer summarized who we were and the reason for our presence in the North Rupununi, signed off, and spun around on his stool giving us a big grin. Exchanging parting comments and leaving the studio, we encountered the instructor for tourism who had taken us for a tour of his classroom. He'd heard Jacob's comment about loss of language and had brought language texts for both Arawak and Warrau "I'm sorry. We have nothing for Carib," he said to Daisy. Tabitha and Jacob accepted the Arawak workbook with eagerness and thanks. The instructor offered Candacy the Warrau workbook, which she accepted with another glorious smile. What generosity in sharing these valuable publications with our group.

When we returned to Rock View after a full tour of the Bina Hill campus and residence halls, we were all energized. We studied the dinner menu with delight: garlic rice, baked chicken, sweet cassava, and cucumber salad. It wasn't as varied as at Surama but still proved a satisfying meal.

That afternoon, I'd dealt with a critical issue when the airline company called. "Hello, this is Air Services Limited in Georgetown. We have a pickup in Surama and will collect you there," said a young woman with a pleasant voice. It was back to challenges of communication and transportation.

"Excuse me, but we have tickets from Annai. We're there now at Rock View," I said in a level voice.

"Oh, that's fine, we can still pick you up in Surama," she replied.

"That's not the point. We have no road transport to Surama and no money in the budget for what you're asking. There are five of us. I request that our ticketing arrangement be fulfilled with a pickup from Annai."

Author self-portrait

"Just a moment, let me talk to my manager." The four young people had overheard the exchange and moved closer to learn how this would end.

"Ma'am, my manager said we'll make a second stop and collect all of you from Annai."

"Thank you. I understand that this might take a bit more time and fuel and I appreciate the honouring of our original agreement. We look forward to another good flight with your company tomorrow." I looked around and saw the young people smiling. I continued, "It's just another demonstration of the communication and transportation issues as key challenges everywhere in Guyana. Remain firm and polite until you get the service you deserve."

Our final morning in Region 9 was to be birding in the nearby Pakaraima Mountains with the guide Hendricks, but we weren't really prepared for highland hiking. Instead, we opted to spend more time as explorers around the immediate area. Based at Rock View for a day and a half had given us time to learn about how this private tourism enterprise evolved. We had heard about the industry from a British-born person who had fully embraced Guyanese life. Colin had built a successful business and helped develop tourism in a land that was now his beloved home.

With the Akawini trainings so close to the end of my posting, I wouldn't have time to return to the village to do a debriefing. There would be an election of all toshaos and a general meeting in each village in Guyana the week after our return. In preparation for this occasion, I asked each person to share a portion of the trainings with their community.

Tabitha had said, "I'll discuss the staffing arrangements at Surama and also talk about how Rock View and Bina Hill are run."

Daisy said, "I'll tell them about the purpose and benefits of ecotourism and all the basic objectives we heard about."

Jacob said, "I'll chair the meeting and fill in details about the buildings and the local youth groups."

"Candacy, what will you talk about?" I asked.

After a moment, she said, "I'll talk about how the village council and the tourism management committee must work together to make tourism successful."

I was beyond happy with their responses. I then cued the young people about transportation arrangements for getting home. Our flight to Ogle was just the first of the next day's travel challenges. "I'll arrange for taxis to take us from the airport to the Cuso office for a quick meeting with Vanessa, as she requested. Jacob will stay in Georgetown with his father."

Daisy said, "I'll stay in Parika with relatives there and won't cross the Essequibo with you."

I said, "That's fine. I'll give you enough passage money to get to Akawini later." I looked over at Candacy and Tabitha and said, "We can't get to Akawini before dark and will overnight in Charity."

I'd contacted Tristan earlier about accommodations for Tabitha and Candacy in Charity. He said, "My family will be staying with relatives for the weekend and all of you are welcome to stay with us."

"That's most generous, Tristan, but I know you'll be crowded. I'll just drop the girls off and will make reservations for myself at a hotel in Charity and get back to Georgetown the next day. Candacy and Tabitha will have money to help pay for their food and enough to cover river passage to Akawini."

While waiting for our plane at the airstrip at Rock View in Annai, I shared money matters with the trainees, so that they understood our investment in them. "It was 33,000 dollars for the flight for each of us, one way. That's a total of 330,000 in your money—$2,200 in Canadian or $1,650 in US dollars. Cuso is also covering all travel costs for departing from and returning to Akawini and has paid for all our meals. Surama and Rock View provided free accommodations and guide services. I've left tips from my own funds." There was silence as all four absorbed this information about the costs for this kind of experience.

While carrying our bags closer to the airstrip and watching for the plane, we saw a young man with a cowboy hat in camouflage cloth ride up. I realized this part of Guyana shared the gaucho culture of this continent. The South American style of horsemanship, in turn, followed the US cowboy culture that started in the 1870s after the US Civil War.

We all sat quietly lost in our own thoughts. Candacy, Daisy, Jacob, and Tabitha would soon return to their world of the marshland and waterways of Region 2 and whatever their futures might hold in the ecotourism industry. The drone of engines interrupted our daydreaming as the plane approached and landed with propellers still turning. We boarded and dropped our luggage with the load of backpacks at the rear of the plane. We bent our heads and eased sideways to find a seat while wedged in with the adventure trekkers from Surama.

We roared down the airstrip and stared out at the world we had just experienced. Gaining altitude, the savannah and surrounding mountains gave way to the lush green of the rainforest laced with ribbons of roads and rivers. Everything we saw now held new meaning.

While we sliced upward through clouds and peered down at them in their fluffy glory, each of us was lost in our own thoughts. An hour later, we felt the start of descent and saw the grid of fields and settlements of Region 4 with Georgetown's suburban residential grid, the tall buildings of downtown, and the coastal hotels in the distance. Sunlight sparkled on the Demerara and the Atlantic.

When we disembarked, I flagged taxis to carry us to the Cuso office for our brief meeting with Vanessa. While the young people spoke with her, I copied the documents that they had requested: the Bina Hill Institute application form, information on wildlife clubs in Guyana, and Adel's Region 2 birding checklist.

I heard the murmur of conversation with Vanessa but focused on the task at hand as it was midday with much travel ahead of us. We also stopped briefly at my apartment where I collected a book called *Birds of the World* that I wanted to donate to their AWG library. I distributed notebooks and Cuso pens for each, which I wished that I'd remembered to pass out before the training session.

Since I sewed for relaxation over the months, I'd accumulated a variety of cloth bags that I'd modified for daypacks with inner pockets plus outer mesh pouches for a water bottle and whatever else. There was also my stash of bandanas in various colours. I invited each person to take a daypack and a bandana as a personal memento from me. Presto! Everything was scooped up with smiles and thanks. I also grabbed bush clothes for an additional day out of Georgetown.

Soon we were on our way and first dropped off Jacob at the hotel with his father standing in front. The toshao and I exchanged formal greetings. Jacob stunned me when he scooped me up for a big hug—not only once but twice in the presence of his stern father. "Thank you!" he said in a tone that I knew came from very deep. Days later, when I'd returned to Georgetown and reported on the training sessions in greater detail with Vanessa, she told me that, unbeknownst to me at the copying machine, she'd received the same huge and heartfelt hug from Jacob.

Now, with Jacob settled, the girls and I piled back into a taxi and headed for Stabroek Market and the Demerara water taxi. Then it was road travel to Parika where Daisy left us with hugs all around. I handed her travel money back to Charity and extra money to top up her phone. "Let your family in Akawini know you're back safely."

Candacy, Tabitha, and I hoisted our bags and took the long walk through the Parika warehouse onto the stelling and found a speedboat just about to depart. Only the front seat was available, and the water looked choppy with tidal action. "Are you two ready for a rough ride?" I asked. Candacy nodded.

"Rough can be fun," said the indomitable Tabitha.

Speedboats at Parika ready to ply the Essequibo estuary

"Let's go!" I said as we climbed aboard with the hatch closure sliding down while we stowed our bags and donned our life vests. The boat pulled away from the stelling and started to buck and heave its way across the estuary, dodging islands, and the direct hit of waves from the Atlantic. Passengers rolled down the vinyl flaps on each side to keep us dry. At one point, with the atmosphere growing stuffy, I called out, "Air!" and somebody opened the hatch over the steps so that a gust of ocean breeze filled the cabin. “Thanks!” I said as others murmured relief.

We reached Supenaam and negotiated the platoon of touts to find a taxi for Charity. I had booked a hotel room and bought food in Parika as I knew no restaurants would be open when I arrived at night.

I’d alerted Tristan and his extended family of our estimated arrival in Charity. Everyone was sitting on the balcony of a large house near the main road to greet us.

“You’re back safely,” said Tristan coming down and helping Tabitha and Candacy with their bags. I briefly summarized the training and handed the young women money for their return trip plus funds for topping up phones and contacting their families.

I turned to Tristan and, with a shaky voice, asked him to convey thanks to Latoya and his whole family for their gracious hospitality the many months of my visits to Akawini. “It was our pleasure to have you stay with us,” said Tristan as we clasped hands and exchanged smiles. I hugged both young women wishing them well. Tabitha and I looked at each other one more time and hugged again.

When I reached my spartan accommodations in Charity, I stretched out on the bed and stared at the ceiling. There had been little time for me to have an official debriefing, but the radio interview at Bina Hill Institute, the readiness to report on the training at the upcoming village meeting, and the eagerness for application forms for Bina Hill was revealing. I parted with these young people with enormous satisfaction and great hope for their future and that of their community. I slept well and caught a taxi the next morning for my return to Georgetown.

Before departing the country, I’d arranged to have coffee with Goldie. I hadn’t seen her since my return to Guyana. Two more Cuso volunteers had been assigned to VYC after me. The first departed the country within two months of her arrival amid controversy during my first posting. The other fulfilled her mission with the National Career Guidance program under VYC’s oversight during my second posting.

Goldie paused as she sipped her coffee and looked at me. “I know your first assignment with us in Georgetown wasn’t your favourite. We had some difficulties. Thank you for assisting. It helped.” I was touched that she had acknowledged without negativity my greater attachment to my later work in the interior.

I'd also stopped by the backhouse office of the birding group in Georgetown to say goodbye. Andy was alone, except for the two rescued squawking toucans. I told him about the mismanagement of funds for the initial eagle effort in Region 2 the previous year. He looked sad and said, "You see what kind of people I have to work with." I felt relieved that now he knew what had happened. I doubted that he even heard that I'd returned to Guyana. Did he have news about the Crested Eagle? I never asked.

I accepted the misappropriation of money that I'd lost in my first investment in ecotourism in Guyana and the failure to repay the balance of the money for gas during my second sojourn. It was tuition paid for my training in the school of life. I wouldn't have spent my funds if I couldn't have afforded to lose them. People with limited access to money sometimes handle it, for even mutually beneficial projects, based on their own definitions of what is justified.

In my final days in the country, I'd received bits of news from the villages. A new toshao was elected in Wakapoa. Lloyd stepped up again to serve as deputy toshao providing continuity of leadership. Representatives from the Ministry of Public Telecommunications arrived to assess the feasibility of installing a tower on School Island. Lydia had made progress with the Cuso agricultural assignment in the territory.

In Akawini, the toshao was re-elected. This meant that he would remain at the rudder of everything happening in the village, especially the ecotourism venture, and retain his moniker of Captain.

Toward the end of my time in Guyana, I also began uncoupling myself emotionally from people and places where I had deep attachments and would be leaving with sadness. Jessica and Eon had come specially to Georgetown the final week of my stay. They made reservations at a restaurant that hosted a formal dinner once a week. Their funds stretched only for travel out of Region 2 and back, plus our dinners, so I paid for the wine. Eon had brought his guitar and serenaded me with his finished song, "Miss Sugarbin." There was applause from Jessica, me, and all the other smiling diners when he concluded on a heartfelt note. Jessica and I blinked away the tears.

I invested in a small digital camera for Chris living up Akawini Creek with his family and asked Jessica and Eon to please deliver it. He was a logger, hunter, and master of GPS and had said that he would document the eagle nests and possibly even Harpy Eagles and Crested Eagles. He was also now on the village council and eager to help in developing ecotourism.

A few days later, and my final night in Georgetown, I stepped out on the balcony of my apartment with a tot of rum in hand. I looked across at the Cuso office in the century-old former hospital building. I took a slow, deep breath and inhaled the pungency of tropical vegetation late in the day. It was the golden hour, and I knew what was coming. Soon a flock of Scarlet Ibis winged overhead from feasting on the Atlantic mudflats to the northeast. They were off to their roosting site on the east bank of the Demerara where they would be red specks in thick foliage. I revelled for the last time in the brilliance of their plumage silhouetted against the clear blue sky.

The brief period that I was with the Akawini youth was the highlight, the finale of my assignment. All that we experienced together could be a turning point in the lives of not only these young people but many whom I'd encountered in my two stints in Guyana. What we'd shared may well have helped in clarifying for everyone—including me—values, dreams, and a way forward.

The next day, I flew like an eagle on my way home reflecting on my improvised bases in Guyana. I'd said farewells to my friends at Adel's and in the villages. I'd wound down my Georgetown life, including a final long conversation with Vanessa. I was now winging my way back to Canada and would soon touch down in the South Okanagan Valley of British Columbia.

When I nested back home in Penticton, the egg of memoir began to form and hatch, and the fledgling idea took flight in the stories that I've shared. May this inspire future flights for all who wish to spread their wings in new directions.

EPILOGUE

Since my departure from Guyana in July of 2018, Eon and Jessica left their Region 2 base two months later and returned to Georgetown full-time. They married in 2021and are creators of Singing Chef Adventures, a tour company that explores Guyana through the mediums of food, music, culture, and history.

In June of 2019, Guyana was named one of the top ecotourism destinations in the world by Conde Nast Traveler, Travel and Leisure, National Geographic, and international travel organizations. In the same month, Cuso International closed operations in Guyana after fifty-seven years of service to consolidate its efforts in other regions of the world. ExxonMobil continues to be controversial as front-page news in Guyanese newspapers.

Volunteer Youth Corps continues its work in Georgetown. Wakapoa got a telecommunications tower. To date, there is no confirmation that Akawini youth made it to Bina Hill Institute for training in ecotourism. However, Vanessa Thompson is now working with another Canadian organization—World University Service of Canada or WUSC. A current project focuses on empowerment of Indigenous youth and may return to Cuso's endeavours in this effort.

While in Guyana, I was in the space between cultures with tugging from each to reach the other. We were on a bridge or perhaps balancing on a tightrope. Tallying local skills celebrated creativity and increased communication and confidence within communities.

Sometimes I now find myself drifting back to an idyllic scenario of an extended, simpler life in the hinterland. Guyana's bounty of birds taught me to take flights of fancy. I see myself gliding on the waterways in a dugout canoe with a small engine like Ivan's. I envision myself at home in a custom-made treehouse near one of the villages. Birds live in trees, so why not me? It's both a benab and an eagle's aerie built of local wood, bamboo, and thatch.

I've found design and construction services for the mechanics of a borewell, a composting toilet, and rainwater harvesting as sustainable infrastructure. There's a small-scale solar grid and wind turbine. I've hung my hammock with its mosquito net and commissioned Lloyd's son Mario in Wakapoa and Dameayon in Akawini to build basic furniture out of local wood, bamboo, and reeds. My nest is filled with local basketwork and woven cloth.

I've crafted an East Indian chula like Latoya's for cooking as well as Eon's Oven John of mud and local block and brick. There's a small shade house with waist-high gardening boxes out of repurposed old wooden boats. The boxes are irrigated with Eon's Easy Irrigation Pump drawing water from the nearby wetlands. I've ferreted out how to have a twenty-first century treadle sewing machine and teach sewing skills as well as handcraft and technology training especially for local women and children. And, yes, I hold out hope for cell service and internet connectivity in all the hinterland villages.

Author and guide Marcy on Turtle Mountain

No, I wouldn't go as far as the legendary naked Nazi with a remote life up a creek, but I would craft a life akin to the Eastern elder retreating to the mountaintop to live out life in a more barebones, contemplative manner. Elder? Guru? Crone? I would still embrace community and welcome the return of its acceptance of me. I would live a life that splices what I cherish of my Global North ways with the natural beauty and bounty, wisdom and cordiality of the Global South. A dream? Yes. It's a scheme for existing between worlds and cross-pollinating values, skills, and the sheer joy of living at peace in the natural world. In focusing on the small in a particular location, perhaps there's a spark that can ignite a flame of fulfillment.

How does all this wandering of my mind pertain to the life that I constructed in Guyana and am now sharing in written form? Perhaps I'm following the habits of the Crimson-hooded Manakin nestled in the comfort and beneficence of the rainforest. I'm also learning the habits of the Crested Eagle perched in the high country scanning the rainforest and wetlands below. The eagle's purpose is to secure prey. Mine is to pray in prose for drawing attention and perhaps even response to other ways of being, doing, and having.

ACKNOWLEDGEMENTS

I'm grateful that Cuso International provides opportunities for enhancing lives of both those in partner organizations worldwide such as VYC and Cuso volunteers themselves. I thank Cuso staff at all levels and donors who've supported my postings with interesst, funds, and equipment.

I embrace Cuso colleagues and Guyanese friends, neighbours, and those in organizations and villages where I worked. Peter Bouchard in Georgetown and Shyamkumar Puravankara in Kerala helped equip me to become a better birder.

Special thanks to Jessica Hatfield and Eon John who proved the glue that pieced this tale into a panoramic whole. Their talents, contacts, and zest for life were crucial to my second posting. Further thanks to the toshaos and village councils, and especially the families in Wakapoa and Akawini who let me hang my hammock in their homes.

It takes a supportive community to write and publish a book. As my story unfolded in written form, friends reviewed the manuscript and provided priceless feedback. Thanks to Linda Belote, Susan Burack, Susan Butruille, Phil Hall, Lona Manning, Neill McKee, Shailaja Nair, A.M. Andino Rochon, Anne Romanow, Jan Sheltinga, Ann Silversides, and Rayleen Williams. Special thanks to Dale King who has read this book from partial draft to final proofreading.

My Penticton writers' groups—conducted by published author Julie H. Ferguson—provided great response to my fledgling efforts. Julie adopted me as a special project and helped me learn the art of memoir. Without Julie, there'd be no book.

Editor Joyce Gram had the unenviable task of guiding me in revamping my skills in teaching English along with having written and published in the areas of business, technology, and academia. Writing memoir was a whole new world of communication.

Jim Bisakowski did a masterful job of turning the forty-year-old batik that I crafted while working in the Bahamas into the cover design. Sincere thanks to Bruce Butler for guiding me through parts of the Kindle Direct Publishing process.

Returned Cuso volunteers Nancy Edwards, Wendy Nordick, and Marian Dodds—all crafting their experiences into memoirs—are my online writing group. Climbing the mountain to publishing has been emboldened by our exchanges.

Apologies to anyone who may feel forgotten in this catalogue of appreciation. I'm humbled and honoured by all who've encouraged and participated in my sharing this journey where I was gripped by Guyana in wondrous ways.

AUTHOR BIOGRAPHY

Merle Kindred is a retired educator, administrator, and international volunteer. Her overseas life includes assignments in the US Virgin Islands, Jamaica, the Bahamas, India, and Guyana. She has published and presented on her work internationally.

Kindred lives in Penticton, British Columbia, Canada. She is writing another memoir on over a decade in and out of India as a volunteer with the Centre of Science and Technology for Rural Development, an NGO in Kerala.

She sold her final gas-powered vehicle in 2008. When it's mild, she walks and cycles. In winter, she walks and uses a bus.

Author at home in Penticton (© Photos by Pharos)

Made in United States
North Haven, CT
13 January 2024

47422724R00139